DISPATCHES FROM LABRADOR

Life on the Mista Shipu

Robin McGrath

BOULDER PUBLICATIONS

Library and Archives Canada Cataloguing in Publication

McGrath, Robin, author
    Life on the Mista Shipu : dispatches from Labrador / Robin McGrath.

Articles and essays previously published in *Labrador Life*.

ISBN 978-1-77523-457-9 (softcover)

    1. Labrador (N.L.)--Description and travel. 2. Labrador (N.L.)--Social life and customs. 3. Labrador (N.L.)--History. 4. Labrador (N.L.)--Biography. I. Title.

FC2193.4.M38 2018   971.8'205   C2018-903913-2

© 2018 Robin McGrath

Design and layout: Todd Manning
Editor: Stephanie Porter
Copy editor: Iona Bulgin
Printed in Canada

Excerpts from this publication may be reproduced under licence from Access Copyright, or with the express written permission of Boulder Publications Ltd., or as permitted by law. All rights are otherwise reserved and no part of this publications may be reproduced, stored in a retrieval system, or transmitted in any form or by any means, electronic, mechanical, photocopying, scanning, recording, or otherwise, except as specifically authorized.

We acknowledge the financial support of the Government of Newfoundland and Labrador through the Department of Tourism, Culture and Recreation.

Newfoundland Labrador

We acknowledge the financial support for our publishing program by the Government of Canada and the Department of Canadian Heritage through the Canada Book Fund.

For Tshaukuesh,
and in loving memory of Kantuakueshish

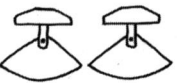

An Introduction to Labrador vii

LIFE ON THE COAST
Old Smoker: A Labrador Ghost Ride 3
Fiddle Making in Labrador: A Historical Look 7
One Pilgrim's Progress in Labrador 11
Wooding: The Chore That Warms You Twice 14
Labrador Christmas Trees 19

JUSTICE
Above the Law: Grenfell's Magistracy in Labrador 27
The Newfoundland Ranger Force in Labrador 33
Murder, They Wrote: Early Accounts of Intentional and
    Unlawful Killings in Labrador 40
Apenam Tanien Pone: First Judge of the Innu Nation 47

FOOD
"Full and Plenty": Life at North River. 53
The Labrador Larder 57
Bread, the Staff of Life 62
For the Love of Mushrooms 66
Wild Arctic Char: An Epicurean Delight 70
Alexander by Any Other Name 74
Dandelion: A Spring Tonic 77
Wild Potherbs from the Labrador Garden 81

NATURAL HISTORY
Summer Splendour: Labrador Wildflowers 87
The Grey Jays of Labrador 91
Carnivorous Plants of Labrador 96
The Weird and Wonderful World of Labrador Bats 99
The Versatile Porcupine 104
Celebrating the Spruce 109
The Beauty of Birches 113

VISITORS AND SOJOURNERS
Keeping Kool with Jens Haven 121
Sir Joseph Banks: the Chateau Bay Naturalist 123
Strathcona: A North West River Love Story 127

The Follow-On Bartletts of Turnavik 132
L.A. Learmonth: A Northern Man for Life 137
Richard White: Trader and Ethnographer 142
Frank Banikhin: The Matjas Herring Man 147

LABRADORIANS AT HOME AND AWAY
Victor Croucher: The Boy with the Giant Cod 153
Anauta: Labrador's Grey Owl 156
Ernie Lyall: The White Man Who Wasn't 161
Labradorians in the Great War 166

ON LAND AND SEA
Labrador Snow Slides 175
Sea Stacks, Cairns, and American Men 180
Fata Morgana: A Looming Phenomenon 184
The Greatest Light Show on Earth: Auroras in Labrador 188
The Voice of the Iceberg 194

PEOPLE OF THE INTERIOR
Playing for Keeps: Innu Checkers as Spiritual Struggles 203
Elizabeth Penashue's Labrador Walkabout 208
Francis Penashue: the Man Behind the Activist 212
St. Anne's Green Cathedral 216

LIFE AND DEATH
Layman's Language: Medical Terminology in Labrador 221
Labrador's Granny Midwives 227
Miles Frankel: The Travelling Doctor 234
Marvellous Moss: The Patriot's Renewable Resource 238
Healing Sweat 244
Bush Medicine and Home Remedies in Labrador 249
Labrador Burial Practices in Ancient and Modern Times 255

L'ENVOY
What's in a Name: Labrador Ducks and Dogs 263

Index 268

An Introduction to Labrador

In 2006, I had the opportunity to move to Labrador. My husband, who had just come through a bout with cancer and was more than ready for a change, had been offered an interesting job there and I knew enough about Labrador to realize that both the job and the place would suit him admirably. That was reason enough.

Although a native of Newfoundland, I had spent much of my working life in what was then the Northwest Territories, now Nunavut. My children jokingly referred to my research trips to the Arctic as my "millionaire's holidays," and I was quite aware of the advantages of being cut loose from urban life, away from cellphones and supervision and the demands of a rigidly hierarchical society. Although I hadn't chosen Labrador for myself, I was happy enough to be there for a time. As a writer, I thought I could do my work anywhere.

The job was to begin August 1, so my husband headed out and I was to follow a month later once I had settled up the sale of our house on Conception Bay. When word trickled down to me that I would be welcome to accompany Innu environmentalist Elizabeth Penashue on her annual trip down the Mista Shipu, or Churchill River, I jumped at the chance. What better way to be introduced to my new home in Labrador than to immerse myself in the country in the company of people who have thousands of years' experience of it?

I arrived in Goose Bay on August 22, and 36 hours later was climbing into the bow of a canoe at Churchill Falls, paddle gripped firmly in hand and a minimum of gear cushioning my knees. I knelt to take my first stroke into the wilds of Labrador. Eight days later, I emerged at Gull Island, bruised and fly-bitten, with aching muscles and a tremendous respect for the Innu people and the river that is the heart of their homeland.

Back in the early 1990s, Elizabeth Penashue went to jail for protesting the low-level flying of NATO aircraft over traditional Innu lands. Years later, she received an honorary doctorate from Memorial University for her initial activism and for her ongoing efforts to educate non-Innu and Innu alike about the spiritual bond between Innu and the land.

One of Dr. Penashue's methods of education is to take any willing participants—children, elders, religious leaders, politicians, or journalists—and lead them into the bush so they can experience what it is like to live in and off the land.

On this, her 10th educational trip down the Lower Churchill, Elizabeth was accompanied by 14 souls. Most of the travellers were Elizabeth's younger relatives (husband, sons, a niece, and some of their spouses and children), but there were two unrelated young Innu men who were along for the adventure, and three naive and inexperienced white folk: a lawyer, a dietician, and me.

I hasten to say to those who are shaking their heads at our utter folly that I did not consider myself inexperienced, nor did the other non-Innu. The lawyer, a former triathlete, and the dietician, a horsewoman of note, had whitewater experience in the Yukon. I had often canoed in northern Ontario with my children years before, and had, more recently, put in 10 days in a winter camp near Natuashish at a Mushuau Innu Gathering.

None of this had prepared we three *akaneshau* (as the Innu called us) for the hard labour of controlling a canoe in a strong current with constant headwinds and heavy loads. Nor did it do anything to mitigate the sheer terror of plunging into rapid after rapid, the only alternative being to climb the sheer sides of the river canyons and hike through thick, unmarked woods while braver paddlers shot ahead.

Each night we stopped and pitched camp. It takes time, hard work, and considerable experience to construct an Innu-style camp. Tent poles have to be cut, spruce boughs collected, the stove assembled, snares set, tea boiled, and supper prepared.

There are small complications. Traditionally, Innu left their tent poles at their camp sites for future use, but nowadays, non-native fishermen come along and burn them for firewood. It makes for extra work. It takes several men about half an hour to locate and cut the cross beam, longer to trim the 26 to 30 smaller poles needed to support the large canvas tent.

There is also the problem of water. I'm not sure at what point I realized that the monstrously vast body of water hurling downward toward Gull Island was all polluted. Back in the old days, you just dipped your pannikin in the river, but today, the water of the Lower Churchill is contaminated with mercury. Innu will not drink it, nor would I. Our camps all had to be as close as possible to feeder streams, and it took some effort to fetch water from these branches.

Food was also an issue. There was lots of baloney in the grub box, but that didn't have much appeal for me. Instead, I expected to manage on the constant fish diet I had been used to in the central and western Arctic.

It wasn't until we reached the halfway point on Lake Winokapau on the fourth or fifth day that I suddenly understood why nobody was eating fish. Far up on the bank, in letters too small to read from the river even with binoculars, was a sign from the hydro company, warning us not to eat more than one fish a week. Apparently, the mercury that was in the water was also in the fish.

On day six, after a particularly trying series of rapids, all the younger men went fishing and we had one glorious meal of trout. We also ate boiled beavers, roasted porcupine, and a few other of the Creator's gifts, but I can't say I was impressed with the amount of wildlife we saw on the Churchill.

In fact, I believe I saw more wildlife in my late lamented garden in Beachy Cove than I saw in eight days in the Labrador wilds. I could count on my fingers the number of birds I heard on the river, and while I did get a brief, thrilling glimpse of a mother bear and cubs, and a couple of moose, I wasn't about to jettison the baloney, just in case.

Intellectually, I had always understood that the boreal forest—the adaptation of tundra to woodlands—is almost empty of life. As you head south from the North Pole, you leave behind the berries and lichens that sustain rabbits and partridge, caribou and muskox, but you have not yet reached the woodlands' nuts and shrubs that feed the deer, moose, and other animals.

To know this is one thing, but to experience it is something else. In the course of eight days, I saw a patch of redberries that would not make a decent pie, a few squashberry bushes, no blueberries, no chanterelle mushrooms, no mountain sorrel, not a rabbit or a partridge, almost nothing to feed 15 people working hard and travelling fast.

The few animals the men shot were young, small, and inexperienced. They made a nice change from baloney and bannock, but they would not have gone far if we had lost our gear in the rapids.

At night, packed into the big tent with nine of the Innu, I shed the aches and pains of the day. The desultory talk between my bedmates, who would throw in a few philosophical questions in English for my amusement, was as good as a lullaby. Elizabeth would say her prayers in Innu Aimun, and one night after a hard fall on the rocks that wrenched her knee into a swollen ache, she sent her daughter-in-law for a smudge with which she purified herself.

Innu are prodigious snorers, and the glorious chorus was like a symphony orchestra with one soloist who hit a series of three notes so sweet it could make you cry. A lifetime victim of nightmares, I had only sweet dreams for eight nights in a row and slept like a contented baby the entire time. Which doesn't mean I wasn't glad to see Gull Island.

I came off the river having learned that this huge land, this enormous body of water, is far more fragile than my own aging and unreliable carcass.

A week after my return, I was back to normal, bites healed and bruises gone, ready to settle in to life in Goose Bay and get back to my desk and down to work. The problem was that much of my previous work was centred on "home," and my home wasn't really Labrador. I didn't know enough about the place to write about it, and I wasn't sure that I could carry it off even if I did. Labrador is very, very different from Newfoundland and very different from the more northern parts of this country also.

Its geography is varied, its languages are complex, its history is unique. It was more foreign to me in many ways than Ottawa, London, or Jerusalem.

Canoeing the Churchill River highlighted for me two of the things that became most important to me during my decade in Labrador: the people and the land. I have in my time there met some of the nicest, bravest, most interesting people I've ever known. My involvement with Elizabeth Penashue and her husband, Francis, was my ticket into a part of Labrador that most people never see. They took me into the country, to the sweat lodges and remote beaches, and into the homes and tents of their friends and relatives. They included me when they went to religious services, baby showers, and funerals, and I went with them on berry picking and fishing trips. Quite a number of the articles I eventually did manage to produce about Labrador, as well as a handful of poems, were a direct result of these experiences, and I am immensely grateful to have had such good friends.

It took some time for me to appreciate the spruce forests of Labrador. The interior, where Goose Bay is situated, is all sand. I was afraid to go into the woods as I had at home because without the sound of the sea to guide me, I was sure I would get lost. And it was all so empty and silent. In Cape Dorset, I had seen hillsides covered in Arctic hares; in Cambridge Bay I hiked into valleys occupied by herds of muskoxen. In Coppermine and Rankin Inlet, the lakes seethed with char. I was used to the seasonal appearance of huge numbers of caribou, seals, even ground squirrels and lemmings, as well as swans, snow geese, and birds of all sorts. Labrador seemed incredibly empty in comparison.

Eventually, I did get used to it and even to like it. And I also discovered that the land isn't quite so empty and barren as I had first thought.

The essays and articles included here are much as they were when I first published them, but a few have been tweaked, either to reflect my grammatical preferences rather than those of the editors I had, or occasionally to correct elements that I later found to be erroneous. For example, I originally wrote that there were three carnivorous plants in Labrador, when in fact there are at least four. My original article on the Labrador war veterans contained an incorrect account of Malcolm McLean's return to North West River, which I based on information recorded by Elliott Merrick, later corrected by Anne Budgell.

While in Labrador, I regularly wrote for the quarterly magazine *Labrador Life*, and I would like to thank my editor, Bert Pomeroy, for allowing me to range so widely in the pages of his magazine. Occasional readers, such as John Joy and Susan Felsberg, prevented too many errors from slipping into the public eye, and I also owe a debt of thanks to the numerous people who allowed me to interview them on various subjects. Above all, I wish to thank Elizabeth and the late Francis Penashue, and all the Penashue offspring, including the grandchildren, for the experiences they shared with me for more than a decade. Their kindness, thoughtfulness, and generosity made my stay in Labrador emotionally and intellectually rich and satisfying.

LIFE ON THE COAST

Old Smoker: A Labrador Ghost Rider

One of the favourite ghost stories on the Labrador coast concerns a spectre called Old Smoker, a spirit who is known throughout Labrador. Whenever there is a snowstorm, Old Smoker is said to be out with his dog team, ready to lead any lost soul to safety. Once the traveller is safe, Smoker disappears and leaves no track or trace of his komatik or team.

Accounts of the appearance of Old Smoker come from all parts of Labrador, and even the Northern Peninsula of Newfoundland. He's appeared in Bluff Head, Rigolet, Ticoralak, Cartwright, Lodge Bay, Frenchman's Island, Open Bay, Battle Harbour, Partridge Bay, Black Bird Bay, Swile Cove, Diver Tickle, and elsewhere. Some believe that these appearances are all the same figure, while James Burdett asserts that many Smokers haunt our shores.

There are a number of theories about the origin of the name "Smoker." John C. Kennedy posits that the origins of Old Smoker lore may be related to the Newfoundland and Labrador lexicon, in which wind-driven rain or snow is said to "smoke." He also suggests that the legend of Old Smoker "resembles Stith Thompson's motif of a person transformed," like the devil who disappears in a puff of smoke.

John E. Hood, writing in *Legends of Newfoundland and Labrador*, claims that "smoke" is also a local name for moonshine, so the person who made moonshine was called Old Smoker. Storyteller Dale Jarvis says that "smoke" was "a deadly concoction" of spruce cones, yeast, and sugar.

The most likely origin of the name is that it is derived from a man by that name. James Smoker, an Inuk, was listed in the census for Reed Brook compiled by Battle Harbour's Anglican minister George Hutchinson Reed in the winter of 1863/4. Smoker resided there with a family of eight, and his descendants were still around into the 20th century.

One of the most famous stories of Old Smoker, told by Tommy Davis, relates how James Smoker's daughter Jane had a racket with her husband, John Dyson, one day. To cool off, Jane "went to sit out on the chopping block for a while." Those inside the house heard a dog team drive up and stop before going on, and that was the last they heard of Aunt Jane for the rest of the day. She walked into the house just before dark and claimed that she had gone for a dog-team ride to Battle Harbour with her father. Battle Harbour was a good hundred kilometres from Open Bay, and her father had been dead for years.

Printmaker Bill Richie is one of a number of artists who has tried to capture the elusive image of Old Smoker. His large watercolour "Ghost Trail of the White Eskimo," which is displayed in the outer waiting room of the provincial courthouse in Happy Valley-Goose Bay, depicts the ghost as a man dressed in white, sitting sideways on his komatik, with a pipe in his mouth, literally smoking. Background information from The Rooms Provincial Art Gallery further identifies the picture as a "colour graphic of a scene from the legend of Smoker Gillingham."

Gillingham, like James Smoker, was a real man and can be traced through the census as well as the court records. Gillingham came across the Strait from Newfoundland in the 1930s to set up as a trapper but soon got in trouble for breaches of the game laws and for liquor infractions. How Gillingham came to be known as the White Eskimo is a matter of debate.

Like "smoker," the phrase "white Eskimo" has several possible meanings. Some, like Harold Horwood, believe the name referred to Gillingham's ability to live like an Inuk, but others suggest it related to Gillingham's white clothes, komatik, and dogs. Jarvis claimed that even his moonshine keg was white, so he was nearly invisible in the snow. When the Rangers tried to chase Gillingham while he was making his moonshine deliveries, "it was like chasing a ghost."

Although Horwood's novel *White Eskimo* paints a portrait of Gillingham as a heroic figure, Hayward Haynes of Nain knew Gillingham and said he was a "dude"—a city slicker who didn't know how to survive in the bush—and that "lots of times people had to help him out."

Rev. F.W. Peacock, who also knew Gillingham, suggests he was a more complex personality. Peacock depicts Gillingham as lustful, quick to anger, and overly fond of drinking but a capable hunter and traveller and "always gentle and kind to children." Jim Saunders, who was along when the Ranger Frank Mercer went to arrest Gillingham for the murder of Mark Kennitok, claimed that Gillingham had been a policeman himself once and that he "respected the uniform and he went with Mercer, no trouble at all."

Gillingham, like many doomed to haunt this earth after death, came to a sticky end. Legend has it that, possibly addled by his own moonshine, he fell off a fish flake, broke his back, and lingered in agony for three days. John Hood claims that his last words were "Lordy, Lordy, God! I don't want to go to hell. Let me drive my dogs along the coast to the end of time. I'll make up for all the bad I've done."

This deathbed redemption would certainly explain why a fox poisoner, bootlegger, and murderer would be a helpful ghost, leading the lost to safety, rather than a malevolent ghost, scaring people to death.

The story of Old Smoker greatly resembles a well-known American legend about a cowboy who "has a vision of red-eyed, steel-hooved cattle ... being chased by the spirits of damned cowboys." Lyricist Stan Jones heard the story when he was a boy, and in 1948 he composed the famous song "Ghost Riders in the Sky," which urges, "Cowboy better change your ways or with us you will ride, / Trying to catch the devil's herd across the endless skies."

In more recent times, the mythic, horse-mounted cowboy has morphed into the vigilante Johnny Blade, a spectral stunt motorcyclist played by Nicholas Cage in the film *Ghost Rider*. Labradorians have, to some extent, modernized Old Smoker too, though his transportation is more suited to the Labrador landscape than a motorcycle would be.

Uncle George Oliver claimed that the reason Old Smoker isn't seen as often in modern times is that "the old bugger got a Ski-Doo and he don't know how to drive it." Singer John O. Heard, in his ballad "Wreck of the Two-Five-O," suggests that Smoker had taken to driving an Arctic Cat: "But he's not the man he used to be, / Since the government put 'en on U.I.C."

Whether his preferred mode of transportation is a dog team or a Ski-Doo, Old Smoker is still occasionally seen, and frequently invoked to keep restless young travellers close to home when the weather threatens. Whoever he is, Old Smoker is still doing penance out in the Labrador wilderness and is the kind of ghost we look forward to seeing.

Fiddle Making in Labrador: A Historical Look

Memorial University School of Music's 2011 tour of "Choral Traditions of the Labrador Inuit," dedicated to the memory of Uncle Jim Andersen of Makkovik, has brought attention to the central part the fiddle has played in the musical traditions of Labrador. It is well known that the Moravian clergy who came to Labrador in the 1770s brought violins and brass instruments to teach their music to Inuit converts. Less well known is the probability that the fiddle actually predated the arrival of the Moravians in the north.

Meteorologist Lucien M. Turner, who spent two years on the Quebec-Labrador Peninsula, from 1882 to 1884, reports that "the only musical instrument [he] observed among these people was a violin of their own manufacture, made, of course, in imitation of those they had seen used by the whites." He goes on to describe it as "made of birch or spruce, and the two strings are of coarse, loosely twisted sinew. The bow has a strip of whalebone in place of horsehair, and is resined with spruce gum. This fiddle is held across the lap when played." Turner bought the instrument in question from its owner and was astonished at "the facility with which she made the various notes on such a crude imitation of a violin."

E.W. Hawkes, who collected artifacts in Labrador for the Geological Survey in 1914, also obtained what he called "a characteristic specimen of an Eskimo 'fiddle' ... a rude box with a square hole in the top, three sinew strings with bridge and tail-piece, and a short bow with a whalebone strip for hair." He recorded that most Inuit fiddles have only one string and opined that this three-stringed one "must be a rude imitation of 'fiddles' seen on whaling ships." Richard Harrington, in the 1950s, photographed an ingenious fiddler in Hudson's Bay who had made his instrument from a large ham tin.

In the 1970s, anthropologist Eugene Arima looked at a dozen museum examples of the Inuit fiddle from the Eastern Canadian Arctic and came to the same conclusions as previous visitors, that "the form was a result of early European contact and a case of cultural diffusion rather than independent invention."

More recent work by Dr. Beverly Diamond, however, suggests it is quite possible that the Inuit invented the *tautirut*, or Inuit fiddle. While similar to a zither found among the Sami of Finland and the three-stringed "fidla" of the Orkney Islands, the *tautirut* is not directly descended from either and may well be an Inuit invention. Diamond argues that most cultures that used the bow and arrow for hunting quickly discovered that these implements were capable of producing sounds as well as providing dinner.

Labrador's love affair with the European violin may have been rooted in the traditional *tautirut*, but it certainly took hold with the introduction of European fiddles. Rev. William Peacock reports that in 1821, Moravian Brethren began to train two Inuit violinists at Hebron, and from that time on, "stringed instruments became an integral part of the Church worship." He added that although the first two fiddlers were taught by Moravian musicians, subsequent violinists were taught by their fellow Inuit, and this tradition of Inuk teaching Inuk to play stringed instruments continued.

According to Dr. Hans Rollmann, violins were regularly donated to the Labrador missions and were also for sale in the Moravian stores, which may account for the fact that a tradition of European-style violin-making did not take root locally. Herman Onalik, who lived near Nutak, used wood from cigar boxes and spruce he found himself to fashion violins, the tone of which, according to Peacock, "although perhaps not equal to that of factory made instruments, was acceptable and pleasant." None of Onalik's violins have been known to survive.

Fiddles brought in to assist in producing church music were often considered inappropriate for purely recreational use, and this may have stimulated a limited production of local violins. According to Marion R. Hardy, writing in *Them Days* from her mother's papers, by 1893 there were five violinists in Red Bay capable of playing accompaniments to church music and Temperance meetings, but "the violins were for the church use and not to be played for dances." However, some of the Red Bay fiddlers "made their own instruments from a pattern," and at least one of those violins survived.

Herb Brown, who ran the Birches Gallery in Happy Valley, found the back of a violin discarded in an abandoned cabin in Dove Brook in the 1980s, and salvaged it simply because it was so beautiful. The violin appears to be handcrafted, the back hollowed out with a crook knife.

Tommy Davis saved part of the old violin his great-grandfather brought over from England in the early 1800s, and his brother Frank reported that their father, John, a master boatbuilder, made violins also. According to Isaac Dawe, the sound of John Davis's violins "was better than one come from the factory." Frank Davis speculated that a few people began to make violins after they had gone out of fashion, because when most people stopped playing violins, they weren't stocked in the stores any more.

It is a pity that the apparently ample supply of factory-made violins stunted the development of a Labrador tradition of violin-making because Labrador tonewood is particularly suitable for high-quality musical instruments. According to Dr. Ze'ev Gedalof, a geographer at the University of Guelph, luthiers have long known that slower-growing trees make better instruments, and high latitudes, thin soils, and northern aspects contribute to slow growth.

Terry Newman, a tonewood supplier based in Goose Bay, is well aware of the northern advantage when it comes to making violins. His company, Musical Forests Inc., has been harvesting, preparing, and selling tonewoods since 1998. "The Labrador spruce in particular is of a very high quality for use as tonewood, being very tight grained and having a very desirable specific gravity to weight ratio [with] excellent perpendicular and horizontal stiffness," says Newman. "This kind of spruce is very hard to find today in Europe, the USA and other parts of eastern Canada because of centuries of large-scale commercial harvesting, but Labrador was spared such a fate." Newman harvests his wood selectively in winter to reduce the impact on the environment and to maximize the quality of the product.

Along with the tightness of grain, mineral content in the heartwood of trees is important in tonewood. Dr. Gedalof, a mandolin player himself, points out that the mobilization of minerals varies by element, so you have to know local conditions to choose the best harvest time. "One study of beech showed that lead concentrations were actually higher in the heartwood during winter than summer, but the opposite relationship was found for zinc and cadmium," he reports. Newman has found that winter harvesting is best for Labrador tonewoods because the minerals present in the wood move toward the bark between December and the end of January.

Although builders of both Inuit and European fiddles may not have made extensive use of Labrador tonewoods in the past, it is likely that full advantage will be taken of our northern forests in future years. "There are still an ample number of large old growth spruce trees in Labrador," says Newman, "and with a more sensitive approach to harvesting, there may well always be spruce in Labrador suitable for tonewood purposes."

One Pilgrim's Progress in Labrador

Miriam Igloliorte Lyall of Happy Valley-Goose Bay is an avid collector of books and her living room is full of works by and about Labrador. Miriam inherited her collecting bug from her mother, Susie Igloliorte of Hopedale. "My mother was a real 'saver,'" explains Miriam, as she shows off some of the prizes of her collection, inherited from her mother. Books on her shelf include several Inuttut works, including a New Testament, printed for the use of the Moravian Mission in Labrador in 1876, a "Geografi" text published in 1880, and a handwritten, abridged translation of *Pilgrim's Progress*.

Miriam's *Pilgrim's Progress* is an unusual item. Written in brown and blue ink, and hand-bound in cardboard, the text has been decorated with tiny 2-centimetre-high illustrations, similar to the illuminated letters that adorn sacred scrolls and text. There is no indication of who wrote the book, but Miriam's mother received it from her husband, Matteus Igloliorte, who got it from his brother.

The date 1937 is written inside the cover of this fascinating little book, but the work almost certainly predated that time. Several pages have been carefully cut away, and even part of the title page is gone. Back when hunters made their own ammunition, paper was in such short supply that missionaries forbade people from using holy scripture for packing cartridges. However, it wasn't uncommon for desperate hunters to trim excess margins from hymn books and prayer books and to remove the endpapers from any text they could get their hands on. Miriam's book could well predate the Bible and geography text she treasures.

Originally written in 1678 in England, *Pilgrim's Progress* was composed by Rev. John Bunyan while he was in jail for violating the Conventicle Act, which forbade religious dissenters from holding services outside authorized churches. Like all allegories, the characters, setting, and actions make sense on the surface, while also signifying a second level of events and ideas that present a deeper moral problem. Such a work is designed both to entertain and instruct those that read or hear it.

The plot of the story is fairly simple: a man called Christian finds himself troubled by an enormous burden and goes on a quest to rid himself of his heavy pack. His journey takes him through places such as the Slough of Despond, the Hill of Difficulty, and the Valley of the Shadow of Death. On the way he meets characters with names like Pliant, Civility, Legality, and Help, until eventually he reaches the Celestial City and the straps of his burden break and fall away.

Christian's burden is his knowledge of his sins, the people he meets are the personification of Christian concepts, and his journey is the Journey of Life.

Pilgrim's Progress is thought to be the most influential book ever written in the English language. It's unclear when it first came to Labrador, but it was known in Greenland in the early 1800s and was almost certainly known in the oral tradition in Labrador not long after. It was first published in the Labrador Inuit dialect in 1900 in a translation by Rev. Christian Schmitt. A syllabic version, done early in the 19th century by Rev. Maurice Flint, is still in print and is widely known across the Canadian Arctic.

The idea of life as a journey probably appealed to Bunyan, who was a peddler and an itinerant preacher, and it had a similar appeal for missionaries, who were often sojourners far from home. Among the First Nations of central Canada, the story of Handsome Lake, the 18th-century Mohawk prophet, is clearly based on the episodic structure of *Pilgrim's Progress*.

According to Dr. Hans Rollmann, after Labrador Inuit began adopting surnames in 1893, Bishop Martin reported that "one Inuk started calling himself 'Ingergajok,' meaning 'Traveller,' since he identified strongly with the biblical notion of being a pilgrim without permanent habitation on this Earth." The figure of the pilgrim had particular relevance for people from a nomadic hunting and gathering society.

Rev. Michael Gardiner, who served at St. Jude's Anglican Church in Iqaluit for many years, reported that, in the 1980s, Flint's translation of *Pilgrim's Progress* had modest but constant sales among his congregation and was frequently quoted and discussed in church. The late Rev. Francis Buckle thought that "students who had attended the IGA school in Cartwright—including young people from the Frenchman's Island to West Bay—would be somewhat familiar with the book, especially older folk." When Buckle wrote his autobiography in 2010, he called it *One Pilgrim's Journey*.

Bunyan claimed that the story of Christian the Pilgrim came to him in a dream, a dream of freedom of the soul, not the body. The dream vision probably had great appeal to the early Inuit Christians, as it did to people around the world. The detail of *Pilgrim's Progress* is specific to 17th-century England, but the larger design of the work is universal, accommodating any culture.

More than three centuries after it was written, *Pilgrim's Progress* is available in over 200 languages. It has been adapted as an opera and a radio drama, is the basis of numerous films, has been put to popular music, and has been abridged and condensed for children. Versions of it are available as a computer game, a graphic novel, and a Classic comic. It has appeared as a narrative tone poem for solo organ and as a story told in words of one syllable. At its most popular, the only book that outsold *Pilgrim's Progress* was the Bible itself.

Of all the versions of *Pilgrim's Progress* that exist in libraries and collections around the world, Miriam Lyall's version is unique. For Miriam, it connects her to her own direct ancestors, her mother, her father, and their relatives who have passed away, but it also has a more universal importance. Worn and faded, the tiny illustrations of this handwritten book document an ancient culture, a nomadic life of dog teams and igloos, hunting and fur clothing, a life that is far older than the story it tells of one man's journey through this world.

Wooding: The Chore That Warms You Twice

It used to be said that every Labradorian was born with an axe next to his cradle. The axe was necessary to break ice for drinking water, to clear track for travel, to chop holes for winter fishing, and, most important of all, to prepare wood for the fire. Without an axe—be it stone or metal—it would have been impossible to sustain life in this country. Wilfred Grenfell said that the poorest man he ever met in Labrador was one who didn't own an axe.

Back before European settlement became common, Inuit generally used stone lamps and sea mammal fat to heat their igloos, huts, and tents, but the Innu always relied upon wood fireplaces and still use wood in the tin stoves that warm their tents. Many settlers also mitigate the cost of electricity by relying on wood stoves and fireplaces, particularly the newer airtight steel stoves that are so fuel-efficient. Wood stoves mean wood has to be cut and split, and these are skills that have not yet been lost, even to younger men and women.

The history of wooding in Labrador goes back to the early years of settlement. In the 18th century, Captain George Cartwright employed five wooders, who seem to have been the untrained young labourers who supported the work of his coopers, furriers, sealers, and smiths. Wooding could be a very hazardous undertaking, and Cartwright described a wooding trip he supervised in October of 1774, where one man cut his foot with a hatchet, another got lost and spent the night alone miles from the camp, and Cartwright himself suffered an attack of rheumatism. On another occasion a party of Cartwright's wooders broke through the ice in St. Lewis

Bay and nearly drowned, and they seem to have suffered frozen toes regularly. One of his wooders was once snowed into a cabin and could only escape by climbing through the chimney.

Women had a hand in preparing firewood as well. When men were away hunting, it was the women who gathered wood and cut it up to keep the family warm and fed. Grenfell recorded that, in his early days in Labrador, a widow with seven children at Stag Island cut all the wood her family needed to burn through the winter, as well as 3,000 feet of planking, which she sold to feed her children.

Elizabeth Goudie reported that at Mud Lake in the 1930s, they burned about 10 cords of wood between September and April, wood that her husband felled and brought home in July and August but that she cut and split. That's almost 400 cubic metres of wood to be cut and stored before the snow came, while she also had to care for five small children. Her son Horace, the oldest at 10 years of age, helped her with getting the split wood under cover in the woodshed.

Grenfell's memoirs are full of references to axes and firewood because it was difficult to obtain either, and because without wood to heat his hospitals, his work as a medical missionary would have been brought to a halt. The scarcity of coal also meant that wood was often used to fuel the ships on which he held clinics. The staff of the Grenfell Mission had neither the time nor the skill to maintain a good supply of firewood; they obtained it from the people they served, often exchanging it for used winter clothing that had been donated to the mission. Sometimes they paid cash for their firewood and, in the 1930s, Jim Goudie always used to cut a thousand "turns" of wood to sell to the hospital at Mud Lake each spring. A "turn" was as much wood as could be carried by one person at a time, in this case usually a length of tree about 12 feet long.

The Hudson's Bay Company and other fur traders also exchanged goods for firewood supplied by local people, and William Andersen Sr. told *Them Days* magazine that his family also sold wood to the Moravian Mission. Occasionally, the trade went in the other direction, such as when firewood was one of the forms of payment made by Newfoundland fishermen to the Labradorians who looked after their premises over the winter months.

When retired forest technician Louie Montague was a very small boy in the 1940s, his grandfather taught him "how to get wood and what kind of wood to get." In his memoir, *I Never Knowed It Was Hard*, he recalls that when he was a little older, his father bought a gas-powered stationary wood engine, ordered in from Nova Scotia, so that Louie and his brother Russell could hire on to saw wood for other people. "We'd saw the wood down by the shore where it had been boomed home and then people would use the horse and cart [belonging to the Grenfell Mission] to haul the wood up to their house and split and pile it." They were paid by the stick or turn, and the money went to help the family.

As Louie recalls, "Every spring we went to Three Mile Point and cut a thousand sticks of wood for the hospital; everybody did their share, like a sort-of poll tax. We hauled the wood out to the shore and then the Mission took it home in the summer, either towed in booms or loaded in their scow. We did that for years and years, me and Russell and Father." In return, they would get clothes from the Mission clothing store, or milk and eggs in the summer that in winter went to feed the children in the school dormitory.

Wooding was what William Andersen Sr. called one of the four main occupations of self-employment, along with fishing, hunting, and trapping. It was a way of life for men like Louie. "In our school years," Louie said, "we'd come home from school and work at wood and on the weekends, we'd work at wood; we'd go in the wood path over across the lake [Little Lake] in March or so; take the dogs over in boat, take them in the wood path to haul the wood out to the water edge to be boomed home in August, then load the dogs in the boat and bring them home again. It was hard work, the komatik bogging down, taking dogs back and forth. Father made sure we worked."

Today, with electric heat in most homes and gasoline-fuelled generators in winter cabins, the need for enormous stacks of firewood has been reduced, but Labradorians still love the heat of a properly fired wood stove. Elder Jim Learning recalls that he was about 12 or so when he began cutting wood. "I was a skinny little kid, so maybe I was a bit older than usual," he explains. "You start out carrying wood, then you pick up an axe one day and begin splitting it, and then you go out cutting trees. And there were no Ski-Doos or chainsaws," he adds. "It was all done with dog team and an axe." Wood was cut in the fall, and stacked into teepees to dry for the following winter, so there was always two seasons' of wood on hand.

Wood was essential to the Learning household when Jim was growing up as the eldest of nine children. "We had an oil stove for heat, but a woodstove for cooking. Mother made bread twice a week, and through experience she was able to get a good even heat for the hour needed to bake it. I guess she was making bread from when she was seven years old."

When asked what type of wood he favours, Learning is quick to answer. "Spruce is best. It's predictable, manageable with an axe." Fir and poplar? "Don't waste your time," he responds. "They burn like paper, a quick heat that doesn't last." Birch is nice, he concedes, but it's hard to split and full of knots. Tamarack is good but rare. Spruce that had been through a forest fire is best of all, hard and dry and burning evenly, perfect for making bread.

Learning cuts his wood in winter, around the margins of a large marsh, going in from the edge and working his way out so that he doesn't leave a mess. He used to stack his poles into teepees to dry for the winter, but at his home near Otter Creek, the ground is unstable and his stacks fell down. Now he has a platform to stack and dry his wood. He enjoys the work and says it keeps him busy. Cutting wood is different now with chainsaws and multi-vented airtight stoves, Learning explains. "In the old, leaky stoves, you always had to have two junks, one to keep the other going. With the new stoves, you can burn just one big junk—you don't even have to split the wood now."

The secondary combustion of smoke in the new generation of wood stoves means that if fed properly seasoned wood, there is less ash to clean up, no creosote buildup, and the labour of cutting and stacking fuel is halved. Furthermore, heating with wood can be up to six times cheaper than burning oil or gas, and it is considerably safer. Today, Labradorians can enjoy the pleasure of wood heat without the hard work that it once entailed, although as Henry David Thoreau noted more than a century ago, it still warms you twice—once when you cut it and again when you burn it.

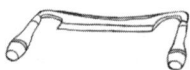

Labrador Christmas Trees

In a land bursting with evergreens, the Christmas tree holds pride of place in the homes, schools, and other institutions of Labrador once December rolls around. However, the phrase "Christmas tree" has special meaning in Labrador, where it is applied to three related but different traditions.

It has often been suggested that Wilfred Grenfell introduced Christmas trees into Labrador. According to an article by D.W.S. Ryan, it was 1905 when "Sir Wilfred Grenfell brought Santa Claus and the Christmas tree to northern Newfoundland and Labrador." Grenfell also claimed that "Christmas Day in Labrador was very little different from any other day in the year." These claims are at best exaggerations.

With regard to feasting and church services, Christmas in Labrador was celebrated much as it was in Newfoundland but there were few Christmas trees in Newfoundland until the 1930s, while the tree was a cherished tradition on the north coast of Labrador long before that.

Florence Grant Barbour of Blanc-Sablon, whose family wintered in Trinity, Newfoundland, in the early 1900s, recalled, "We did not have a Christmas tree [in Newfoundland]. It was not the custom in that day." Gladys Stone Ivany, who was born in Random Island in 1906, told her niece Patricia Pike that the first Christmas tree in her childhood home was erected in 1910. Sheila Hynes of Port Hope Simpson, who grew up in Newfoundland, reports that they had no Christmas tree at their Twillingate home in the 1920s, although she saw one at the school in Bluff Head once she moved to Labrador.

For many Newfoundland families it was the Americans who made Christmas trees popular in the 1940s. However, the decorated Christmas tree had been introduced into Labrador more than a century earlier by the Moravian missionaries, who brought the custom from Germany prior to its being popularized in England by Prince Albert in the 1840s. In archives in Labrador and Germany, there are literally dozens of historic photographs of Christmas trees in Labrador Inuit homes and Moravian churches, schools, and mission houses taken in the 19th century.

These trees were decorated with handmade ornaments but also with glass balls (or what Rosie Ford of Nain called "Christmas bubbles"). These glass ornaments were imported from Germany by the missionaries. H.G. Schneider, writing about Christmas trade at Hebron in the 1880s, describes seal oil and fox furs being traded for soap, tobacco, and flour as well as "coloured paper and many glittering decorations for the Christmas tree."

In Labrador, glass Christmas ornaments were greatly treasured family heirlooms. Rev. Peacock recalled that, when he lived in Nain, the Inuit families would decorate their trees with "glass baubles that had been in the family for four generations."

According to all accounts, every house in each Inuit community and many on Labrador's south coast had a tree, and there were also trees in the schools and churches. Homemade decorations were cherished, and many of these ornaments are still favoured today in Labrador homes. Thorwald Perrault had a homemade eight-sided star from the 1880s which he was still using a century later.

Traditional ornaments could be as complex as the Moravian star or as simple as the wings, feet, and tail feathers of a ptarmigan. Robin Goodfellow-Baikie recalls that her trapper husband, Vivan, would take a quill from an eagle or raven and blow up the bird crops to use as ornaments, and often even hung the heads of the partridge on the tree.

Miniature mitts and boots, redberries or dogberries strung on thread, stars made from cigarette or chocolate-bar foil, and whitewashed tree cones were all common. Anything that glittered would be saved for the tree, including bullet casings, fur tags, and cellophane candy wrappers. In later years, staples from milk bottle tops were saved and looped into chains, and egg cartons were cut and painted to make bells. The tin strips and keys from bully-beef cans were cleaned and pulled out into spirals to hang on the tree.

Some Christmas ornaments acknowledged special occasions. Peacock recalls that one householder in Nain hung a dried fish on the tree, "the first caught by a small girl in the family." Often, "dolls would be positioned under the tree and at the end of the holiday they would be put away until the following year."

According to nurse Millicent Blake Loder, in Hopedale in the 1940s, these "boughten" and homemade ornaments would be supplemented with "home-made cookies, ribbon bows and small candles which were lit at night and carefully watched."

While she was in Hopedale, Loder was also introduced to the second type of Labrador Christmas tree, the Advent tree, a Moravian tradition unknown on the island portion of the province. The Advent tree, as described by Sharon Edmunds, is a small tree, 2 or 3 feet high, which is collected by the eldest child in the family on the day before Advent Sunday. The tree was decorated and the following day the child would find a few small treats and gifts under it.

Children would also give small Advent trees to their godmothers, grandmothers, or midwives. According to Loder, each child she had delivered "would bring a little tree with a gift on it: a pair of slippers, a partridge, or a pack of cookies." After seven years of delivering babies, she said her living room "looked like a tiny forest at Christmas."

Sybella Nitsman of Paul's Island said children would give the midwife who delivered them "little trees with the tops covered with candies, matches, and homemade gifts." Suzie Pottle of Rigolet told *Them Days* magazine that "[w]e'd tie grandmother's parcels to a little tree and take them up to her." Edmunds says that the custom of giving an Advent tree to your "old woman" was common up until the 1960s, but "in recent years, no more than a few people practice the tradition."

The third type of Labrador Christmas tree is an organized party, called simply a Christmas Tree, at which presents are given to all the children of the community. Wilfred Grenfell introduced the practice of holding Christmas Trees to northern Newfoundland and parts of the Labrador coast, but it was already a common occurrence on the north coast.

Early Moravian records document the community gift-giving, and Doris Peacock, who moved to Nain in the 1930s, said there were two big trees in the church at Christmas, but that "a third tree was brought in on Christmas Eve, decorated with presents for all the children ... The Christmas tree was fitted into a stand which was wound up and rotated, turning the tree around gradually as it played a tune like a musical box."

Grenfell was known as a huge advocate of Christmas and he often liked to play the part of the jolly elf himself. In his account of "How Santa Claus Came to Cape St. Anthony," he describes his first Christmas Tree party. Naturally, he had to work it into a story about a desperately injured boy, a life-saving journey, and a last-minute appearance by "Sandy Claws," designed to wring the heartstrings and loosen the purse strings of his wealthy donors in America. After that, Christmas Trees were held in dozens of communities on the Northern Peninsula, organized by the doctors and nurses of the Mission.

Grenfell would have had the world believe that "few of the children here had ever possessed a toy, and there was scarcely a single girl that owned a doll." The presents at the Grenfell Christmas Trees were often second-hand toys donated to the Grenfell Mission. It was Grenfell's habit to exaggerate the poverty in Labrador in order to increase donations, and while it was true that some people were in dire need up until World War II, things were never quite so bad as the good doctor suggested.

Lydia Campbell, writing of her childhood in the 1830s, recalled the snow sleds and "pretty snowshoes" and deerskin shoes "all painted so pretty" that her father bought from the Innu for her and her sisters at Christmas time. An article in *The Evening Telegram*, by a writer identified only by the initials L.A.W., says that, in 1887, there were "no shops or stores near in this part of the world, so the presents and keep-sakes, little tokens of love and friendship, must be made by their own fair fingers, and as they are not to be seen by the owners till the Christmas morning, it requires some little maneuvering to keep them out of sight."

While many Labrador children may have lived lives devoid of "boughten" toys, most remember fondly the toys that were made for them by doting parents and other adults. Louie Montague, in his memoir *I Never Knowed It Was Hard*, recorded that into his 80s, he continued to make "toys similar to those he received as a child," including spin tops, windmills, bows and arrows, slingshots, and spinning buttons. Louie also made carved wooden ornaments which were very popular at Christmas time—miniature snowshoes, paddles, kamiks, and other objects suitable for the tree. These would be similar to the "tokens of love and friendship" referred to by L.A.W.

During World War II and after, the Allies provided toys to children in Labrador through an organized Christmas Toy Drop. Today, Air Labrador and Rotary sponsor a program called Santa to the Coast, so the spirit of the Grenfell Christmas Trees continues. The boughten pocket knives, pennywhistles, and rag dolls have been replaced by video games and Barbies, but they come as supplements to the simple wooden toys and ornaments that decorate the Christmas trees of Labrador, not as substitutes.

JUSTICE

Above the Law: Grenfell's Magistracy in Labrador

Tom Marshall, as Minister of Justice and Attorney General, wrote in 2005 that the law "reflects and helps shape the society out of which it springs," so that although the history of Labrador is tied to that of the island portion of the province, Labrador has "from earliest times had its own unique legal traditions."

For thousands of years, Labrador's Aboriginal people had their own systems of dispute resolution, which involved everything from song duels and head-butting matches to shunning, banishment, and even execution. European-style justice wasn't introduced until the 18th century, when the British government gave the governor of Newfoundland the authority to appoint justices of the peace and surrogate judges. The surrogate judges were usually captains of naval vessels, such as Captain Thomas Adams of the sloop *Niger* who was appointed in Labrador in 1765. Justices of the peace were often commanders of forts, such as Alexander Ged of York Fort who was appointed in 1771.

According to historian Hans Rollmann, the 1769 Order in Council that permitted Moravian missionaries to establish themselves in Labrador also permitted them to become justices of the peace, "a right which they never practiced since they did not want to sit in judgement on their fellow Inuit brothers and sisters."

Because of the size of the district, and its sparse population, there wasn't a lot of work for judges in Labrador, except in the summer months, when thousands of Newfoundland fishermen flooded onto the coast, so the Labrador courts were discontinuous and there was no resident judge in Labrador until Confederation with Canada.

Although there were no sitting judges, there were justices of the peace who could issue warrants of arrest, administer oaths, try civil cases, and hold courts of record. There were also magistrates who dealt with lesser crimes such as assault, battery, larceny, and embezzlement. Magistrates could not try cases of rape or murder, but they could impose fines of up to $100 and imprison offenders for up to six months. Two or more justices of the peace, sitting together, had the same powers. Justices of the peace and magistrates were allowed to retain part or all the income from fines as recompense for their work.

Justices of the peace and magistrates were usually drawn from the educated classes of European heritage, such as missionaries, doctors, Hudson's Bay traders, and teachers. Aboriginal justice workers were unknown in Labrador until the appointment of Jerry Sillett, who was sworn in as a justice of the peace in the church at Nain in 1968. Jim Igloliorte was later appointed as a lay magistrate and became the first Aboriginal provincial court judge in 1981.

While missionaries like Rev. Henry Gordon tended to do their work quietly and without fanfare, medical missionary Wilfred Grenfell was anything but shy about his judicial work. As with his medical practice, he mined his court experience for stories to promote his mission and himself.

Appointed first as a justice of the peace in 1899, and later made a magistrate, Grenfell used his legal position with two ends in mind—eliminating the sale of liquor on the coast and raising funds to support his numerous enterprises. He did the first by refusing liquor licences and prosecuting bootleggers, and the second by acting as agent for the shipping insurers Lloyd's of London.

The liquor trade was Grenfell's key target in court. In the 1890s when Grenfell first arrived, Labrador was legally dry, but homebrew and stills for making moonshine were common. According to J. Lennox Kerr, Grenfell "asked that law officers be sent to the coast during the fishing season," and one magistrate was stationed at Cartwright, but "he was known to be a drunkard and of little value." Therefore, once authorized as a justice of the peace, Grenfell did not hesitate to use his authority to suppress the production and sale of alcohol.

Any biography of Grenfell will confirm that he was a devout teetotaller, and most mention that he "sought out and prosecuted mercilessly those traders who carried and sold drink." In his autobiography, Grenfell wrote that he hated the liquor traffic "with a loathing of [his] soul." He called alcohol the "curse which is throttling England," a "glaring demon in [their] midst." Grenfell recognized the right of a man to "degrade his body with swallowing alcohol," but believed he did not have a right to "lure others to their destruction for money." Not surprisingly, he often used his judicial position to pursue vengeance upon liquor traders.

Fullerton L. Waldo, writing in 1920, described Grenfell's judicial decisions as "luminous with a Lincolnian light of acumen and sympathy," but few modern justices would wish to emulate his methods. Grenfell disdained red tape and let "the jot and the tittle ... take care of themselves." Furthermore, he claimed that "a man's own soul is a matter more important than an ordinance," so if he judged the law inadequate, he simply ignored it. Grenfell himself wrote that "even if the judgements arrived at had been rather more equitable than legal, yet disputes had been ended, wrong-doing punished, and the weak had been time and again helped to get right done them." Grenfell believed that he was better able to establish what was right and what was wrong than those who drafted the laws.

W.R. Moody, writing about a charge laid by Grenfell in 1905, noted that a constable sent to assist him used the excuse of serving a warrant to illegally search the house of a fisherman while the owner was on board the *Strathcona*, appearing before the court. When the irate man found out, he returned to the *Strathcona* to complain, and was rearrested. The charges were eventually dismissed, but no doubt the constable was following orders on this and other occasions in service to Grenfell's war against liquor. There would have been very little recourse in those days for a fisherman who defied the magistrate or the constabulary.

Grenfell's stand on barratry, or the wrecking of ships for their insurance, was equally above the law. As early as 1893, the famous ship insurers Lloyd's had asked Grenfell to act as their agent in Labrador, but the Mission Council disapproved on the grounds that this might put them in conflict with the fishermen they were mandated to serve. However, in November of 1902, when the barquentine *Bessie Dodd* was reported as wrecked at the entrance to Hamilton Inlet, and sold as a total loss for $80, Lloyd's contacted him again to investigate the situation on their behalf. In fact, as Grenfell soon determined, the ship had run aground on a flat, sandy beach less than 150 feet from the wharf and the only damage to her was a broken steerage chain.

The ship and cargo were insured for a total of $35,000, and it was obvious that, for her size, she was unable to carry the amount of cargo that was listed on the bill of lading. The *Bessie Dodd* was taken back to St. John's, and, according to Kerr, upon arrival Grenfell charged her skipper, George C. Jerrett, with barratry. What followed was a highly publicized trial, with both the captain and owner going before the Supreme Court.

The proceedings were given broad newspaper coverage and over 1,000 spectators were on hand for the sentencing. Suzanne Sexty, who reconstructed the case from newspaper accounts, wrote that "the judgement noted that there were a number of heavily insured foreign-going ships frequenting the coast of Labrador where the remoteness of the locality made the risk of detection of a crime comparatively slight." The defendants were sentenced to four years' hard labour in the penitentiary in St. John's.

According to Kerr, Grenfell's prosecution of the *Bessie Dodd* case drew the ire of local merchants, who felt Grenfell was profiting from his threefold work as trader, magistrate, and doctor, but the result for Grenfell was all good. He was paid by the insurers, who also presented him with a gold watch and an appointment as a Lloyd's agent. Further, he got the kind of publicity he always craved, and he "was more pleased at having removed Jewett from the coast, for the trader had been selling liquor, and Grenfell had long tried to get proof of this."

Although the court records from Grenfell's cases appear not to have survived, incidents of barratry in particular tended to make the newspapers, as was the case of the *Violet M.*, which sank off Englee in 1901, insured for $3,900 by Union Marine. Grenfell convinced one of the crew to turn witness, and the owner, Samuel Moulton, was sentenced to two years in the penitentiary.

Grenfell also intervened in the case of the schooner *Kimberly*, on her way to Mud Lake with Salba Dominic, a Lebanese trader, in 1907. The crew of the tug *Ethel Jean*, of the Grand River Pulp and Lumber Company, took possession of her cargo, much to the dismay of the trader, who claimed the goods weren't salvage. Grenfell apparently ruled in favour of the *Ethel Jean*, forcing the trader to go to St. John's to find a lawyer to help him retrieve his goods. Since traders often carried alcohol as well as household items, Grenfell would have been more than willing to prosecute on very thin evidence. Susan Felsberg recalls that the Mud Lake women "were roped in to launder the wet clothing inventory from the wreck." Pieces of the *Ethel Jean* remain on the shores of Mud Lake to this day.

Although the illegal possession and sale of alcohol and insurance fraud took up much of Grenfell's court time, other problems came before him as a magistrate, usually ones connected to fishing. In 1905, two parties at Indian Harbour claimed exclusive ownership of a bawn; Grenfell divided it between the two disputants. Disagreements over the possession of trap berths were common and sometimes even led to assault charges, which Grenfell had to resolve. Domestic assaults occasionally came before him, and in one case the guilty husband was sentenced to cut 1,000 turns of wood for the church at Makkovik. The husband cut the wood, but made his wife carry it from the woods to the landwash.

It has been said that Grenfell frequently overstepped his authority in his actions as a magistrate. A small book by professor of theology Jerome Davis, who worked for Grenfell in the summer of 1917, recounts how Grenfell sent Davis to arrest a man accused of rape, "a great big six-foot-three fisherman with powerful muscles." Rape was one of the crimes that magistrates were not allowed to try; his authority was to lay the charge and send the man to St. John's. Instead, Davis and the accused boarded the *Strathcona*, where Davis "acted as court stenographer and took down the proceedings of the trial." The man was convicted and placed on probation, the most Grenfell could do to punish him, as there was no correctional institution in Labrador at that time.

Although judges travelled regularly to Labrador or were resident there after Confederation, justices of the peace were still available to the public into the 1990s. A notice in the *Labradorian* in April of 1976 identified four justices of the peace in the Happy Valley-Goose Bay area: Garfield Warren, Aubrey Battcock, Harold Ford, and Jim Kelland. There were also justices of the peace in many of the coastal communities. Today, government policy is to limit the appointment of justices of the peace to personnel in the Supreme and Provincial Courts of the province. Marriage commissioners have been created to provide services in this one area.

Holding court in stages and on board ships as Grenfell did sounds romantic, but it was rough justice and not always equitable or even legal. Today, the administration of justice in Labrador has been put on a much more professional footing than in Grenfell's time. Magistrates who were sitting when the law changed were upgraded to judges, and those judges who did not have law degrees were given the opportunity to go to law school. There are now permanent Provincial and Supreme Courts in Happy Valley-Goose Bay and a Provincial Court in Wabush. All the judges travel on circuit to smaller communities, bringing justice to the people, justice that is not only done but is seen to be done.

The Newfoundland Ranger Force in Labrador

In 1932, burdened by war debt and operating under the restrictions of the Commission of Government, a new police force modelled on the Royal Canadian Mounted Police was proposed for Newfoundland and Labrador. The aim of the Newfoundland Ranger Force was to increase the efficiency of the Royal Newfoundland Constabulary, who would continue to operate in the larger towns, and to provide better service from smaller communities in more rural areas, including Labrador, which was where the first six Ranger detachments were established. Three years later, the Ranger Force was up and running, with from 51 to 72 members, trained, uniformed, and hard at work for the next 15 years.

The all-male Rangers were exceptionally educated peacekeepers; they had to have a minimum of a Grade 11 education (high for the time) and be in top physical condition. The Rangers attracted highly qualified recruits, in part by stressing their association with the Mounties, but also with the Royal Newfoundland Regiment, borrowing their crest and hiring as first head Ranger Leonard B. Stick, a veteran of Gallipoli and Beaumont Hamel.

Rangers administered not just justice but social services as well. Their responsibilities included acting as game wardens, collecting customs and other fees, acting as wreck commissioners, inspecting logging camps, fighting forest fires, issuing relief payments, arranging medical treatment, escorting mental patients to hospital, enforcing criminal law, acting as deputy sheriffs, and supervising the maintenance and construction of public roads, wharves, and breakwaters. They also investigated suspicious deaths and fires, acted as truancy officers, and organized adult education programs, and in the case of accidents, took charge of rescue and recovery efforts. They were often called upon to administer emergency medical treatment such as pulling teeth and delivering babies.

All these extra duties meant that the Rangers came under the jurisdiction of the Department of Natural Resources rather than the Department of Justice, with responsibility for reporting (in writing) to six different government departments. This was why the entry qualifications demanded such a high level of education. A Ranger needed to be exceptionally fit, but he also needed to be highly literate and articulate. Given the difficulty of bringing offences before a court in Labrador, Rangers tried to deal with most problems without criminal prosecution, but, when necessary, they took cases to a magistrate and then acted as crown prosecutor and court reporter.

Once World War II started, the Rangers were declared an essential service so that they could not resign to join the military; thereafter, they became recruiters for the army, located and returned deserters, enforced rationing and blackout orders, and reported on enemy submarines and aircraft along the coasts. Rangers were expected to attend public meetings and report what was discussed to the appropriate commissioners and, when the Confederation referenda were held in 1947, they operated the polling stations.

Labrador initially had five established detachments, which eventually became nine, as communities consolidated or relocated. Larger communities were more likely to be assigned detachments. Of 204 Rangers in the whole country, at least 46 served in Labrador at some point in their careers. The busiest stations were Nain, Hopedale, and Battle Harbour, and the six Rangers who served in three or more Labrador detachments were Frank Mercer, Walter Rockwood, Gladstone Guzzwell, John Howard, William Mullally, and Earl Brazil. Brazil, the only Labrador-born Ranger, had been born at Battle Harbour.

One of the chief duties of the Rangers throughout the country was the issuance of welfare, the despised but coveted "dole." Rangers determined eligibility for the 6 cents a day able-bodied relief, a responsibility that weighed heavily on almost all the men forced to make the decision to refuse or cut off payments to families that were on the verge of starvation. When the Department of Public Health and Welfare ordered that able-bodied relief not be issued during summer months, regardless of the actual circumstances, some Rangers refused to comply. A Ranger in one community was threatened with being fired for issuing dole, and another was told that since he had issued relief contrary to orders, he would be held personally responsible to repay the money. Many others were reprimanded for refusing to follow orders to deny dole, but none were actually dismissed for refusing to obey orders.

The issuance of relief in Labrador was a particularly complex circumstance. When the Ranger Force took up work in Labrador in 1935, relief for Inuit was generally left in the control of the Moravian missionaries, while Innu dole eligibility was in the hands of Father Edward O'Brien. Since the Moravians relied on Inuit parishioners for locally available supplies for the Mission itself (wood, labour in the gardens, fresh game and fish), they were well aware of the availability of food and other necessary provisions, but they were also able to call on financial assistance from overseas for their congregants.

The Innu, unfortunately, were not in the same situation. Although Rangers had by then established detachments throughout Labrador, Innu relief remained the responsibility of Father O'Brien. Unusual weather conditions in 1937 were such that, by 1938, several large groups of Innu were starving but receiving no relief. When O'Brien, who wintered in Carbonear, inquired of the Rangers whether rumours of starvation were true, he was assured that the condition of the Innu was fine. However, a Ranger had mistakenly sent Innu in his area on to Voisey's Bay where, he assured them, there were plenty of caribou. The supplies they were given were inadequate for the trip, but those who refused to go were denied any relief, so most opted to comply. At Voisey's Bay, no work was available, there were no caribou, and relief had not been provided. The Innu hunters and their families turned back to Davis Inlet and arrived in an emaciated condition, for which O'Brien blamed the Rangers.

A guerilla skirmish, played out in the columns of the *Daily*

News, quickly turned the public against the unfortunate Rangers, whom O'Brien described as "nit wits wearing the symbolic dress of authority." In a letter addressed to Hon. J.C. Puddester, commissioner of the Department of Public Health and Welfare, O'Brien described starving children being force-marched in the teeth of a raging blizzard in "a journey of approximately fifty miles," an intolerable hardship under deplorable conditions. A few years later, when an epidemic struck the same group, nobody relied on the Rangers for help—it was a group effort by the Moravians, the Roman Catholics, and the Grenfell medical people that assisted the Innu in stopping the deadly illness from progressing.

The liquor trade was another target of the Ranger Force. Obtaining liquor of any sort was made deliberately difficult in the early 20th century in Labrador. It was against the law to make or sell alcohol, although people did both when they could get their hands on a supply of berries or raisins, and it was illegal for Aboriginal people to consume it. Down on the coast, it was not hard to smuggle liquor in from Quebec, but farther inland or on the north coast, alcohol was generally only available from American fishermen trading over the sides of their boats.

Usually, the Rangers didn't try to push the limits of the law, particularly as some of them enjoyed a snort themselves. Tim Roberts recalled for *Them Days* magazine an occasion when a couple of thirsty Rangers paid his father a visit and bullied him into getting out his jug. When they left, having obtained what they wanted, one Ranger managed to get tangled in drying traplines. When Roberts called out for his father to bring a knife to cut the snared Ranger out, the angry fisherman took a big splitting knife and off came every one of the 13 brass buttons of the Ranger's uniform jacket, "right from the neck to the tail," thereby saving the traps and exacting revenge upon at least one Ranger.

Josh Burdett recalled word getting out that he had been making moonshine from blackberries. Knowing that he was likely to get a visit from the Ranger, his father got a bottle of the wine, replaced half of it with strong tea, and buried the rest of the bottles. When the Ranger tasted something that was more like cold tea than the strong moonshine he was expecting, he was disgusted. It was the last time the Burdetts ever shared wine with anyone, as sooner or later the word would leak out.

Labradorians thought that, like liquor laws, game laws were "made to be broken." During the Depression of the 1930s, the once-prolific caribou herds were decimated by overhunting and disease, and the beaver was almost extinct, so it was hardly surprising that starving people did not hesitate to kill and consume even threatened species. Miriam Hamel reported that when she was a girl in Sandwich Bay, she always got nervous if the Ranger came around when she was preserving seal meat or porpoise, for fear that he might think it was beaver, or bear out of season. Most of the Rangers were unfamiliar with the dark wild meats Labradorians often ate. The Rangers laid wildlife charges but rarely imposed severe fines, because nobody had money to pay them and incarcerating poachers was expensive.

Constable Leslie Chaffey was the first Ranger to reach Labrador, in October of 1935, where he set up the one-man Battle Harbour post. Chaffey arrived at Battle Harbour aboard the *Kyle*, along with two years' worth of provisions and construction materials for a small detachment. Since it was already heading into winter, Chaffey was fortunate to be able to engage a team of five carpenters, who were passing through on their way to another community. They got the building up in three days. Although it was possible for the Ranger to live at the detachment, Battle Harbour Rangers generally boarded with a local family, as the detachment was only equivalent to two small rooms, and according to former Ranger Nathan Penney, with an income of $2 a day the billet money gave a boost to the local economy.

Probably the best known of the Labrador Rangers was Frank Mercer, whose place in history was secured when Harold Horwood fictionalized him in his novel *White Eskimo*. Originally from Bay Roberts, Mercer was 22 when he went north to Labrador on the *Kyle* in 1934. His first posting was Hopedale, after which he moved on to Makkovik, Nain, Hebron, and Cartwright. Later, he retired after serving in three different police forces, and returned to Labrador as Commissioner.

The Rangers and their families were not immune to the troubles that plagued other people in Labrador, including the results of isolation, food shortages, and bad weather. Walter Rockwood and his wife lost their baby son, David, to an epidemic of whooping cough while stationed in Nain in the fall of 1944, and their older boy, Robert, fell into a coma and was medevaced out by the US air force during the same outbreak. Robert recovered but lost his hearing as a result of the illness.

Three Newfoundland Rangers died while on duty, one from falling through the ice, one from a motorcycle accident, and one who got lost on patrol and died of exposure. None were in Labrador, but Corporal John Hogan spent seven weeks in the Labrador bush with an injured companion after bailing out of what they thought was a burning plane on their way from Goose Bay. Other than losing 30 pounds, he was unharmed, surviving on spruce tea, marsh berries, and rabbits he was able to snare.

No doubt some Rangers suffered what today would be identified as post-traumatic stress disorder from dealing with deranged and desperate people during those hard times. Their roles in rescue and recovery were also enormously stressful. The Rangers had to help retrieve the bodies of 147 passengers and crew who died when the SS *Caribou* was torpedoed and sunk by a German submarine in 1942, and in 1946, they had to cope with 27 victims of a Belgian airliner crash. After searching for days to find the crash site, they had to pull the decaying bodies out of trees, and search, identify, and bury them in the heat of summer.

Although five of the first six Rangers originally posted in Labrador had northern experience, and some ran their own dog teams, most of them, and virtually all those who followed, depended a good deal on local drivers and guides. Detachment #6, Battle Harbour, was responsible for the area from Murray Harbour to Charter Bay, including Belle Isle, an enormous geographic area. The Rangers hadn't the time needed to attend to their own dogs and familiarize themselves with the trails. Joe Palliser, Gilbert Saunders, and Rod Williams, among others, were dog-team drivers and guides who often worked for the Rangers. Wallace McLean guided them also, but he was so "ronk" (religiously observant) that he wouldn't take money for bringing the Ranger from North West

River to Happy Valley on a Sunday.

Joe Palliser worked as a driver for the Rangers for five years and had some difficult trips in very foul weather. He used to travel from Bob's Brook to North West River and back, for $2.50 a day, which included the use of his team, his komatik, and his dog's traces. If they were snowed in, his pay dropped to $1.50 a day, but as he said, in those times, "if you could get a job like that you'd manage pretty good."

Today, the Ranger detachment at Battle Harbour is a museum, the only built heritage remaining of the old Force. The Union Jack still flies over the post and visitors can see what a bare bones operation it was. On display are a variety of artifacts and storyboards, as well as a Ranger uniform and Nathan Penney's typewriter. All reports had to be typed in triplicate, and Penney's daughter Mavis explained that each detachment had only one typewriter, which was fine in a one-man detachment such as Battle Harbour. Where more than one man was posted, the typewriter was available according to seniority, so Penney saved his salary to buy exactly the same model, which he took with him when he moved from one posting to another.

Despite the occasional disagreements caused by poaching and alcohol, most of the Rangers were well liked and well regarded in Labrador. They were really the first government representatives most Labradorians had ever dealt with, and people were grateful for the help they received. In return, the Rangers appreciated the assistance they got from the people they served and did their best to represent local problems in a balanced and fair way. It was a case of mutual respect that helped both sides through a very difficult period in our history.

Murder, They Wrote: Early Accounts of Intentional and Unlawful Killings in Labrador

Murder in Labrador is as old as the land itself, but as the sobriquet "The land God gave to Cain" indicates, often as not the murderer escaped to a less desirable place to avoid retribution. In traditional times, the intentional killing of one person by another was often tolerated, depending on the circumstances. Killings and revenge killings abound in the old Inuit legends, and even up to quite modern times, murders often didn't come to the attention of the authorities, though they were often immortalized in the oral tradition.

The history of murder in Labrador is generally thought to begin with the deaths of Moravian missionary John Christian Erhardt and six of his crew in 1752. Although most Europeans at the time would have considered the deaths murder, it's not unlikely a modern jury would find the deaths the result of manslaughter, or even self-defence. Numerous Inuit had by that date been kidnapped by European explorers, and even Augustin le Gardeur de Courtmanche admitted in 1714 that when the Inuit attacked and killed Europeans, "it is only by way of reprisal."

According to E.W. Hawkes, writing in 1916, in cases of the murder of an Inuk, it was traditionally the duty of the relatives to avenge it, but although retribution could be delayed, it was never forgotten. "In the meantime, the murderer may be treated by the relatives of the deceased as if nothing had happened: a situation which is unthinkable to us, but which does not conflict at all with Eskimo ideas."

Ignoring a murderer in one's midst may have been unthinkable to Hawkes in 1916, but prior to that, it was often the only thing a community could do, even when both perpetrator and victim were European. In a 1783 memorandum to the Earl of Dartmouth, proposing that the British government appoint him as governor of Labrador, George Cartwright gave as an example of crimes that went unpunished due to the lack of an appropriate authority a case where "a master drove a sick servant out of his bed to work, and he immediately died as he was turning fish upon the beach." In another instance, "a headman knocked a fellow servant down with a billet of wood and killed him on the spot."

One of the early accounts of Europeans killing one another in Labrador is recorded in what is known as "The Moss Diary." Moss, whose first name does not seem to have survived, was an employee of the Slade Company at Battle Harbour between 1832 and 1837 and during that time he kept a detailed diary in which he recorded weather, work assignments, local news, and other items of interest.

On Sunday, February 26, 1833, Moss recorded that a group of Inuit had arrived with a letter from Timothy Craze, Joseph Bird's agent and manager at Francis Harbour, saying that a crew at Seal Islands had reported that one of their men, Joseph Score, had gotten into an altercation with their cook, John Ellvert, and had murdered him. Apparently, Score had accused the cook of using his hatchet, and when Ellvert denied it, Score had struck him with the weapon, breaking the haft, and then followed up with a blow from another hatchet haft. Ellvert died three hours later.

The real problem for the manager was what to do with the offender, who could not be sent out for arrest and trial until after breakup of the ice in June or July. Mr. Craze had no means of holding him prisoner until then, and Score had no means of escaping. There is no follow-up report of how the dilemma was solved, but more than likely, Craze and the other members of the crew did what Inuit had done in traditional times, which was to give the accused his freedom but to watch him very carefully until there was an appropriate opportunity to take action.

The opportunity arrived that summer when the Labrador Court of Sessions held a circuit on the coast, and according to a transcript made by Augustus Lilly and Christopher Curran, Score was charged, and the sheriff of Labrador was paid 7 shilling for bread and 2 shillings for "a pad lock and staples" so that the prisoner could be confined on board the schooner *Belinda* prior to being taken to St. John's for trial.

According to Lilly and Curran's transcript, the court also had to deal with a case at Chimney Tickle "to inquire into the particulars of a murder said to have been committed at the Camp Islands," where sufficient information was obtained to apprehend John Gallivan on suspicion of having murdered Edmund Cleary; Gallivan was taken into custody and incarcerated on board the *Belinda* with John Score.

Both prisoners were delivered safely to St. John's, where they were tried. John Score was found not guilty of murder but was convicted of manslaughter and sentenced to six months' incarceration. John Gallivan must have also been tried, as there is a report of his being delivered into custody, but all further reports of him have disappeared from the court records.

The year 1833 seems to have been a particularly violent season on the Labrador coast as three men were murdered at Domino that year as well. Joseph Hackett and Thomas Fitzgerald were charged with the wilful murder of Edmund Power, John Brady, and William Fitzgerald. At trial, Fitzgerald was acquitted; Hackett was found guilty and sentenced to death, but sentence was respited or postponed.

In the early days of contact between Aboriginal people and Europeans, the murder of Aboriginal people by their own was not of much concern to the European administrators, but when the victims were of European heritage, it was a different matter. When an Inuk named Pualo killed a European settler, William Reed, and his half Inuit son, in the area of Adlavik Bay south of Makkovik, nothing could be done about it. However, the Moravians considered Pualo "a murderer and a hardened sinner" and refused to have dealings with his family, who were only welcomed into the community after Pualo died in the winter of 1855. In effect, Pualo and his dependents were expelled from the community.

By 1880, the government was sending a small mail steamer along the coast as far as Hopedale, and crimes such as murder were more likely to be confronted. The Moravian Brethren at Hopedale reported that an Inuk by the name of Ephraim had murdered his son-in-law, Philip, and took steps to arrest the man. Ephraim was suspected of having already murdered his first wife by having thrown her over a cliff into the sea, so the community was not surprised when Philip's wife, Nancy, admitted that Ephraim had shot her husband through the head and threatened her if she told.

According to the *Periodical Accounts*, Brother Bourquin led a group to the site of the murder on an offshore island, examined the body, gave it a Christian burial, and when Ephraim refused to accompany them back to the mission, tied his arms with cords to compel him. Ephraim subsequently admitted to the murder of Philip, while maintaining that the death of his first wife was unintentional—he had "held her over a cliff to frighten her, until her jacket gave way, when he tried in vain to save her."

Ephraim's confession did not solve the community's problem; it exacerbated it. As the *Periodical Accounts* put it, "The question as to the disposal of the criminal now came before us with all its perplexities: we could not release him, and in our circumstances it was impossible to keep him in custody all through the winter until the road [the sea] to Newfoundland would be open next." Fortunately, it happened that, despite the lateness of the season, William Bartlett's steam launch at Turnavik West was still active, so the Moravian schooner *Meta* was relaunched and the prisoner conveyed to Captain Bartlett's care.

Ephraim was subsequently tried for the murder of Philip in St. John's, with Brother Bourquin, Nancy, and William Ford travelling down to Newfoundland to testify against him, and he was sentenced to be hanged. According to William Gosling, "the sentence was afterwards commuted to imprisonment for life." Given the conditions of the penitentiary in St. John's at that time, life was not long and Ephraim died while incarcerated, in 1886.

By 1893, murder was being taken much more seriously, especially when it was mass murder. An Inuk known as Thomas Brown was believed to have murdered four members of his family at Benjamin Cove. The fishermen who discovered the bodies sent to Hopedale for the Mission doctor, Eliot Curwen, who determined that they had probably been poisoned with hemlock. Hemlock is common in parts of Labrador and can easily be mistaken for Scotch lovage.

An inquest was held and Brown was eventually arrested, but not for the murders. According to Curwen, "having insufficient evidence to take him on the charge of wife murder they have arrested him on the charge of a doubtful crime that he committed 12 years ago, convicted him and sentenced him to 4 months imprisonment ... in order to take him out of the way for a time; the end aimed at may be all right but the means adopted is unjust."

As was the case of Ephraim, Brown was thought to have murdered his first wife and child, but nothing was done about the matter at the time. However, people remembered, and watched him carefully, and were not surprised when he apparently killed again. Wilfred Grenfell, writing in the Moravian *Periodical Accounts* at the time, claimed that at least five murderers were known to the authorities "from their own confession to the missionaries" and it must "encourage crime when it is known that no attempt whatever will ever be made at punishment." Charging Brown with a lesser offence at least got him out of the community while the process of gathering evidence went on.

Any unexplained or sudden death, especially that of a young woman, will always spark speculation and gossip. Such was the case when Marguerite Lindsay, a summer volunteer with the Muddy Bay boarding school near Cartwright, disappeared on August 4, 1922. Apparently, the 26-year-old woman from Montreal had gone for a walk alone and had not returned when expected. An intensive four-day search turned up nothing, and the case remained a mystery for almost a year. Speculation was that Miss Lindsay had slipped on the shoreline and drowned, her body being pulled out to sea, although there was also talk that the Mission dogs had got out of their pen and torn her to pieces. Rev. Henry Gordon, who wrote an account of the death, seemed more intent on asserting that "foul play was not involved" than in actually answering questions about the circumstances of the young woman's disappearance.

Almost a year later, trapper John Martin, following what he thought was a fox track, found signs of a body in the snow and some days later, with the help of two friends, dug the young woman's corpse out of the bank of a frozen brook about a quarter mile from the school. An autopsy performed by a doctor from Battle Harbour revealed that she had died from a bullet through her breast. The body was transported to St. John's for further examination, and Vital Records listed the cause of death as "Gunshot."

Speculation after the fact suggested that Miss Lindsay had taken a loaded pistol along on her walk in the hope of shooting a partridge or marten, although she was not known to have made a practice of this. Nothing in the newspaper reports indicated that the gun had been retrieved. The trappers who found her had been in Fox Harbour at the time of her death, so no suspicion fell on them, but they claimed after to have had disturbing dreams "about women and babies" between the time they found signs of her body and actually digging up her remains.

A magistrate's inquiry at Cartwright didn't uncover any other evidence, but gossip suggested a love triangle, a possible pregnancy, and a murder. The story persisted long after those involved were dead, and in 1994, singer Harry Martin put lyrics and music together to give voice to the story, in a popular song called "Somewhere beyond the Hills." The narrative line is suitably vague, with secrets "silenced by the years" and "suspicion on the winds":

> Someone said somebody knew, but when he spoke he lied,
> Others said they saw them talking on the day she died;
> When the darkness found her she was silent, cold and still
> And the body lay somewhere beyond the hill.

While in most cases, employers, friends, and relatives might be expected to press for answers, the circumstances of Miss Lindsay's death seemed only to spur all involved to suppress what little was known about the tragedy. Members of her family, including her brother who was an ordained minister, went out of their way to declare themselves satisfied with the rather vague findings of the inquiry, and the same was true of the Grenfell Mission and its supporters.

Whether the death of Marguerite Lindsay was a murder, a suicide, or an unfortunate hunting accident will never be known, but it is clear that the lack of information from the official autopsy and investigation fuelled the local imagination when it might have put to rest concerns about the death.

Accusations of murder were made and dismissed against the white trader Esau Gillingham in the winter of 1936 when the body of Inuk Mark Kennitok was found to have what appeared to be a bullet hole in its forehead. Ranger Frank Mercer, with the help of a dog team driver, hauled the body over the Kiglapait Mountains from Okak to Cartwright, where it was examined by Dr. Lionel Forsythe of the International Grenfell Association, who determined that Kennitok had died of alcohol poisoning following a drunken fall.

Mercer then went all the way back to Okak to arrest Gillingham, who was eventually tried on a charge of supplying illegal alcohol to a native, found guilty, and sentenced to six months' incarceration. The distance Mercer and his guides covered for the case was approximately 2,500 kilometres and took two months. Gillingham served three months of the sentence, but the charge of murder never quite went away. Like the other accused murderers, Gillingham had a reputation for occasional violence; nevertheless, he was immortalized, deified even, in the novel *White Eskimo* by Harold Horwood. Gillingham died some years later when he apparently drowned on the Gander River.

Today, with air travel, forensic evidence, and province-wide policing, suspicious deaths are not ignored, nor are suspected murderers allowed to roam free. Greater care is taken in distinguishing accidental deaths and manslaughters from murders, and police do not release the names or circumstances of murder/suicide victims. The days when Cain could clobber his brother with a rock and escape into the wilderness have long gone. And despite the numerous stories of unpunished murders, most Labradorians would agree with Rev. F.W. Peacock, that murder in Labrador is infrequent, despite the fact that "the opportunities for murder without detection are manifold."

Apenam Tanien Pone: The First Judge of the Innu Nation

The Innu people went into mourning in June of 2007 when they lost a dynamic leader. Apenam Pone, who has been called the First Judge of the Innu Nation, died after a sudden, catastrophic stroke at the age of 56.

Apenam was born out near the Grand River Rapids, the son of Daniel and Penash Pone, or Poon as it was sometimes spelled. He lived in the country with his parents and seven siblings until he was 13 years old, when they moved into the community of Sheshatshiu. Despite having little formal education, Apenam had an insatiable curiosity and a thirst for knowledge that stayed with him throughout his life.

Apenam's introduction to the Canadian justice system was not propitious. As a young man, he got caught up in the cycle of drinking and substance abuse that has so plagued his people, and one evening a stone-throwing incident ended with a woman dead and a very frightened and grief-stricken young man in jail. Tried for manslaughter, Apenam was found not guilty, but he was never entirely sure that he had not contributed in some way to the death. He also never forgot the terror and confusion he experienced as a prisoner in a judicial system that did not speak his language or understand his values.

After a considerable struggle to achieve lasting sobriety, Apenam returned to his home community of Sheshatshiu, aware that he had been given a second chance at making something of himself. It was then that he began his great life's work—to assist others, young and old, so that they would not be trapped forever in their addictions. He worked primarily at the Innu Uauitshitun Alcohol and Drug Awareness Program and for almost 25 years he listened, counselled, intervened, and took the hand of anyone who was ready to begin the lifelong journey to peace and sobriety.

It was specifically in the area of justice that Apenam Pone worked hardest. It was his gift and his challenge that he felt a personal bond with each and every Aboriginal prisoner caught up in the justice system in Canada. He created sentencing circles for Innu communities, he established sweat lodges at the Charles J. Andrew Youth Treatment Centre and at the Labrador Corrections Facility, and he acted as advocate for prisoners going into court, visited them in jail, advised lawyers and judges on Innu tradition, and worked tirelessly to try and bring a conservative legal system into balance with the reality of Aboriginal life today.

Although Apenam Pone saw Aboriginal people, and youth in particular, as his constituency, he did not confine himself to working with Innu. He welcomed lawyers and judges, doctors and teachers to participate in sweat lodge ceremonies, and it was his hope that one day sentencing circles would be adopted by non-Innu in the justice system. "We participate in your system, so why shouldn't you participate in ours," he often said to non-native people. John Joy, now a provincial court judge in Labrador, wrote in 1996 that the expectation of Apenam and other Innu was to see a complete Aboriginal justice system operating in Labrador within five years.

By 2001 Apenam Pone was still waiting, but tirelessly continued to pursue his day-to-day work. That year, the Law Society of Newfoundland recognized Apenam's contribution to the justice system and presented him with an Award of Merit. Recognition such as this was important to Apenam, not for himself but because he thought it was important to acknowledge the work done by Aboriginal court workers, advocates, and translators. At the time of his death, Apenam was in the process of applying to become a Marriage Commissioner and a Commissioner of Oaths, as a step toward being appointed as a justice of the peace.

Apenam was a tireless hunter who provided good country food to elders and those in need. He believed that eating from the country strengthened people and helped them live a balanced life. At his funeral, his friend Kirk Lethbridge quoted from Matthew 25.35: "For I was hungry and you gave me meat, I was thirsty and you gave me drink, I was a stranger and you took me in, naked and you clothed me, sick and you visited me, I was in prison and you came unto me." Apenam Pone lived by that directive. He never allowed basic needs to stand in the way of sobriety and if it meant putting food into peoples' mouths or a roof over their heads before they could deal with their emotional pain, he did it. He was a model of practical Christianity, which he saw as absolutely compatible and parallel to traditional Innu values.

Apenam's early history was not something he expected others to forget, and one of his coping strategies was to remind people of his own painful past. He spoke about his history of incarceration and the reasons for it when he addressed youth, in the hope that frank discussion would help others to speak out about their problems. Apenam used the sweat lodge as a vehicle for releasing those trapped inside their silence. "When you talk about your pain, and you share it with someone else, you feel relaxed," he explained, "and you sleep better because of the heat and everything." He used sweating to treat both physical and emotional ailments, believing both needed attention.

Apenam was preparing the hot rocks for the Sunday afternoon sweat at the Charles J. Andrew Youth Treatment Centre when a stroke felled him. A young man who was assisting him drove him immediately to the RCMP station across the road and the police quickly summoned an ambulance. Apenam was medevaced to St. John's, where it was determined that his stoke was progressive. He knew exactly what had happened to him and was able to speak with his wife and children before he died several days later. It was typical of him that some of his last remarks were jokes, intended to assure his family that he was not afraid of what he was facing.

"The justice system has lost a tireless worker and an honoured friend," said Labrador Affairs minister Tom Rideout. Apenam credited his wife, Lynne Gregory, and Father Paul Charbonneau of the Brentwood Treatment Program in Windsor, Ontario, with giving him the courage to face his addictions. Leaders such as Peter Penashue now credit Apenam with giving them the immediate and vital assistance they needed to get sober. It is a chain of support that will be Apenam Pone's lasting legacy to his people.

FOOD

"Full and Plenty": Life at North River

Josh Davis is alert and cautious as he steers his boat out the mouth of North River into Sandwich Bay on a warm August day. Each spring, melting ice carries sand down from the interior and deposits it in banks at the mouth of the river before the current cuts a new channel into the salt water.

Overhead, companies of geese head upriver to feed, while on the surface of the water, families of eider ducks bob and fatten up on the shellfish below. When the tide goes out, the numerous mussels and clams are evident, and on the offshore islands, the bakeapples are ripe. Darting schools of sand lances thrive in the shallow water.

Margaret Davis, who moved to North River in 1948 with her trapper husband, Percy, told *Them Days* magazine that at that place "there was full and plenty of everything." The same was true a century earlier, and it is still true today. North River, just 14 kilometres north of Cartwright on the edge of the Porcupine Strand, seems to teem with wildlife and edible plants.

Although it was never a large community, North River was always considered a favourable spot for a dozen or more families to settle. Trapping provided the primary income for settlers, who went after foxes, ermine, muskrats, otters, and beaver, but there was also a small amount of commercial salmon fishing, particularly in the 1930s when the collector boats were icing down the fresh fish.

The real attraction of North River was not its commercial viability, however; it was the availability of such a wide variety of food to be harvested for personal use. At North River and on the nearby islands are berries of every kind, as well as alexander, beach peas, roseroot, and willows, all of which are edible.

Trappers travelled to the Mealy Mountains to hunt caribou, but black bears, partridge, rabbits, tinkers and turrs, grampus, gull eggs, and rock cod were all locally available for the pot. Seals were an important part of the North River diet.

In the summer of 2007, Matthew Beaudoin led the excavation of a Métis sod house at North River, believed to have been built by Charles Williams and his Inuit wife in the 19th century. Most of the 7,000 artifacts recovered related to food and cooking and provided a fairly clear picture of how people survived. Mammals, birds, fish, and shellfish were all represented in the remains found in or near the house.

In the graveyard out on the point, the stones tell the story of the settlement. The marker for Charles Williams, the man who built the sod house, identifies him as a native of Plymouth, England, who died June 23, 1829, aged 71. Since life expectancy at that time was only 40 years, Williams obviously had good genes, a healthy lifestyle, and good luck.

Not all Williams's relations were so fortunate. When the Spanish influenza epidemic hit Labrador in 1918, 13 of the people of North River died, five of them members of the Williams family. Other graves record a father and son drowned together, and a small child killed by dogs. Family names include Sheppard, Pardy, Davis, Mesher, Martin, Heard, and Goodenough. Written records also identify unmarked graves as belonging to Elsons, Burdetts, and others. The most recent marker belongs to Margerite Martin, who died in 2012.

According to Clarice Hopkins, her great-grandmother, an Inuk by the name of Salome, died of tuberculosis and was buried in North River in 1850. Her great-grandfather, John Burdett, who originally came from Derbyshire, was so in love with his wife that he never remarried. When he passed away 33 years later at Sandy Hill, he asked his children to bring his body back to North River so that he could be buried with her.

Although the Spanish influenza epidemic decimated the families at North River, life went on. Mrs. Keddie, the industrial worker at the Grenfell Mission, recorded in the 1930s that she was calling at North River to collect "a fine family of Eskimo dolls and handiwork of Mrs. Jim Williams." According to Chesley Lethbridge, Dorothy Williams was also known as "very gifted with a needle and sewing machine" and her daughter Ena's work was "the very best." Ena usually won any craft competition she entered.

The 1940s brought the war to Labrador and very nearly changed North River in a major way. When the surveyors went looking for a suitable location for an air base to serve the planes going overseas, they narrowed the choices down to two flat, sandy places: North River and Goose Bay. Goose Bay was chosen because, unlike North River, it is exceptionally fog-free.

By 1960, trappers were still being drawn to the area. Solomon Davis and Kirby Walsh, both 19 years old at the time, went up the river by canoe to trap fur as their forefathers had done. They didn't do particularly well, but they lived on partridges and enjoyed themselves immensely. Before they left, they wrote a song, "Our Flour Is Almost Gone," about their experience, one of a number of songs that has been composed about North River.

Late in the 1960s, the Newfoundland government, as part of the resettlement program that eliminated thousands of small communities all around the province, moved the people of West Bay to North River. A few years later, it was North River's turn to resettle, and the population was split between Cartwright and Rigolet.

However, Labradorians have strong emotional ties to their original homesteads and are reluctant to abandon them. Long practitioners of transhumance, they often "shift" from one community to another according to the season. A number of the people who have homes in North River have small homes in other seasonal communities as well. There are currently houses on both sides of the river, and although the population fluctuates according to the weather, there is usually some movement in and out of the place.

A large hole near Charles Williams's sod house, identified as the site of an early pit saw by Absalom Williams, is another indication of why North River was so attractive to early settlers and why it still attracts people today. There is good timber in the river valley, enough to provide materials for shelter and for heat. "Living in the woods was strange at first," said Margaret Davis, but she soon got used to it.

Cecil Bird, who has one of the dozen or so summer homes at the river, has an active sawmill behind his cabin, which he uses for boat building. Lew and Doris Davis, who usually summer in Packs Harbour, also set up a sawmill in North River and liked it so much there that they built a substantial house as well. An old sawmill established by the late Mercer Davis still sits, abandoned but undisturbed, back from the shore.

Over in the graveyard, the mosses and lichens slowly creep over the fallen tombstones, obscuring the names and dates inscribed on them. Pea blossoms, fireweed, yarrow, and arnica flowers nod toward the beach, where the tracks of an old dog wolf cross those of a caribou stag. Out on the water, Josh Davis heads cautiously back into the mouth of the river. The stag, swimming across to the other side, finds a convenient sandbar on which to rest and watches the boat as it slowly passes by. The residents of North River continue to live in peaceful coexistence.

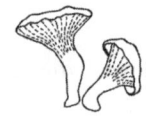

The Labrador Larder

A Newfoundlander who taught in Happy Valley in the 1960s tells a story of a wedding he attended in Rigolet. Rev. F.W. Peacock, who was to perform the ceremony, had invited him along and told him that there had been talk of a special treat at the wedding feast. The teacher made the journey, fantasizing all the while about the wonderful food he was going to eat. Imagine his dismay when the "treat" turned out to be several cases of Puritan meatballs, a meal the locals found a welcome change from their usual diet of smoked salmon and roasted venison.

To the Aboriginal people of Labrador, not very many years ago, the whole country was one big larder. Fish and game, birds and berries, roots and seeds all contributed to the nourishment people needed to sustain life. For the fishermen and whalers from Europe, however, Newfoundland and Labrador was a wasteland. They carried almost all their food with them from home and when it gave out, they starved.

A few of those thousands of seasonal visitors, however, chose to settle in the New World, and they quickly learned from their Innu and Inuit neighbours how to locate, harvest, and eat local food.

Labradorians, unlike Newfoundlanders, eat a wide variety of locally available animals, including beaver, porcupine, lynx, loons, ducks, turrs, seabird eggs, and even squirrels. You have only to try a slice of Elizabeth Penashue's "beaver baloney" to become a convert. Unlike its English namesake, beaver baloney is a delicious mix of different parts of the animal, stuffed into the stomach like haggis and smoked over a slow fire.

Porcupine, swinged of its quills and baked in the oven, is a delicacy that would be appreciated by any gourmet. Caribou, of course, was eaten by anybody who could beg, borrow, steal, or shoot a gun. Moose, which were fairly recently introduced into Labrador, are said to be a poor relative of their Newfoundland counterparts but are becoming more popular as the caribou herds continue to decline.

The Innu *mukashan*, a sacred feast of caribou bone marrow and fat, has often been likened to Holy Communion, but it tastes far richer and more delicious than any wafer of flour paste, and the attendant calories help ward off the cold Labrador winters.

This isn't to say that the original inhabitants of Labrador turn up their noses at imported food. Tea, for one thing, is considered to be an invaluable addition to the traditional Labrador diet. Both Innu and Inuit historically made and drank infusions of plants such as Labrador tea and juniper, but most of their hot liquid intake consisted of meat or fish broth. Today, the teapot rules in most Labrador households, regardless of ethnic origin.

Bread and other baked grain products are probably the most important European import into the Labrador diet. Hard tack, also called ship's biscuit or Hamburg bread, was a staple of the fishermen who came from Europe and was still widely eaten up into the 1950s. According to Peacock, it was even used for making homebrew. Ship's biscuit was so hard that one manufacturer in St. John's packed a hammer into the top of every barrel he sold. Aboriginal people quickly learned to like European bread and biscuits and developed their own ways of cooking them.

In the 19th century, corn flour, or Indian meal, was often distributed by the government on the island, but as there was little or no government ration in Labrador, people managed as best they could with the flour issued on tick by trading posts. During the depression years, "dole bread" made from cornmeal was universally hated. To be seen eating yellow doughboys, or bread made from coarse brown flour, was a source of shame.

In Labrador, hunters and trappers made their own bread, usually in the form of flummies, cooked on a damper or frying pan. It could also be wrapped around a stick and cooked over an open fire. Depending on how it was cooked, a flummy might be called a damper dog, and if it had pieces of salt pork added, it would be called a pork bun.

Permanent housing brought about the widespread consumption of soft, home-baked bread in Labrador, but by 1956, even that was a little different than it was in the rest of Canada. The Enrichment of Flour Regulations demanded that all white flour sold in the province had to comply with prescribed standards, which included added vitamins. As the province was a limited market, only a small number of flour mills such as Robin Hood and Cream of the West were prepared to take on the added expense of vitamin enrichment and specialized packaging. These regulations impacted competition between manufacturers, but the enriched flour also greatly reduced the incidence of rickets and malnutrition on the island and in Labrador.

Bread, whether formed into loaves, stove cakes, pastes, or dumplings, all required a little fat to be palatable. Animals were, of course, an obvious source of fat, but in the early days of the fishery, the fat most often used on bread and fish was olive oil, usually called sweet oil. Shipwrecks off the coast have yielded many examples of olive oil amphorae—large, round-bottomed clay jars used for shipping goods—and salvaged free-blown bottles of English origin have also yielded traces of olive oil.

Lieutenant Griffith Williams, in the 1750s, complained about the high cost of olive oil, which had to be imported to England before being forwarded to Newfoundland and Labrador. "The fishermen could not do without it to cook their salt fish," wrote Williams. Oil was often smuggled in through St. Pierre from Cadiz and France to avoid the extra taxes.

George Cartwright, writing in 1778, was hugely relieved to discover that American privateers who had raided his premises at Sandwich Bay had "forgot[ten] a puncheon of olive oil." Later that spring, he had to dig his way through huge snowdrifts to get at the remaining olive oil he had hidden in his salt house.

Lambert de Boilieu, who was working for an English trading firm in St. Lewis at the same time that Cartwright was homesteading at Caribou Castle, recorded that a settler whose stores had been plundered by a bear came to him for a "small supply" of olive oil.

"How much did he want? Oh! Only about two gallons."

Butter was available, heavily salted, but it was, as Lieutenant Williams noted, "scarce and dear." Once pigs were introduced to the island, salt pork and pork fat became more widely available. Even today, Labradorians believe that a little pork fat, chopped into almost any dish, improves the flavour. The modern trend toward commercial pork rinds as a substitute for rendered pork fat and scrunchions is generally deplored in true Labrador households.

While the Inuit diet favoured fat from seals and whales, most people were unaware that butter in the traditional Labrador diet actually consisted of sea mammal oil also. "Butter" in Newfoundland and Labrador meant margarine, made from sea mammals, while "table butter" was the spread that came from cows' milk.

Prior to Confederation, it was illegal to manufacture margarine in Canada. Under term 46 of the agreement by which Newfoundland and Labrador joined as the 10th province of the Dominion, companies such as that owned by the powerful Crosbie family were allowed to continue to produce their Golden Spread "butter." Eventually, Canadian companies were given the same privilege, but the spread came as an unattractive, white block with a pill of dye that had to be mixed in by the purchaser.

Although the public perception of Labrador is of a meat-eating society, fish was and is important to the local diet and economy. The Inuit and Innu ate all kinds of fish, for millennia, and salt cod was the backbone of the coastal economy for over a century, but salmon became increasingly important in the 19th century as it had higher value and more fat.

Labradorians eat eel, smelt, caplin, sea trout, brook trout, pike, and many other kinds of fish, but today, smoked char, shrimp, and fresh salmon are dominant. Salmon fishing as a sport is a vital part of the tourism industry, but the salmon food fishery is of enormous emotional and political as well as gustatorial importance. The right to catch salmon is a hotly debated topic everywhere in Labrador.

Since the imposition of the cod moratorium more than two decades ago, the availability of salt and fresh cod has been perceived as culturally important also. Pipsik, or dried fish, could be trout or char but was often small cod, boned and notched before being dried for a week or more. Fried cod livers (*shivva*) were a great favourite. Mussels, clams, and wrinkles (periwinkles) were harvested and preserved.

All these local foods were supplemented with rice, beans, and whatever vegetables were available. Inuit traditionally ate the fermented lichen from the second stomach of the caribou. Wild fruits such as redberries, bakeapples, and blueberries are still widely harvested, as are wild mushrooms, alexander, sea plantain, sorrel, and even the tips of willows (*kakajuks*), which in modern times are eaten with molasses.

The practice of cultivating vegetables was introduced into Labrador by Moravian missionaries in the northern communities and by Hudson Bay traders in the interior. On the coast, fishermen from Newfoundland planted gardens near their summer houses. Most of the vegetables grown successfully in Labrador were root crops such as turnips, carrots, potatoes, and parsnips. Chives and rhubarb were widely disseminated and can still be found on long-abandoned homesteads.

Today, in the larger towns of Labrador, you can buy fresh mangos and asparagus even in mid-winter. But good news for the gastronomes is that the local food movement has meant the founding of a seasonal Farmers' Market in Happy Valley-Goose Bay and a renewed appreciation for traditional meats, fish, and wild plants. Mushroom forays at Point Amour and Birch Brook have helped educate the public about the delicious, free delicacies in our woods and barrens, and the collapse of the cod and caribou stocks have Labradorians turning to alternate forms of organic, natural foods.

Puritan Foods still sells plenty of tinned beef stew and meatballs in gravy in Labrador, but you are far less likely to see them served up at a wedding feast, even in the coastal communities. The Labrador palate is getting more discriminating and the Labrador larder is working hard to meet those higher expectations.

Bread, the Staff of Life

Musician Alan Doyle likes to tell the story of the time he asked his mother if she could teach him how to make a loaf of bread. "No, my son," she answered, "I can't. I only knows how to make eight loaves."

There was a time when that anecdote could have been told of most mothers in Labrador. With large families and a high-protein diet of local fish and meat, most meals were stretched out with lots and lots of homemade bread.

Even today, bread and other products made with wheat flour are highly prized in the towns, villages, and cabins of Labrador. With the high rate of diabetes and obesity in this part of the world, more than one nutritionist or nurse has tried to break Labradorians of the bread habit, but with noticeably little success.

Memoirs of life here in the early 20th century, such as those found in *Them Days* magazine, abound with references to bread. Jean Crane remembers going across the river from boarding school in North West River to the Sheshatshiu side, "home to mother's good white bread." Trader Horace Folin used to yearn for the bread his friend Jim Martin's wife made down in Cartwright. Francis Saunders Mueler remembered her Auntie Goodenough's "good homemade bread" at Paradise River.

Most girls in those days learned to make bread as soon as they were tall enough to see down into the flour barrel. Kathleen O'Shea, who came up to Bull Island from Newfoundland each summer to cook for the fishermen, recalled that "[y]ou never seen men eat so much bread in all your life … I'd bake eight to ten loaves those days." She said that keeping up with the bread-making was harder than keeping up with the fish.

Bread, made from flour, liquid, and some form of leavening agent, has been a staple for people since prehistoric times. It sounds simple enough, but that basic recipe allows for a lot of variation. Flour is the ground meal of any edible grain, the liquid can be water or milk or anything potable and wet, and the leavener can be yeast, hops, baking powder, eggs, or beer. Additional salt, sugar, nuts, fruit, herbs, spices, and fats and various methods of cooking the dough produce an infinite variety of breads.

In Labrador, all-purpose wheat flour bread has always been preferred, most often with water, fat, yeast, and a little salt and sugar. Additives are usually restricted to raisins and molasses or bits of pork fat to make pork buns.

The method of cooking varies considerably, though. Bread is generally baked in a conventional oven, but when people are at their cabins or camps, they often bake it in a frying pan or on a griddle. The late Flossie Oliver recalled her mother making bread outdoors in an iron pot—the coals were put into a hole in the earth and then piled over the lid of the pot, which is how it was done when people had only open fireplaces in their houses.

Since Central Labrador is blessed with an infinite amount of sand, the Innu have perfected the art of baking bread even without a pot to put it in. You build a hot fire on a sandy beach, and when the fire dies down, you remove the cinders and dig a hole, place the risen dough in it, and cover it with the heated sand. Once the bread is cooked (you can tell it's ready by knocking on it), you simply brush the sand away, or scrape it gently with a knife. Today, some Innu will wrap the raw dough in paper from the flour bag to ensure that no bits of sand remain attached to the bread. The paper scorches but doesn't burn.

Trappers on their trap lines had to haul their flour on their backs, so they were very careful when making bread, which they called flummies, damper dogs, or river cakes. Made with baking powder, these were a form of bannock, introduced to the north by early Hudson's Bay men from Scotland. Bannock can be cooked in a dry frying pan, in a deep pot of oil, or right on the top of the stove or damper. Damper dogs can even be slapped onto the side of the stovepipe—you know the bread is cooked when it falls off the pipe.

Stove cakes cooked with molasses and a few raisins and fried in fat are called "Innu donuts." If the cakes are large, they will not cook through to the middle before turning brown, so often a hole or two will be poked into the buns before they are put in the pan. They are a particular treat and are often cooked up for community feasts, music festivals, and sports events. Innu cooks also make yeast bread in a skillet by letting it make its second rising right in the frying pan, which is then put on the stove. The dough is turned several times while it is cooking.

As new yeast strains, such as instant yeasts, have made it easier for people to make more exotic breads at home, there is a recent interest in what are generally called "artisan" breads—loaves that include seeds such as sesame, flax, and caraway, or nuts and herbs, as well as whole wheat or rye flour.

Roberta Benefiel is the rare Labrador-raised woman who didn't learn to make bread at home. Her mother arranged her week so that she made bread while the children were in school, and "[t]hings had to be done when they were supposed to be done," with washing on Monday and fish on Friday.

"Any time Mom ran out of homemade bread before bread-making day," says Benefiel, "she would buy 'bakers' bread from the Hudson's Bay store and Dad hated it. I did too. If there had been a bakery here in Goose Bay that made what I consider good, hearty bread (heavy, seeded, and crusty), I likely wouldn't have been so interested in learning to make my own."

Making artisan bread at home is relatively easy now, as many Labrador stores carry not just better yeasts but also whole wheat flour and flours from rice, corn, almonds, rye, and other grains. A small selection of gluten-free breads can often be found in the frozen food sections of larger stores.

Today, bread is commercially available throughout Labrador. Small bakeries such as Dot's in L'Anse-au-Loup, Joe's in Labrador City, and Uncle Ern's in Happy Valley-Goose Bay supply local and coastal customers, while most of the larger supermarkets have in-store bakeries that produce a variety of breads and buns as well as sweet baked goods.

However, there's still a ready market for homemade bread in Labrador, and it quickly sells out at bake sales, summer markets, and fundraisers. There's nothing quite like the traditional three-bun loaf of fresh white bread to trigger happy memories of childhood and home.

For the Love of Mushrooms

Imagine walking your dog through a spruce-wooded trail and discovering gold—not the gold that King Midas starved for, but gold with a flavour to rival ambrosia: golden apricot-scented edibles, free for the taking; gold that can fill your belly, fight off disease, and improve your love life; the gold of a flush of chanterelle mushrooms.

Well, that last claim may be just wishful thinking, but scientists have recently proven what mushroom enthusiasts have always known—mushrooms are good for you. It has always been thought that while mushrooms are a flavourful addition to any diet, they haven't much nutritional value. Recent reports, however, say they are high in antioxidants and vitamin D, which are both useful in fighting off cancer, and the more wild and exotic the mushrooms are, the better they are for you.

For well over a century, Labradorians have been enthusiastic fungus-eaters, far more adventurous than their Newfoundland brethren, who still look askance at wild mushrooms. Inuit were traditionally opportunistic eaters, and poisonous mushrooms are virtually unknown above the treeline, so that segment of Labrador's population has always consumed puffballs and other fungus. Those living in the boreal forest, however, are a little more cautious.

According to theological historian Hans Rollmann, the earliest European record of mushrooms in Labrador is probably found in Moravian Andreas Schloezer's manuscript account of Jens Haven's 1765 exploratory journey to this part of the world. His manuscript includes observations of mushrooms, and he specifically mentions that mushrooms were particularly abundant in Chateau Bay and he found "small black and yellow mushrooms" near Davis Inlet.

Emma Dicker Voisey, who was born in Rigolet in 1884, used to pick mushrooms with her children nearby at Voisey's Bay. "She never let us go and pick [them] unless she was with us," her daughter Rose Spurvey reported in *Them Days* in 1997. "She knew the kind that was poison and the ones that was good to eat. She showed us which ones to pick. I believe there was brown ones, kinda like the ones you buys in the store, cut 'um up like onions, fry 'um in the frying pan. Oh, I loves mushrooms."

Kate Austin Merrick, the subject of the 1942 biography *Northern Nurse*, claimed that Wilfred Grenfell had once had every mushroom on the island of Indian Harbour analyzed and all but one was found to be edible. The nurses at the station gorged on the mushrooms, but their Newfoundland schooner captain wouldn't touch them and claimed they would all be poisoned. "He s'posed he'd have to work the ship alone all the rest of the way home like some blinking Ancient Mariner," said an amused Merrick.

Most of the wild mushroom eaters found in Happy Valley-Goose Bay or North West River have roots on the coast, where boletus mushrooms are consumed enthusiastically. According to Harold Hamel of Cartwright, they are fried up and then mixed with bread and water to make a sauce. Jemima Learning recalled that they were plentiful around Dumplin and Pack's Harbour, where they would fry them up in pork fat or butter or stew them.

In the Labrador cookbook *Caribou Cakes*, Learning remembers one time when her niece Myrtle found a big patch of mushrooms but had nothing in which to carry them home. She stripped off her petticoat and tied it around the waist to make a bag. "I couldn't resist," she told her aunt. "They were too good to leave behind."

Red-skinned boletus mushrooms grow particularly well out on the coastal islands, and the late Doris Saunders recalled that you had to get them early to avoid worms. Her father wasn't so picky, though, and he often used to "come home with mushrooms and peel the skin off of them and throw 'um in the pot when Mom had a soup on—you'd have to take your spoon and scoop the worms off the top."

If the idea of inadvertently eating a worm has no appeal, then the mushroom to look for is the chanterelle. The chanterelle is the most popular edible mushroom in the province, in part because of its fine flavour, texture, and keeping qualities, but also because it does not bear a resemblance to any of the poisonous species and is therefore easy to identify and safe to consume. Chanterelles rarely get worms, and the dry, sandy soil of the interior of Labrador seems to discourage the slugs which distress some mushroomers.

Dr. Wieslaw Rawluk, a veteran doctor at the Labrador-Grenfell Health Centre, is an avid mushroomer. He enjoys large boletus, which he slices, dips in beaten egg, and breads like Wiener schnitzel. However, his real enthusiasm is for the lovely chanterelle, which is particularly abundant on the Goose Bay air base. Most mushroomers treat the locations of their patches as if they were state secrets, but Dr. Rawluk claims there are so many chanterelles on the base that there's more than enough to go around.

"My heart bleeds," Dr. Rawluk says, "when I think of all the wonderful mushrooms being ignored in Labrador." However, he also urges caution, as even experienced pickers can make mistakes. According to the doctor, when the German Air Force was in Goose Bay there were several very serious cases of poisoning because the Germans believed they knew more about mushrooms than any local person could.

Chanterelles are unique in both appearance and flavour, which makes them a favourite of the novice mushroomer. When they are cooked, their slightly peppery taste disappears, but they retain the delicious flavour and scent of apricots as well as their delicate colour. They are rarely eaten raw. They can be dried, pickled, preserved in oil, fried in butter and frozen, or eaten fresh in season, in a variety of dishes. They go particularly well with eggs, salmon, or chicken, but can be used in place of supermarket button mushrooms in any cooked dish.

Foray Newfoundland and Labrador, an annual mushroom survey based in the Humber Region, split its program between Gros Morne National Park and the community of L'Anse-au-Clair on the Labrador Straits in 2005. Thirty-five participants converged on the Point Amour lighthouse, where they identified 144 species of mushroom, including truffles that were so humble in appearance that most of the collectors mistook them for rabbit droppings.

Chanterelles could never be mistaken for anything as ordinary as rabbit buttons. These apricot-coloured fungi begin life as small convex funnels, pushing up out of the mossy or spruce-strewn earth. They are initially round and compact, but soon they stretch up, developing irregular umbrella-type caps that, if allowed to grow, lift up at the rim to become shallow convex saucers. The gills have irregular, branching folds, and the stem tapers toward the base. They can usually be found in Labrador from mid-July to late August, or about two weeks later on the island of Newfoundland.

All mushroomers have their own theories about why chanterelles are so populous in certain areas. As a novice picker, this author was told to look for old homesteads and search downhill from the abandoned wells. Many mushroomers believe that chanterelles like the vibration of footsteps, which distribute the pale yellow spores most efficiently, so they stick to the pathways and carry a stick to lift the lower branches of trees when hunting. In Labrador, some theorize that the low-flying military aircraft of 5 Wing Goose Bay had the same effect as regular footsteps, which is why the base is now such a rich field for gatherers.

While Inuit, Métis, settlers, and come-from-aways all have a history of eating mushrooms in Labrador, what about the Innu? Elizabeth Penashue, when asked if Innu traditionally eat mushrooms, was circumspect. "The only mushrooms Innu eat come on a take-out pizza," she replied.

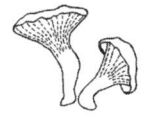

Wild Arctic Char: An Epicurean Delight

Since 1981, the Torngat Fish Co-operative Society has been involved in the small vessel Arctic char harvest, processing high quality frozen and smoked char at their fish plant in Nain, making this incredible Labrador delicacy available to commercial consumers. The demise of wild salmon stocks, and the disinclination of some people to eat farmed salmon, has led to a re-evaluation of northern char as a suitable replacement for discerning eaters.

Arctic char goes by a number of names. Its scientific Latin name is *Salvelinus alpines*; in English it is often referred to as sea trout; in Innu-aimun it is *shushashu*; and in Inuttitut it is called *isiugalittâk* or simply *iKaluk*, which means "fish," just as cod is called "fish" by Newfoundlanders to indicate its importance to the culture. Char's appearance varies as much as its name. The flesh can be anything from deep red to pale pink, its dark brown back can have a greenish coloration, and its mature weight can run from 0.2 to 4.5 kilograms. Landlocked char can develop in a dwarf form and mature when they are merely 8 centimetres long, yet the stock in Burnt Lake, in Southern Labrador, is famous as a trophy fish.

Char breed and hatch in fresh water, and unless they are landlocked, they migrate to the sea between two and five years of age. It is when they are building up their tolerance to sea water that they are most often caught in the river estuaries. Traditionally, Inuit built stone weirs at the mouths of the rivers to trap the fish and speared them with trident-shaped leisters. Both men and women participated in weir fishing in the spring, and it was often a time for feasting and celebrating the return of the sun.

Manasse Fox recalls that his parents used to tell the story of how a group of women were weir fishing for char at the mouth of the Annainak River when they were threatened by a polar bear. An old man who was with them put a spell on the bear and turned it into rock, which to this day can be seen at the base of Mount Sophie, just across the bay from Nain.

As unlikely as it seems, there was once a time when fish buyers and distributers considered char to be an inferior fish. In the Rigolet area, for example, the Hudson's Bay Company preferred to buy cod or salmon, which had higher commercial value, and char was purchased only as dog food. Although Inuit preferred char to cod for personal consumption, the traditional spring char fishery would be interrupted by the commercial cod fishery, which was a source of cash or credit.

A few fishing families, such as the McNeills and Lyalls of Island Harbour Bay, harvested char and pickled it for export, but according to Patricia Lane, the market for their fish "was specifically sought out for them and was not generally available." Individual char fishers not only had to locate a buyer, they had to arrange for shipping as well, because the larger merchants wouldn't touch it.

Northern Aboriginal people have always recognized the superior qualities of char and for centuries have made it an important part of their diet. Both salmon and char have similar nutritional value, but even when wild salmon was widely available, many people preferred char for its mild taste and delicate texture. A steady diet of salmon tended to become tiresome, but char had staying power.

Today, when it is almost impossible to buy wild salmon, the choice is often between farmed salmon and wild char, and it's no contest. Farmed salmon has twice as much fat as wild salmon or char, three times as much saturated (unhealthy) fat, a third more calories, more sodium, less calcium, and fewer minerals.

While wild char, hatched and fed in the cold, clean waters of northern Labrador, are considered to be the most nutritious fish in the world, even farmed char is regarded as a superior product because it is easier on the environment than salmon farming. Char farms are land based, and high density living puts less stress on char, which, unlike salmon, are used to close quarters when they overwinter in freshwater lakes. Char living close to other char are actually healthier than char given more space.

Although the high fat content of char makes it well suited for smoking, Inuit across the Arctic generally prefer to air-dry this fish, a method that is still widely used on the north coast of Labrador. To make *pipsey* or *pitsik*, the backbone or rack is removed, and the flesh is sliced through almost to the skin, after which the fish is hung to dry, flesh side out, for two or three days. In the high Arctic, where there is 24-hour daylight, the fish quickly responds to sun and wind and develops a deliciously chewy texture. Often, it is just partially dried before being fried or packaged for the freezer.

Farther south, below the treeline, the fish takes longer to dry. In the Labrador cookbook *Caribou Cakes*, Rose Michelin of North West River said it took her mother up to 10 days to dry *pipsey*, which would be brought into the house in the evening. Tama Winters of Happy Valley-Goose Bay said, "You got to have a little bit of wind. If you got no winds the maggots get at it."

Smoked char is now very popular in Labrador but it was unknown in Hebron when Leonard Budgell was posted there with the Hudson's Bay Company in the late 1930s. Budgell used "blackberry vines," probably *Empetrum nigrum* or crowberry bushes, to smoke the fish. To hot-smoke fish, you put the source of the smoke close to the fish, which cooks as it develops a smoky flavour. To cold-smoke it, the smoke is funnelled from 5 metres or more distance, so the fish is preserved but retains its raw texture.

Smoked char is considered a great treat throughout Labrador, and many Labradorians have a smokehouse, often made from an old refrigerator. The fish plant in Nain cold-smokes much of its char, vacuum packs it, and freezes it for sale. The Torngat outlet in Happy Valley-Goose Bay sometimes carries smoked racks, a local favourite and an economical way to get your smoked char fix. Consumers love to feast on the flesh that clings to the bones after the char has been filleted.

According to Wade Kearley, Arctic char stocks appear to be healthy in Atlantic Canada. However, these stocks spawn almost exclusively in the rivers and lakes of the north coast of Labrador, and most of the commercial catch comes from a 200-kilometre stretch of coast between Voisey's Bay and Hebron Fjord. Sea-run char usually breed only twice in an average 15-year life, so it wouldn't take much to damage the population. There are no regular surveys; management is based on catch rates. Labradorians will have to hope that the fisheries managers know what they are doing, because if the char eventually goes the way of the cod, it will be a cultural tragedy for Labrador and a culinary tragedy for the world.

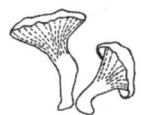

Alexander by Any Other Name

One of the traditional foods that has fallen from use in recent times is the green *ligusticum scothicum*, known as Scotch lovage, sea lovage, or Scottish licorice root. However, there is one place in Labrador where it is eaten regularly and that is Battle Harbour, the famous historic fishing capital. Alexander, as Scotch lovage is called in Labrador, grows all along the shore at Battle Harbour and it is not unusual to see residents picking shopping bags full of the greens for Sunday's boiled dinner. They often have requests for it from older people living back in Mary's Harbour and nearby settlements.

Alexander was thought to be native to Scotland, but it actually grows naturally in salt marshes, on cliffs, and on the beaches along the coasts of North America, from New England up right through the Arctic, Greenland, and Northern Europe and Asia. It prefers salt water but will grow in river mouths where the salinity exceeds 0.1 per cent.

Although people elsewhere tended to eat the root of the plant, residents of coastal Labrador probably acquired their taste for alexander from the men who came over from the Hebrides, where it was generally boiled as a green or eaten raw in salad. Sailors used it as a treatment for scurvy, and no doubt it served the same purpose in Labrador, particularly on the outer islands, where the season isn't long enough for cabbages to head up.

Captain George Cartwright certainly recognized the plant when he encountered it southwest of Rigolet on June 9, 1771. In his diary he noted that he named the small river where he found it Alexander River for the "abundance of that plant growing on its banks."

Alexander tastes like parsley and is best eaten when it is young, as it develops a fairly pungent flavour as it blossoms and grows. It was formerly used by herbalists and doctors to disguise the taste of unpleasant medicines. Gerald Pye, who works at Battle Harbour, admitted that he generally likes greens but never developed a taste for alexander as it was simply too strong for him, but other residents, like Nancy Smith, are fond of it. As a child, Nancy used to have to pick it every Sunday for her mother, and she now feeds it to her own children and grandchildren.

One resident of Battle Harbour reported that his grandfather ate only the stems of the alexander, cooked up like asparagus. The stems were traditionally considered a good substitute for angelica or celery, and the seeds were used in pickles. The root was often used as a substitute for chewing tobacco.

Many people argue that the alexander at Battle Harbour is better than that in Happy Valley-Goose Bay, or even Red Bay. Pearl Pye, in an interview with *Them Days*, said that she stopped eating alexander when she moved from the coast because "what's up home is not so strong as what's down here." Even in Battle Harbour, the alexander at Acreman's Point is preferred to the alexander along the boardwalk. Cindy Gibbons, who visits regularly from Red Bay, boils it up and bags it for the freezer. She said that in Red Bay she used to have to walk a mile or more to collect alexander, while in Battle Harbour it is only a few steps from her door.

Alexander is everywhere on Battle Island and guide Nelson Smith often gets tourists to try a taste of it. In places, it grows next to cow parsnip, which it resembles, but alexander is darker and smaller, with reddish stems, and the flower is flatter than that of the plant known as hemlock in Labrador. Both alexander and hemlock belong to the Umbelliferae or parsley family.

On a recent visit to Battle Harbour, I was able to try alexander, and found it a delicious addition to the larder. I used it liberally as a garnish and added it to soups and stews as well as fish. Alexander is being marketed in Quebec to fancy restaurants and fine grocery stores, and harvesters can expect up to $6 a pound for their efforts.

With the increasing interest in the local food movement, alexander is likely to develop a renewed popularity. Delicious, beautiful, accessible, healthy, and free—what more could you want from a vegetable?

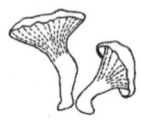

Dandelion: A Spring Tonic

Few wild plants elicit such disparate reactions as the common dandelion. Gardeners groan when they see the cheerful yellow blossoms appear in their otherwise immaculate lawns, and gourmets lick their lips as they anticipate a steaming plate of fresh greens. Goose Bay is on the northern border of the dandelion's natural habitat, and though it has taken a while for it to make its mark on the town, it has found a home and is here to stay.

The *Taraxacum officinale*, as dandelion is properly called, can be found all over the world, and it is remarkably successful at establishing itself in lawns, meadows, and disturbed soil. The plant can regenerate if even the tiniest bit of root is left in the ground. Furthermore, it produces abundant pollen and nectar to attract insects, and even without pollination, it can produce viable seeds. Each seed has a parachute that can carry it long distances and it has a tiny grapnel at the top to latch on when it settles and germinates in soil.

Common dandelion was introduced to North America by early settlers from Europe, probably in the 1500s. It is unclear when it reached this province, but Sir Richard Bonneycastle wrote in 1842 that "[t]he dwarf dandelion (*Leontodon taraxacum*) is one of the most difficult of the garden and field weeds to eradicate here [in Newfoundland]; I have seen a hay-field literally white with it when in seed. Its root is sold at St. John's, in spring, by children who gather it in the gardens and fields, and in the absence of other fresh vegetables, after a long winter, it is relished as a salad."

The common dandelion had almost certainly reached coastal

Labrador by that time. Henry Homfeld, who worked as a cooper for John Rorke, told his daughter Meta that when he lived on Venison Island in the 1870s, cabbages would not head up due to the shortness of the season, so in spring they would eat dandelion. Meta reported that growing up as a child in Hamburg, "[w]e often cooked dandelions because father had learned to like them" in Labrador.

It's interesting to note that Meta Homfeld's mention of dandelion is the only reference to the plant in the first 20 volumes of *Them Days* magazine, and no mention of dandelions is made in any of the Labrador cookbooks that can be found in the Melville Public Library.

Despite this lack of documentation, the dandelion plant was and is consumed in a variety of ways in both Newfoundland and Labrador. The most common cooking method is to pick the dandelion leaves before the plants flower and boil them up in salted water. Some diners sprinkle vinegar on the greens, while others prefer butter, but everyone agrees that dandelions boiled with salt meat and root vegetables are acceptable at any table. Carrots and turnips sweeten the greens and the salt enhances the flavour.

Educator Otto Tucker reported that the second stage of growth for the dandelion is as delicious as the young crowns. He suggested one should pick the unopened flower buds, fry them in butter, season them with a little salt and pepper and serve them on toast or as a side dish. Dr. Tucker dubbed this delectable recipe "the Bishop's mushrooms" for the similarity of their texture to little button mushrooms.

A quick check of my own family cookbook produced recipes for dandelion bacon salad, dandelion dip, chicken livers and dandelions, dandelion stir-fry, weed balls with dandelion and parmesan cheese, and dandelion quiche.

The natural drink to accompany any dandelion feast is, of course, dandelion wine. It takes a bit of work, but the results are worth the effort. The wine is made from the petals only (to avoid the bitter taste of the dandelion milk), and the lovely clear yellow colour of the wine is enough to lift the spirits.

After the meal, a cup of steaming dandelion coffee is in order.

The pioneer writer Suzanna Moodie describes how this was made by chopping the roots into small pieces and dry-cooking them in a cast iron pan, but the roots can also be roasted under a grill and ground like regular coffee. This caffeine-free drink went out of fashion for a time as it was an unpopular substitute for the real thing during World War II, when German submarines disrupted shipping. However, it made an enthusiastic comeback when the hippie generation began to take an interest in health food in the 1970s. Dandelion coffee is now available commercially and consumers find that the taste is very similar to real coffee, particularly when prepared as a latte.

The word *officinale* in *Taraxacum officinale* means that the plant has a medicinal use, and according to John Crellin, a medical historian at Memorial University, dandelion was a popular natural medicine. Commonly used as a spring tonic in Newfoundland and Labrador, he asserts that "for some people, the culinary rite of eating a plate of dandelions was as much a celebration of spring as a health rite." Dandelion was an ingredient in popular patent medicines such as Dr. Wilson's Herbal Bitters, which also included mandrake and alcohol, and dandelion milk was thought to make warts disappear.

The list of ailments the common dandelion is said to cure includes everything from eczema and acne to hepatitis and heart disorders. It is also thought to relieve gallstones, constipation, jaundice, and insomnia. The one attribute of dandelion that is not readily identified in Newfoundland and Labrador is, according to Dr. Crellin, its diuretic properties, a curious omission considering that the plant is often referred to locally as a "piss-a-bed." It is also known in this part of the world as a "dumbledor" or a "faceclock."

The medical missionary Wilfred Grenfell promoted dandelions for nutrition, even though he admitted that the meat-only diet of the Labrador Innu and Inuit produced strong and vigorous people. Botanist Peter Scott claims that dandelion is "an excellent source of calcium, potassium and vitamin A," not to mention vitamins B-1, B-2, B-5, B-6, B-12, C, E, P, and D. The dandelion is higher in beta-carotene than carrots, higher in iron than spinach, and it contains phosphorus, magnesium, and zinc.

Even northern artists have found a use for the dandelion. Inuit embroiderers from the central Arctic have found that when prepared with alum, dandelion gives a beautiful magenta dye, and when it is prepared with iron, it gives a grey-purple colour.

Will any of this dandelion lore be a consolation to the lawn-proud Labrador homeowners of Spruce Park and Hamilton Heights? Maybe not. But even the most hard-hearted gardener must feel a brightening of spirits when the icy fist of a Labrador winter releases its grip and allows a few of those cheerful yellow heads to pop out of the ground. Dandelion, taken internally or merely observed with the eye, provides a tonic for the body and the soul.

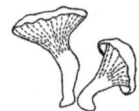

Wild Potherbs from the Labrador Garden

Invasive species are one of the problems of modern life. Anyone and anything can move around the globe easily in this high-speed age, and whether it is purple loosestrife or zebra mussels, most non-native plants and animals cause trouble to the original inhabitants.

Despite hundreds of years of non-Aboriginal habitation, however, relatively few exotic or introduced weeds have become established in Labrador, and those that have taken root—such as the dandelion—are usually restricted to areas of human habitation.

One welcome plant that has made its way across eastern North America and into Labrador is the *Chenopodium album*, known locally as lamb's quarters. Elsewhere called fat hen, goosefoot, or common pigweed, lamb's quarters is a rather inoffensive garden weed, easy to pull up and delicious to eat.

John Hicks, a teacher at Mary Queen of Peace Middle School in Happy Valley-Goose Bay, was delighted to discover a whole field of lamb's quarters on the Grand Lake Road one summer. "I'm essentially lazy," Hicks says. "I like to harvest without moving around too much. When I'm tired of tilling my potatoes, I just sit down and fill a bag full of greens without having to stir."

Whether Mr. Hicks is lazy or not may be a matter of some debate, but nobody would describe Joyce Pye of Grand River Farm as anything but energetic. A vivacious woman in her 70s, Mrs. Pye is a relentless weeder. Lamb's quarters go straight to the chicken coop for the hens to feed on.

According to John Osbourn, Happy Valley-Goose Bay's favourite bus driver, "They've got a right nutty flavour, absolutely delicious. I've been telling everyone about them," he said after his first feed of lamb's quarters.

Intrigued by this sudden enthusiasm for eating weeds, I hauled out my *Culpepper's Complete Herbal* to familiarize myself with this delicate little plant. The entry wasn't helpful. Culpepper describes lamb's quarters, which he calls Arrach or Orach, as "so commonly known to every housewife it were labour lost to describe it." Fortunately, other sources were more forthcoming.

Chenopodium album takes its Latin name from the Greek *khenopodium*, meaning goosefoot, which is the general shape of the plant's leaf, and *album*, meaning white, because the soft, mid-green foliage appears to be dusted with a flour-like substance.

In Labrador, lamb's quarters can stretch out to as much as 1 metre in height. They are most often found in flower beds, newly tilled ground, construction sites, or roadsides. Part of the same family as beets and spinach, they are edible both raw and cooked.

The really intriguing thing about this modest little weed, though, is that it is so good for you. Aside from having all the usual advantages of a fresh vegetable, lamb's quarters are more nutritious than cabbage or spinach and are rich in iron and calcium, as well as vitamins B1 and C.

Like many inhabitants of Labrador, lamb's quarters prefer the inhospitable environment of rocky shores and salt surf. Seaside lamb's quarters, called orach, grow so close to the sea that Euell Gibbons, author of *Stalking the Blue-Eyed Scallop*, says that they are "tender, succulent, and tasty ... slightly impregnated with sea salt with all its healthful minerals." Gibbons reports that he often nibbles the fleshy, ready-salted leaves as he walks along the shore.

The flower of the lamb's quarters is undistinguished, a small cluster of mealy greenish-white blossoms that appear in mid-summer. However, the fruit or seeds of the plant are highly valued. The entry on lamb's quarters in *Native Cookery and Edible Wild Plants of Newfoundland and Labrador* claims that the ripe seeds were used as a cereal by Aboriginal people at one time and that they give "a pumpernickel taste" to breads and biscuits.

Lamb's quarters' seeds, which can be ground and used as flour, have been a part of human diets for centuries, both in the Old and the New World. Lamb's quarters' seeds were part of a porridge-like ritual food found in the stomach of the bog mummy Tollund Man, who was sacrificed around 400 BC in Denmark and only disinterred in the 1950s. Some of the Aboriginal people of North America were probably eating a similar food at the same time.

One of the reasons lamb's quarters has succeeded in establishing itself even in Happy Valley-Goose Bay's gardens is because, unlike other, more aggressive weeds, it is immune to herbicides. The leaf also repels water, so that rain either runs off it, leaving it dry, or else it pools in large drops on the leaf's surface without wetting it. This quality disappears the moment the plant is boiled.

Once the plant has dried out in the fall, you can harvest the seeds by rubbing the husks between your hands and winnowing out the chaff. Caged birds are said to love the seeds, but you might want to save them to dress a salad or add to a pancake. Lamb's quarters can be gathered from early spring up until the first frost and can be canned or blanched and frozen for winter use.

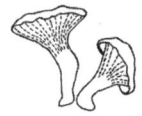

NATURAL HISTORY

Summer Splendour: Labrador Wildflowers

Wildflowers as a tourist attraction don't immediately come to mind when Labrador comes up in conversation, yet if you fly into Happy Valley-Goose Bay in mid-summer, one of the first things you will probably notice is the huge swath of beautiful magenta flowers bordering the airstrip. These fireweeds, known as "salmon flowers" on the coast, as their appearance marks the end of the salmon run, are among the largest and showiest of the 674 species of vascular plants in the 300,000 square kilometres that make up this part of the province.

What is remarkable about wildflowers in Labrador isn't their number or variety but the fact that they grow here at all. Ironically, the thin, acid soil of the Ungava Peninsula is home to many small hardy species that would be crowded out in richer landscapes, so it is possible to get a good look at some flowers that are hard to find in more verdant geography.

Larger flowers, like fireweed, ox-eye daisies (Labrador's only wild chrysanthemum), blue flag (iris), and bog laurel, present themselves willingly to the eye and the camera, but to see the real beauty of Labrador's plants, it is often necessary to get down on hands and knees and take a close look.

Leatherleaf, which flowers early in the spring, is a relatively tall plant, but it hides among other shrubs in bogs and near ponds and it takes a keen eye to spot it. Botanist Peter Scott describes the bell-like white flowers that hang from the new shoots as looking like "thin bone china."

Other tiny blooms that hide from sight are those of the creeping snowberry (also called maidenhair fern), which is found as far north as Rigolet. The fruit that develops from the minute flowers looks like a tiny white egg and tastes like wintergreen. Dainty pink twinflowers, which are often found in mossy woods with the snowberry, sometimes grow in fairly dense patches, but are so delicate that they are easy to miss. Get down for a closer look, however, and their sweet scent becomes obvious. Twinflowers can be found as far north as Okak.

In central Labrador, retired science teacher Betty Anne Fequet leads wildflower walks at Birch Brook Nordic Ski Club near Happy Valley-Goose Bay each spring. Walkers meet for several Saturdays in a row so that they can see the plants at various stages of development. Fequet checks out the trails ahead of time to locate particular species and has a comprehensive slide show for groups of students and for elders who are unable to hike the trails. When asked if she worries about meeting bears in the woods, Fequet says she usually has her nose so close to the ground that she could walk right past a bear and not see it.

The Birch Brook wildflower enthusiasts include the very young and the very old, some of them repeat visitors but others new to the idea of nature walks. With 40 kilometres of cleared trails, there is always some surprise—perhaps a beautiful yellow flower of the carnivorous horned bladderwort or an exotic looking twisted-stalk, a relative of the garden perennial Solomon's seal. If the walkers can divert their gazes away from the flowers now and again, they may also see a nest of baby flickers or a puddle full of tadpoles. As Fequet put it, "One never knows what might be out there. It's all about timing, as many flowers don't last long and afterwards the plants don't stand out."

Deiter Holeiter, who goes on the Birch Brook wildflower walks each year, is interested in all plants and flowers but has a particular affection for the ubiquitous fireweed. However, he doesn't wait for it to gain its unusual height and colour to search for it. Holeiter learned in Quebec to eat the fireweed when it is a very young shoot, steamed with a dollop of butter. The early leaves that appear when the plant is about 12 inches high are excellent salad greens, and when the plant is fully grown and flowering, the stems make a tea that, as Holeiter delicately puts it, is "a friend to old men." The decoction assists urine output for those with prostate difficulties. Aboriginal people used the pith of the stems to make a thick soup.

While the Birch Brook walkers are focused on locating small, hidden flowers, Robin Goodfellow-Baikie always has an eye out for larger, taller plants. For the last eight to 10 years, she has been decorating the United Church in North West River, and while there are plenty of flowers in summer for her to choose from, winters can be a challenge. Sometimes she will dry willow branches, paint them white, and roll them in glitter, but she avoids artificial plastic or silk flowers and, instead, uses pearly everlasting, dried beach grasses, pussy willows, or red osier (dogwood). There are in all 10 species of cotton grass in Labrador, all of which dry well.

"I've not seen dried things to purchase any nicer than Labrador's wild bushes," Goodfellow-Baikie says. At Christmas, she brings in balsam fir (locally called silver pine) which fills the church with wonderful scent. Goodfellow-Baikie regards doing the decor for the church as a real pleasure. "The church enables me to have grand displays that would never suit my little house," she says, and "I find that having to do the decor keeps me looking always for what is happening outdoors."

Goodfellow-Baikie admits she can't identify everything she picks in the wild, but she learns a little more each year and when she comes up against something she doesn't recognize, librarian Isobel Watts can usually help. Isobel is known for her beautiful paintings of Labrador flora.

House lots in Happy Valley-Goose Bay tend to be quite large, so gardeners in the Lake Melville area often leave some of their property for nature to landscape. The pink blossoms of the sheep laurel, the ivory flowers of Labrador tea, yellow hawkweed, purple vetch, and other flowers often move in when gardens receive benign neglect. One gardener was astonished to find that a year after she stopped mowing her backyard, hundreds of hooded ladies'-tresses popped up. These sweetly scented orchids can also be found in late summer along the side of Hamilton River Road, the thoroughfare in the community. Two years after the negligent gardener stopped mowing, she was able to harvest a gallon of redberries without leaving her own property.

Most wildflower enthusiasts are careful not to pick rare plants, of which the Lake Melville area can boast several. As Robin T. Day explains, "Happy Valley-Goose Bay is the warmest part of Labrador and many thermophilus or heat loving species, like Wild Calla (*Calla palustris*) and Bristly Sarsaparilla (*Aralia hisprida*) are restricted to this small area."

There are at least two calla lily sites near Happy Valley-Goose Bay that can be easily spotted from the road, though it helps if you are in a truck or high vehicle, as the guardrails around marshy ponds tend to block the view.

There are several useful guides to Labrador wildflowers available, including Peter J. Scott and Dorothy Black's *Wildflowers of Newfoundland and Labrador*, Alain Cuerrier and Luise Hermanutz's *Our Plants ... Our Land: Plants of Nain and Torngat Mountains Basecamp and Research Station (Nunatsiavut)* and *Botanical Guide: Labrador Straits Common Wild Flowers and Shrubs* from the Labrador Straits Natural Heritage Centre. Serious wildflower enthusiasts may find Robin T. Day's three-volume *Atlas of Labrador Plants* of interest. Visitors can also find location-specific lists, with or without illustrations, at places such as Battle Harbour and Birch Brook Nordic Ski Club.

The Grey Jays of Labrador

In November of 2016, the Canadian Geographic Society declared the grey jay as Canada's national bird, the result of voting in which 50,000 people participated. Strong front runners had included the chickadee, the loon, the Canada goose, and the snowy owl, two of which had actually come in ahead of the grey jay. The experts and ornithologists who made the final decision, however, pointed out that the chickadee, loon, and Canada goose were already provincial emblems. Furthermore, loons and geese migrate south each fall, and chickadees and snowy owls are not found throughout the country. The grey jay is non-migratory and can be found in every province and territory in Canada.

While it is true that the grey jay isn't a provincial bird, a resolution of the Combined Councils of Labrador adopted the grey jay as the official bird of Labrador several years ago. Birdwatchers in Labrador were among those who suggested the grey jay as the official bird of Canada, according to Gordon Parsons of Labrador City, and were overjoyed when their choice was confirmed by the Canadian Geographic Society.

Although not as familiar to city dwellers as the chickadee or even the Canada goose, grey jays are known to most Newfoundlanders and Labradorians who spend even a little time in the woods. My own first encounter with a grey jay was in a campsite in Pistolet Bay in the 1960s, when a daring little bundle of feathers came and boldly snatched a slice of my breakfast toast right off the grill. Today, Happy Valley-Goose Bay is still forested enough to attract grey jays to backyards.

Early accounts of the grey jay in Labrador come to us through the oral tradition of the Innu people, who regarded the bird as an oracle. His cry is said to sound like a knife being sharpened, foretelling success in the hunt. According to anthropologist Frank Speck, writing in the 1930s, the Innu held the jay in high regard partly because it was thought to lead them to game and partly because jays were generous in sharing their cached food with other small animals. If an Innu hunter did not attract the attention of a grey jay, then he was not going to have luck in the hunt.

Numerous Innu stories involve the grey jay, the best known of which is probably the tale of how the grey jay or whiskeyjack tricked wolverine out of a meal of ducks by leading a band of Innu to the pot where they were cooking. That story turns up in Lucien Turner's work in 1894, and a variation recently appeared in *Naskapi Wolverine Legends* written by John Peastitute for the Naskapi Development Corporation.

In the 1960s, Joseph Rich of Sheshatshiu recorded a very old story about two Innu who tortured a jay by plucking the feathers from his whole body. To punish them, the jay called all the Innu together and conjured up a violent snowstorm that blew so hard that people began to run out of food. One Innu man braved the heavy snow to go hunting, and discovered that the storm was only in the locale of their camp.

A century earlier, in 1861, William and Henry Youle Hind encountered grey jays in their explorations of the Labrador Peninsula, and clearly enjoyed the interaction. Henry recorded that the Innu "would never permit the Canadian Jay or Whiskey Jack, which they called Ouich-cat-chan, to enter their lodges, lest they should have pains in the head; but they examined the gizzard of this bird with great care, to see if it contained any fragments resembling the bones of the moose, or any other large animal, in the belief that if such were discovered they would soon kill one of the animals whose bones were figured in it." Henry's brother, William, painted a humorous portrait of himself lounging on a hillside with three jays hovering around his head.

Elizabeth Penashue, when asked about the grey jay, explained that these birds come with a message to say if the men have found caribou. Although the Innu believe it is not good for jays to come into their tents, they are generally respected. "When you put the meat on a scaffold," she explains, "you cover it to keep the whiskeyjack from seeing it, but they are very clever about getting at the meat anyway. When you clean caribou or wabush [rabbits], you put the intestines into a tree for the whiskeyjack. We give him whatever we don't use."

Settlers in Labrador must have developed a love/hate relationship with the grey jay early on. In 1770, the year George Cartwright came to Labrador, he used birdlime to catch two jays on the porch of his house. At first he kept them confined in a cage, but within two days he gave them the liberty of his room and recorded that he was "greatly surprised to see them fly to [him] for food, and familiarly perch upon [his] hand: they even suffered [him] to stroke them with one hand while they were eating pork fat out of the other." On seven subsequent occasions in his journals, Cartwright recorded that jays had "struck up" his traps, robbing him of the martens he relied on for his living, yet he also clearly appreciated the jay, which was the only bird whose call he reported hearing the whole winter.

Although Innu usually don't molest grey jays, when the birds become so active that they interfere with traps, the Davis Inlet band will set what William Duncan Strong describes as "an ingenious device" that catches the bird in a loop of thong. Speck believed this spring trap was a source of food in times of famine but Strong felt that it was employed "mainly as a pastime to amuse the children and punish the saucy jays."

The grey jay, a member of the *Cordivae* or crow family, travels under a number of aliases in Labrador: *Perisorfeus canadensis*, Canada jay, bobby jay, moose bird, meat bird, camp robber, moose robber, venison hawk, lumberjack, whiskeyjack, Wiskedjan, uishkatshan, and Kupanuatjuak. Whatever name they go by, they are irrepressibly friendly and brash little creatures that attract attention whenever they appear. About the size of a robin, and lacking the colouring and crests of their blue jay cousins, the grey jay nevertheless has a number of striking characteristics that make it stand out.

It's most noticeable feature is its fearlessness around humans. Like the bird that stole my toast in Pistolet Bay, jays will take food from almost anyone. Grey jays adapt to human activity in their territory and will exploit it if possible. As their nickname suggests, they are quick to steal meat from hunters, but they do more than that. According to naturalist Candace Savage, if jays find a large carcass that has not been opened, they will solicit the help of other species: "Unable to tear through the tough hide themselves, they allegedly go looking for a wolf, a coyote, or even a person to cut into it for them."

Grey jays have a rich vocal repertoire, which includes a clear whistle *whee-oooh*, the second note being lower, as well as frequent single, quiet *twirks* or *whuits*, contact notes by which each bird keeps track of its family group. It will make a hard chattering or clicking noise when mobbing earthbound predators, and a softly repeated whistle—*hoo hoo hoo*—when predatory birds are identified. Part of their mating behaviour is described as a "whisper song," which, along with their bill-rubbing "kisses" and gifts of food from the male to the female partner, can melt any heart, avian or human.

Grey jays are also noted for their ability as vocal mimics. Their one note is harsh—Cartwright described it as a short, coarse tune—but it can mimic the songs of other small birds, crows, blue jays, hawks, and even people. Mina Hubbard, on her 1905 expedition through the Labrador wilderness, reported that once when they lost the trail, her guide George Elson called out to the other travellers, and "a saucy whiskeyjack answered him from the green woods not far away. It sounded just like a person whistling. 'Just listen to that fellow. If you didn't know his call you would really think it was a person answering you.' He called again and again the answer. Then we heard a shout from the hill ahead."

The grey jay's most notable feature is its ability to overwinter in harsh, cold Labrador weather. Its thick grey and white plumage keeps it warm through the long winters. Naturalist Gary Saunders writes that "in bitter weather it puffs up to cover its feet and legs," and "even its nostrils are feathered." It's frequently cold habitat, of course, explains its preference for high protein, fatty foods.

The diet of the grey jay generally consists of insects, berries, fungi, small frogs, bird eggs and nestlings, mice and shrews, not to mention slices of toast that happen to appear in its territory. They are opportunistic eaters and will adapt to human food immediately. The secret of their success is in the way they store these bits of food, holding them in their throats so that they become covered in sticky saliva, and then caching them above the snow line in trees. The pieces of food are shoved behind a bit of bark, under branches, or inside lichens, and the saliva makes them stick there through the cold months.

The really amazing part of the grey jay's food storage system is that each jay can make as many as 1,000 caches a day in summer, and when winter comes it still remembers where all these caches are. They are what is known as scatterhoarders, which means they don't gather the stashed food together where it might be stolen or discovered by other animals, but instead they spread it out as evenly as possible throughout the forest. Months later, when the snow is down, they can locate these thousands of caches and survive even the coldest weather.

Another major characteristic of grey jays, which mate monogamously, is that they breed earlier than other birds. Their nests are well insulated with tiny twigs, bark, lichens, and even scavenged fur and feathers, as well as things such as cocoons of the forest tent caterpillars, and they might start laying eggs when there is still 1 metre or more of snow on the ground. The female sits on the first egg she lays and keeps it from freezing until she has a clutch. Incubation takes about 18 days, during which time she is fed by her partner.

Grey jays survive the cold *because* of the cold. Harsh winters preserve the food they store, allowing them to breed early and survive longer. The greatest threat to the grey jay population is global warming. If our northern forests heat up, the charming grey jay may be endangered. Hopefully, the environmental activists who voted to make the grey jay our national bird will be able to convince the public that they should work to preserve our cold Canadian winters.

Carnivorous Plants of Labrador

People eat plants, but plants don't eat people—or at least that's the way most humans see the world. When the natural world reverses the usual order of things, as in the musical comedy *Little Shop of Horrors*, we gasp in fright and delight. There's something awful that fascinates us when the alien plant, Audrey II, feasts on Steve Martin's sadistic dentist in that film.

In real life, however, plants do sometimes eat sentient beings. Everyone has heard of the Venus flytrap, but there are equally exotic carnivorous plants closer to home, even in Labrador. In fact, Labrador can boast of not one but at least four insect-eating plants.

The most famous and the easiest to identify is the pitcher plant, Newfoundland and Labrador's provincial flower. Back in the 18th century, Dr. Michael Sarrasin de l'Etang first sent specimens of the *Sarracenia* back to Europe from Quebec, but it wasn't until the 19th century that it caught the attention of Queen Victoria. At that time, the national flower of Newfoundland, and by extension Labrador, was the maidenhair fern, a delicate little plant with a white bloom. However, it's said that Queen Victoria was so mesmerized by the flesh-eating pitcher plant that she substituted the large, red "hunter's cup" for the tiny *capillaire* when our national coins were being struck.

The pitcher plant, as its name suggests, has rolled red leaves that look and act as jugs, secreting nectar to lure the insects in and holding water that eventually drowns them. As bacteria digests the insects, nitrogen and minerals are released which allow the plants to thrive in boggy and acidic areas.

Although the plant looks rather waxy and bizarre compared to most wild flowers, it has its own beauty, and our ancestors appreciated its other qualities. Hunters and gatherers were known to drink the contents of the pitchers, and folk herbalists learned to collect the slightly acidic water to treat infected eyes during outbreaks of smallpox. The pitcher plant is credited with saving the sight of many of our early settlers, who learned how to use it from resident Aboriginal people.

Much smaller, but equally alien-looking, is the sundew, which can usually be found in the same area as pitcher plants. Although the reddish sundew is a saxifragous plant that can grow in rocks, it often snuggles down in a bed of red moss, so it's easy to miss unless you know what you are looking for. Once you find it, it is unmistakable.

The leaves of the sundew have glandular hairs that secrete a sticky substance that traps the insects and that then curl around them to aid digestion. It's rather like closing your fingers over a grasshopper that has landed on the palm of your hand. The secretions look like little drops of dew and it's only when you touch them that you realize that it is not water but something infinitely gooier. The sundew, though inedible, has one very useful property—the gel that attracts flies also kills bacteria. Some Aboriginal groups used it as a medicinal agent.

The third insectivorous plant we can usually find in our bogs and ditches is the butterwort, both the common, *Pinguicula vulgaris*, and the hairy butterwort, *Pinguicula villosa*. The hairy butterwort is found in Labrador but not on the island. The "butter" in its name comes from the greasy coating on the leaves. Insects stick to the surface and then become digested. Smaller than the pitcher plant and larger than the sundew, the butterwort is a relatively anonymous plant and most people will have seen them but not recognized them. The leaves tend to be pale green, almost yellow, and they are curled at the edges as if the plant is dying. Take a close look, however, and you will see tiny black dots of insect remains on the surface. The plant isn't dying; it is thriving and feeding itself.

The horned bladderwort, or *Utricularia cornuta*, has a trap that works 100 times the speed of the Venus flytrap. It lives in boggy peatlands and is hard to spot because its stem and leaves are very inconspicuous. The leaves have small bladders with trigger hairs that suck in prey when they are disturbed.

All of these plants have flowers, though they tend to be relatively short-lived. The pitcher plant has a nodding bloom on a stout stalk, with five petals that fall off after a few days. The tiny sundew sends up a long stalk with a line of blossoms toward the tip that open one at a time. The homely butterwort has a single flower on top of a long stem, like a violet with a backward spur, and the bladderwort, too, has a spur below three yellow lobes.

Although these insect-loving plants have gone through major adaptations in order to digest insects, sentient prey are not their major source of nutrition. Pitcher plants, sundews, and butterworts, like other plants, derive most of their energy from photosynthesis. The insects, however, provide them with nitrogen and trace minerals that are not found in the poor, thin soil of many areas of Labrador. In richer soils, these plants would be crowded out by vegetation that grows more aggressively.

Like the people who live in Labrador, resident carnivorous plants have made a home where most others see only want and scarcity. They love our harsh climate, our poor soil, and our rocky shores, and they thrive here in a way they wouldn't in a softer, more welcoming environment. Labrador is their home, as it is ours, so we should get to know these unusual neighbours and celebrate their unique qualities.

The Weird and Wonderful World of Labrador Bats

One night in the summer of 2017, resident John Joy was reading quietly in his living room in Happy Valley-Goose Bay when he suddenly noticed what he assumed was a bird flying gracefully around the room. He thought a window or door must have been left open, but when he got up to usher the bird back out into the night, it suddenly swooped down into a small model kayak that was on a nearby shelf and he realized he was dealing with a bat.

The bat snuggled down into the nose of the kayak and settled in for a snooze. There was no way it could be dislodged without doing injury either to the animal or the kayak, so Judge Joy laid both outside on his back deck and hoped that they would have parted company by morning. They hadn't. In daylight, the outline of the bat could be clearly seen tucked into one end of the boat.

Bats aren't the first animals that come to mind when you think about Labrador, but as it happens, Labrador might turn out to be very important to the survival of bat populations in North America. One of the people doing research on Labrador bats is local ecologist Sara McCarthy in Happy Valley-Goose Bay.

McCarthy's recent focus has been little brown bats (*Myotis lucifugus*) and northern long-eared bats (*Myotis septentrionalis*), the two species that reside in Newfoundland and Labrador. Listening to her wax eloquent on the diversity and unusual qualities of the world's bat population, it's hard to believe that most people feel only fear and disgust at the very idea of close contact with bats. McCarthy thinks it's fun to work in an area that other people find weird and scary and sees only a unique opportunity to further her already interesting career.

According to the provincial Department of Fisheries and Land Resources, bats are a vital part of the ecosystem. They directly benefit the human population by controlling agricultural pests and insect-borne disease, particularly the mosquito population that can make summers in Labrador such a trial.

Bats can eat 50 per cent of their body weight in insects each day, and a nursing mother will increase that intake to 100 per cent. In fact, it has been estimated that 1 million bats will eat about 700,000 tons of insects annually, saving the agriculture industries billions of dollars a year on pesticides and keeping chemical contaminants out of the environment.

Numerous qualities make bats interesting to a scientist like Sara. Aside from their omnivorous appetites, they are the only mammals that can fly, they can live up to 30 years, and they are nocturnal, so lots of people have never actually seen one. Add to that their remarkable ability to navigate in the dark using echolocation, and what's not to love?

Unfortunately, bat populations around the world are currently threatened by an outbreak of an infection caused by the fungus *Pseudogymnoascus destructans*, which first appeared in a New York cave a decade ago. Named for the white fungus that grows on an infected bat's wings, nose, and ears, white-nose syndrome has spread along the eastern seaboard wiping out bat colonies in Ontario, New Brunswick, Nova Scotia, and PEI, as well as the eastern US. It has recently been found on the west coast of the continent also, so it is possible that bat populations there might crash in the near future.

White-nose syndrome causes bats to wake up during the winter, when they have suppressed immune responses. Affected bats can be seen flying around, desperately trying to find food, when they should be sleeping and conserving energy. If they survive the winter, they often die later from damage to their wings.

It is important to note, however, that white-nose syndrome has not yet been detected in Labrador, so one of the issues facing Sara and her colleagues is to determine whether Labrador's good fortune is the result of simple isolation or if there is some form of immunity among our bats that protects them from the disease.

Bats do not have a very high profile in Labrador. Although little brown bats can often be seen roosting around cabins and sheds during the summer, bats in this province are not generally associated with human habitation. Northern long-eared bats roost alone when they are breeding, usually under loose bark in large trees.

Bats live only below the treeline, so Inuit in Arctic Canada are unfamiliar with the creatures, but even in Labrador, there are no traditional Inuit stories about bats and there is no Inuttut word for bat listed in *Labradorimi Ulinnaisigutet*, the Labrador dialect dictionary. William Duncan Strong, who spent the winter of 1927/28 with the Innu, then called Naskapi, reported that bats were known as far north as Davis Inlet, but he recorded no myths or traditional knowledge about them. Innu, however, have two words for bats: *kuakuatapikushish*, or *upau-apikushish* (meaning flying mouse).

Innu legends about bats don't appear in any published works, but Justine Rich of Natuashish believes that they are not regarded as "good" animals as they can get tangled in your hair. In reality, bats are such good navigators that they are able to avoid contact with people, but the myth persists. Sara McCarthy agrees that bats don't like to be around people very much, as she has to work very hard to catch them.

According to Sara, bats can carry rabies and parasites and can bite, but in some ways we are more of a threat to the bats than they are to us. When she goes collecting bats, she wears new hazmat suits or clothes and equipment that have never been used outside of Labrador to protect the bats from infection.

Labradorian Stanley Oliver says that when he was a boy, his family had a cabin at Welbourn Bay that had a colony of bats roosting in the eaves. The children used to "play" with them, watching them and chasing them around. They had no fear of the small creatures. However, the children of Mud Lake defined "playing with bats" rather differently. Playing with bats essentially meant killing them.

In a production the children from Mud Lake wrote for the Labrador Creative Arts Festival, directed by Ginny Ryan, the children represented both humans and bats, the humans perpetuating the myths that bats should be killed because they suck your blood and carry rabies, while also describing how little boys would torment little girls by chasing them with dead bats. In the play, the argument that won the day and ended the war on bats is the fact that bats eat so many mosquitoes. Without bats, the children could not play outside in Labrador's short summer, so they call a truce and live happily ever after.

Sara has a lot of work ahead of her if the true-life bat story is to end happily. Sara teamed up with colleagues from St. Mary's University to capture commuting and foraging bats from 11 central Labrador sites. Using mist nets and harp traps, they caught, individually bagged, and examined hundreds of bats, checking for parasites, pregnancy, lactation, and, of course, white-nose syndrome. Once processed, the bats were released at their collection sites.

Through their research, the team of scientists was able to determine that up to this point, at least, there is no sign of the disease in Labrador. They were also able to estimate parturition dates for little brown bats and confirm the presence of northern long-eared bats in the mainland part of the province, the first confirmed record of the species in Labrador.

In 2016, Sara was able to establish bat boxes and information panels outside the old log cabin at Birch Brook Nordic Ski Club, one of the collection sites. For many years, the abandoned cabin and sauna owned by the ski club have been a roosting loft for maternal colonies of little brown bats, but they now have world-class bat hotels to lodge in.

Literature available through the Wildlife Division of Lands and Natural Resources can educate people on how to eliminate bats from cottages or cabins without harming them, how to build bat boxes to house them safely, and how to live in harmony with them.

Bats in Labrador or anywhere in North America don't entangle themselves in hair or suck blood. Only 0.5 per cent of bats carry rabies and infected bats do not become aggressive as some animals do.

As for the Judge's kayak-encased bat, an online search soon revealed that bats find it hard to launch themselves into the air from a horizontal position, so the kayak was propped up against the post of the deck and the following night, the bat vacated its borrowed residence, a happy ending for one bat and one human.

The Versatile Porcupine

One of the many things that distinguishes Labrador from the island part of the province is the presence of an interesting and useful rodent, the *Enethizon dorsaturm*, or porcupine. Smaller than their Old World relatives, Labrador's New World porcupines are traditionally cherished as a source of fresh meat and quills for decorating clothing.

Weighing up to 18 kilograms and measuring as much as 100 centimetres tip to tail, porcupines can be found in all the forested areas of Labrador, even in isolated patches of trees as far north as Hebron. However, they are even more common in the valleys that lead down into the Hudson Strait.

In previous times, the Innu, Inuit, and European settlers of Labrador all valued the porcupine for its meat, skin, and fat. The Innu, in particular, always supplemented their caribou harvest with porcupine and other small game. The meat is so delicious that even the most fastidious visitors and settlers welcomed having one for the pot when they had the opportunity.

The Moravian Brethren, writing in 1846, described porcupine as tasting like "very tender mutton." Captain George Cartwright always delighted in getting a porcupine and described catching and consuming them with enthusiasm. Clarence Birdseye, of frozen food fame, spent four years in Labrador and wrote an account of eating a porcupine that was "unexpectedly tender ... in spite of the beast's age and sex."

In the Labrador cookbook *Caribou Cakes*, Horace Goudie gives a full account of preparing porcupine, from killing it to topping it with a paste or pudding. Una Saunders and Jack Shiwak both recall eating roasted porcupine feet, and Sylvia Blake remembers that they also boiled and ate the tail. With the quills removed, the tail was also used as a brush for cleaning combs.

Porcupines were hunted in a number of different ways. Trappers usually caught them in their snares or traps, or shot them. Innu still use dogs to find them, usually up in trees, and often hunters will just knock them out of the tree or chop the tree down. Once on the ground, the porcupine is flipped onto its back and the pressure of a foot applied to the underside stops the heart.

Of course, the problem with porcupines, whether living or dead, is the quills. Despite popular belief, porcupines do not "shoot" their quills, but the loosely embedded quills may drop out when the porcupine shakes its body. The backward-facing barbs are so effective that with the slightest contact they can pierce the skin and remain in place. The barbs are efficient and tenacious to such a degree that medical engineers are studying them to design better, less painful, biodegradable needles and surgical sutures.

Cortland Best of Mud Lake once managed to ingest a 2-inch porcupine quill that eventually worked its way from his gut out through his back. He said the process was painless and he didn't even realize it was happening until it protruded though his skin and hooked into his shirt. A fellow trapper twisted and pulled it out for him. "A quill is like a screw so you got to twist it out the same way as you would a screw," he explained. It would have been very painful if he had tried to pull it straight out.

Trapper Ben Powell recounts, in his book *Labrador by Choice*, how he picked up a porcupine quill while crawling into his tilt one evening. He experienced very little pain, so he ignored it for some days, and by the time he got around to trying to remove it, it had buried itself inside his knee cap. When on his trapline, Powell found animals as diverse as wolves, owls, and weasels dying from porcupine quills and wrote that he believed that "porcupine quills kill more animals in the country than anything else [he knew] of."

George Cartwright was able to witness the efficiency of the porcupine's quills the first time his favourite dog encountered one:

This porcupine chanced to be upon the ground; and my greyhound, which always attends me and had never seen one before, no sooner set eyes upon him, than he struck at him with the same resolution that he would have done at a fox. I thought he would have instantly gone mad. His tongue, the whole inside of his mouth, his nose and face were stuck full of quills, as it was possible for them to be; insomuch that his mouth was gagged wide open, and he was in such agony, that he would have bit me, when I attempted to give him relief.

It took Cartwright and his servant Jack three hours to free the poor dog from the quills, some of which had penetrated through the roof of his mouth and nose and had to be extracted by their points. Once the suffering dog was relieved of the quills, Cartwright "singed the porcupine and made a good soup of it."

Singeing, or "swingeing" as it is often called, is the first necessary step in preparing a porcupine for cooking. The stiff quills are modified hairs coated in keratin, the same material found in human fingernails. These stiff, barbed quills are interspersed with bristles and under-fur. Generally speaking, the long quills are hauled out with an axe and the remaining hair and small quills are burned off. Some people scrape away the blackened skin, while others appreciate the smoky flavour that is imparted to the meat.

The porcupine can be roasted over a fire, baked in a pot, barbecued in tinfoil, or boiled until tender. The cooking time will vary according to the age and size of the animal, but Innu elder Cajetan Rich insists that neither salt nor any other spice need to be added because porcupine is already a "perfect food."

Dillon Wallace, during his 1905 Labrador expedition, recorded eating a porcupine that was so tough it was "just like chewing India rubber," but Mina Hubbard, eating porcupine nearby, declared it "good," despite it being the wrong time of the year for hunting them. Preference is given to the fall catch, when the porcupines have been feeding on berries rather than bark.

While people of all cultures in Labrador appreciate porcupine, the animals are particularly associated with the Innu, who consider it one of the most important spiritual beings of the animal kingdom. Innu share porcupine meat and broth as an informal communal meal or *mukashan*, burning a portion as an offering to the animal masters. Innu John Poker explained that the offering showed respect for the animal; "[t]he fish and the porcupine spirits are the two who most want to be respected." If an animal is respected, it will allow itself to be caught in the future.

Innu also use porcupine for scapulamancy, a way of "obtaining knowledge of the universe besides the common sense method of empirical observation." In porcupine divination, a scapula of the animal may be charred over a flame and studied to determine where the hunters can find future game. The cracks and marks on the scapula are read like a map. The skull of the porcupine, when thrown into the stove, is said to emit a sound or echo that is interpreted to indicate future success in hunting.

The Innu study the habits of the animals they hunt, and according to anthropologist Georg Henriksen, they "know the behaviour of the animals and what they eat by close association with them." He added, "Occasionally some of the Naskapi have had wolves, bears, foxes, porcupines and other animals living in their tents ... the man who kept a porcupine had no feeding problems with it, since the porcupine was satisfied with eating the bark off the poles inside the tent."

The importance of the porcupine in Innu life is evident in the presence of no fewer than 88 words related to porcupine in the Innu-aimun dictionary. Its pervasive presence in Labrador is also reflected in the geographic nomenclature of the place. William Gosling reports that early Portuguese maps of Labrador included the place names Prassel and Baia du Prassel, *prassel* being the Portuguese for "little pig" or porcupine. In English there is the winter community of Porcupine, the Porcupine Islands, Porcupine Bay, Porcupine Creek, Porcupine Hill at Fox Harbour, Porcupine Harbour, Cape Porcupine, and the Porcupine Strand, which the Vikings called the Wonderstrand.

Unfortunately, porcupine place names reflect the presence of these animals in the past rather than the present. Porcupine populations collapsed in Labrador in the late 1960s and 1970s, except in the extreme north. Lawrence Jackman noted in 1982 that many hunters and trappers reported and commented on their disappearance but were unaware that this was a widespread phenomenon, not a local problem. Labradorians attributed the decline to everything from forest fires and wolves to overhunting and a mysterious kidney disease.

Wildlife officer Frank Phillips admits that nobody knows exactly what caused the porcupines to die off. He believes the decline was probably some "bug" or disease, as the small, isolated populations north of the treeline appears to have been less affected. He said that "in the late 80s, there seemed to be a slow comeback but the numbers haven't reached former levels." Tony Williamson reported that porcupines completely disappeared in the Voisey's Bay area but by the late 1990s were starting to come back again.

Today, although the Innu still hunt porcupine for food, particularly since the hunting ban on caribou was instituted, settlers and younger Innu are less inclined to eat porcupine. Two generations have been deprived of seeing roast porcupine on the supper table, so despite their increased availability, the time-consuming process of swingeing and simple unfamiliarity has made them reluctant to try eating this exotic bush meat. A porcupine on the doorstep, which was once a lucky windfall, today is often cursed for chewing its way through cabin door frames, wooden tool handles, and any material containing traces of salt.

The continued improvement in Labrador's porcupine population, an increased appreciation for organic, locally sourced meat, and a return to traditional values, as well as an improved understanding of population collapse and regeneration, could spell an improved relationship between humans and animals in the Ungava. That relationship might well include a willingness on the part of the animal masters to release more porcupines for human consumption. Our respect for both animals and their environment may yet bring nature back into balance again.

Celebrating the Spruce

The year 2014 marked the 40th anniversary of the adoption of the Labrador flag with its white, green, and blue bars and spruce twig. Although the flag has no official standing, it is flown throughout Labrador and appears on car stickers, baseball hats, key chains, Christmas decorations, garbage cans, grave markers, sheds, dog collars, earrings, and dozens of other everyday items.

It is the spruce twig in the upper left-hand corner which makes the Labrador flag stand out. The three arms of the twig symbolize the three founding peoples of Labrador: the Inuit, the Innu, and the European. Its two years of growth represent both the history and the future of Labrador.

Black and white spruce and balsam fir were all three historically called "spruce" by Labradorians. Stands of these trees dominate the forests of Labrador and are often considered of little use except for feeding the pulp and paper industry. However, spruce was an invaluable asset in the lives of settlers and Aboriginal people alike.

Aboriginal people taught settlers how to use spruce and fir to build and heat shelters and to construct canoes, snowshoes, and toboggans. Both groups slept on spruce boughs. Innu people steeped young spruce tips in water to make healing poultices and teas, while the settlers fermented the concoction to make spruce beer, a spring tonic that warded off scurvy.

Although spruce are usually thought to be thin and scrubby, Captain George Cartwright, writing in the 1770s, claimed that where the soil was good and the stands not too thick, the spruce "run clear and tall, and attain substance sufficient for shallop's oars, skiff's oars, stage beams, rafters, longers and other purposes." Because the roots run horizontally, he reminded readers, they "supply proper stems and other particular timbers" for boat building. In St. Lewis Bay, Cartwright found white spruce trees that were "tall, clear and straight; from six to nine feet in circumference."

Labrador settlers on the coast soon learned to use the boughs on their flakes and bawns for drying fish. They also fermented them to make yeast for bread, steeped their nets and sails in a preparation of the buds and boughs to preserve them, and even used the boughs to strain oil out of cod livers. The Innu also taught the settlers to fashion makeshift snowshoes by tying spruce boughs to their feet if they were caught in a sudden snowstorm.

When a Liberator aircraft crashed in -48° Celsius weather 13 miles from Goose Bay in 1943, five of the men aboard survived because one of them insulated their sleeping area from the snow by layering a mattress of spruce boughs, and when they failed to make snowshoes from "catwalk and cartridge belting," Warrant Officer A.C. Johns devised some for them from evergreen boughs and parachute cord. Clearly, he had spent time in the Labrador woods prior to the crash and had picked up a few survival tips.

One of the most innovative and aesthetically satisfying uses for spruce in Labrador is in the construction of a spruce-bough floor. The Innu, over thousands of years, have perfected this practice and maintained it into the 21st century. Without knowledge of this form of construction, it is unlikely the trappers and hunters of European descent would ever have been able to survive a Labrador winter.

Originally developed for lean-tos and teepees, the spruce-bough floor has been adapted to suit the rectangular canvas tent used throughout Labrador. Once the tent is erected, the floor is systematically covered in fir or spruce tips from 6 inches to 1 foot in length, each twig with the butt pushed down into the snow or forest floor and layered the way a bird's feathers are. This produces a smooth, soft surface suitable for sleeping, which is warm in winter and cool in summer. The boughs can be renewed as the needles dry out and fall off and each new layer interlocks with the previous one, preventing the underlying snow from melting in winter and capturing a cool layer of air in the warmer months.

Innu elder Elizabeth Penashue has been making spruce-bough floors since she was a child and is very particular about how it is done. Harvesting the twigs takes almost as long as constructing the floor. The branch is snapped from the tree with an upward motion, and Elizabeth's mother taught her to start at the door and go straight to the corner, making sure that the butt of each twig is pushed well into the underlying surface and the needles point downward. In winter, Elizabeth uses balsam fir under and around the stove because it does not dry out so quickly as true spruce does. She renews the floor every five to seven days.

Forester Louie Montague, who was a trapper in his youth, had been making and sleeping on spruce-bough floors all his life. He explained that on the coast or in the Mealies, where he used to hunt caribou, he used black spruce for making floors because that's what was available, but in the interior, he preferred to use balsam fir. Balsam fir "spreads out nice, it's soft, and it's tidy looking on the floor," he says. Like Elizabeth, he insisted the only way to harvest the spruce tips is to snap them off by hand. "Don't chop them off with an axe, 'cause the axe will go into the tree and it will take a chip out—do it all with your hands."

Louie constructs his floor slightly differently from Elizabeth, with the stems all pointing toward the door. "Some people do it the other way," he explains, "because they say when your tent floor is messy it's easier to sweep out, but my way is the stems toward the door, and put it on about two layers thick."

When the people who settled in Sheshatshiu first moved into permanent housing across from North West River, they were so attached to their spruce-bough floors that they laid them on the planched wooden floors of their houses, just as they did with their tents in the country. In modern times, they have also adapted the blanket of *tshishtapakun* to honour the dead at funerals. Elizabeth Penashue agrees that this funeral practice is "a new thing." She feels it is a reflection of how important the boughs were in Innu life as medicine, insulation, food for animals, and so on.

"People said we should use *tshishtapakun*, not flowers anymore," she explains. Now, when someone dies, she and other mourners put pieces of spruce tip into their pockets when they go to the church to place on the corpse. Often the family will bring spruce tips to distribute to the mourners for this purpose. "It's like people say goodbye, *Nutshimit* (the country), that's your home. You're going home." As the gift of a spruce twig is often accompanied by a kiss, it is very moving to observe the body being embraced by young and old alike and symbolically buried under a green blanket of spruce.

Given all the important ways the spruce has contributed to the ecosystems of Labrador and the cultural lives of Labradorians, it is both appropriate and fitting that it has a place of honour on the Labrador flag.

The Beauty of Birches

One of the regrets I had shifting from Newfoundland to Labrador was leaving behind a beautiful yellow birch in the back of my garden. Islanders call yellow birch "witchhazel," which in itself is a magical name, and I lived at the time at the bottom of Witchhazel Ridge in Beachy Cove. Yellow birches don't grow in Labrador and I was sorry to say goodbye to it.

Fortunately, I found that Labrador was rich in seven other varieties of birch. I quickly developed a great affection for dwarf birches, which are shrubs rather than trees, and thought that if money grew on trees, it would look like dwarf birch leaves with their glossy, leathery surfaces and their ornamental frills. But what really captured my affection were the paper birches that are common throughout Canada but that particularly seem to thrive in the cool temperatures of central Labrador.

Happily, the rather unremarkable bungalow we bought in Goose Bay was blessed with a truly magnificent paper birch smack in the middle of its front lawn. Naturalist Gary Saunders, in his wonderful book *My Life with Trees*, claims that white birch could win a popularity contest due to our nostalgia for "snowy villages nestled among white birches" which have become part of the Canadian iconography. These snowy birches, he writes, are "a sight to soften the most embittered winter-hater."

Paper birches, unlike the dwarf varieties, are of considerable practical use to humans, and I came to appreciate those qualities the longer I lived in Labrador. Industry tells us that the paper birch is short-lived, responds badly to heat and humidity, and is good only for pulpwood or burning, but individual craftspeople love its clean, straight-grained nature. In Labrador, birch was used by the Innu for making snowshoes, as well as assorted useful objects such as spoons and bowls. They square-braided and sewed together thin strips of birch, similar to the shavings Newfoundlanders used as fire-starters, to make hats and baskets.

Settlers found birch useful for making barrels for the fishery, furniture for houses, and dozens of everyday objects such as clothespins, brooms, and salt cellars, but it was particularly prized as firewood. Many Labradorians prefer spruce for the stove, because birch burns fast and hot, but it is so clean and splits so well once it is dry that it's hard to beat. The even heat produced by birch is perfect for baking tricky things such as cakes.

Even if birch wood is easily replaced by fir and spruce, the same can't be said for birch bark. Paper birch is often called "canoe birch" because, until recent times, it was irreplaceable for sheathing canoes. Birch bark has a high oil content, which makes it waterproof and weather resistant. If you see a dead birch in the woods, chances are the wood itself has rotted away leaving the hollow bark whole. That bark, when stripped intact from a living tree, could be secured with spruce root and fir gum to make a light, reliable, mendable boat that would last a surprisingly long time.

Birch bark was used in Labrador and elsewhere by both Aboriginal people and settlers to create waterproof tents and huts. Before canvas or tarpaper was available, a teepee or box structure would be layered over with strips of birch bark held down by longers to make a durable shelter for short- or long-term habitation. Birch bark shrouds were also used by Innu to wrap the dead prior to burial.

Being waterproof, birch bark also made excellent containers for food or drink. I have on my desk a birchbark drinking vessel that has served to hold my pencils and pens for almost 50 years. A bit of the spruce root stitching has been mended with sinew, but otherwise it is as clean and fresh-looking as if it were new. Aboriginal people carried fish, berries, and meat in folded envelopes of birch bark, and they cooked food by dropping hot rocks into stitched birch bark containers.

Various animals in Labrador feed on birch bark. Moose, which are relatively new to the Labrador Peninsula, feed on birch bark in winter, and although it does not fulfill all their nutritional needs, it is important because of its abundance. Porcupine eat the inner bark of the trees, snowshoe hare browse on the bark and seedlings, grouse eat the buds, and small mammals and birds like chickadees and sparrows eat the abundant seeds.

Birch sap has only about one-third of the nutrients found in sugar maples but is said to make an excellent syrup. My father used to tap birch trees when he was a teenager, but I suspect that he was using the sap to make wine rather than syrup. The bark or the sap is also used to make birch "beer," which is a carbonated soft drink popular in various parts of the world. Crush Birch Beer is manufactured by Browning and Harvey in St. John's in the summer months for sale only in Newfoundland and Labrador and Fort McMurray. Birch beer can be brown, red, or clear—Crush Birch Beer is red, like cream soda.

Both the outer and inner bark of the birch is a key ingredient in home medicines as a bitter, an astringent, and an anti-rheumatic. Philip Tocque, writing in 1877, claimed that birch was known in Newfoundland to be beneficial in disorders of the lungs, for treating minor cases of frostbite and burns, and as a "mother's cure-all." It was also employed as a treatment for obesity—infusions of birch bark were thought to "shrink the stomach." It was also said to be a cure for worms, gout, cankers, bleeding gums, skin complaints such as eczema, and a decoction of the leaves was recommended for baldness.

While many home remedies are purely panaceas, birch bark contains glycoside, which decomposes to give methyl salicylate (oil of wintergreen), and it also has a high content of vitamins and minerals, so it may be truly effective as a treatment. According to Saunders, Aboriginal people used birch leaves to treat urethral and bladder infections and boiled the inner bark to heal burns, bruises, and wounds. Their supplies of tobacco were stretched by adding fresh powdered birch wood, but in my experience, smokers will add almost anything to their tobacco when they are running short.

In the winter of 1927, ethnohistorian William Duncan Strong

lived with the Innu and recorded in his diary many instances of Innu children playing by swinging on lodge poles, sliding in the snow, and teasing dogs. One evening he asked some of the children to draw pictures for him, while the other children remained busy "folding the inner skin of birch bark and making designs with their teeth. Some of the children made little birch bark containers, while still others made interesting designs and paper dolls out of the inner bark."

This passage reminded me of an evening when Francis and Elizabeth Penashue stopped by with some of their grandchildren for an impromptu supper. In an attempt to amuse the children, I distributed paper, pencils, and a pair of scissors. Within moments, everyone at the table was cutting, tearing, and folding paper, producing lines of dolls.

I kept those paper dolls and when Elizabeth and Francis visited at a later date, I brought them out and told them about Strong's description of the birch bark toys. A quick visit to the woodshed produced some sheets of bark, and in no time at all, both Elizabeth and Francis were hard at work showing me the kinds of toys they used to make themselves.

Francis began with the simplest toy, one that any child could make. He took a slip of bark, peeled off a thin layer, lifted it to his lips and made a piercing whistle. My sisters and I used to produce the same effect with a blade of grass.

Elizabeth's first product was a remarkably clever float plane, a favourite toy she used to make for her brother George Gregoire. From there she passed on to dolls, quickly cutting out a series of figures: priest, boy, girl, man, woman, and a self-portrait on which she wrote her name with a ballpoint pen.

Francis worked more slowly, fashioning first a small canoe and then a larger one. In the absence of fir gum to fuse the ends together, he worked with a little wood glue, and then using a crook knife, he shaved down a couple of wooden souvlaki skewers to make the gunnels. Once the glue dried, he explained, a boy would sew the ends of the canoe together and then stitch on the gunnels and thwarts.

Justine Rich, from Natuashish, reports that snowshoes were

a favourite item to cut from birch bark, as well as rings of boys and girls. According to Cajetan Rich, when the men brought home lengths of birch for making snowshoes, people would remove the bark so that it slid intact off the log. When these cuffs of bark were cut, the result would be a complete circle of figures. Later, when store-bought groceries were more common, people used the red Purity Hard Bread bags to achieve the same effect.

Elizabeth Penashue said that generally boys cut out animals, while girls cut out people. She did stitch together a toy canoe for me, though, with a birch bark tent tucked into the bottom of it, and she described how the pole was used to work up through the rapids on the river. Francis used some masking tape to hold his canoe together and set it to dry, with a promise to finish it next time he came for supper.

As I was tidying up, I put some of the leftover pieces of birch bark between the pages of a book, and when I found them again several years later, they were still immaculately fresh. Birch bark was actually used as paper in the early contact era, particularly for maps. It was also the means by which missionary James Evans was able to convert whole tribes of Aboriginal people to Christianity in the 1830s. Known as "the man who made birch bark talk," Evans invented the syllabic system of writing, and by marking out the syllabarium with soot on birch bark, he enabled thousands of Ojibwe, Cree, and eventually Inuit to learn to read and write.

Somewhere in Labrador I had seen an example of birch bark biting—a process whereby an artist (usually a woman) produces a pattern on birch bark by folding and biting it to bruise the surface. Think of carbon paper or paper snowflakes made by children in school, and you will have some idea of how this works. The memory of that unlikely craft got me thinking about ways to use birch bark in my own art practice, so the next time I was making a print, I substituted birch bark for actual paper and it produced a clean, neat image that was quickly snapped up by buyers.

Philip Tocque referred to paper birch as "the queen of the forest" for its elegance, but surely its versatility is what gives it such a hold on our affection, that first place prize in the popularity contest Gary Saunders referred to. The birch is beautiful, but it also yields up transportation, shelter, and tools, food, drink, and medicine to nourish the living, shrouds for the dead, as well as toys, prayers, and art to nurture the soul. There's not another tree in the world that can match that record.

VISITORS AND SOJOURNERS

Keeping Kool with Jens Haven

On a visit to the offices of *Them Days*, I noticed that some old bottles, which had been tucked away in a storeroom prior to renovations, had been put on display. I was particularly interested in the old Keep Kool bottles, partly because I remember drinking Keep Kool Orange Crush when I was a little girl but also because I had once found an older and earlier version of the same bottle buried intact in a rock wall I was repairing.

What I noticed about the old bottle is that, unlike the white painted logo of the seal on an ice pan that I had grown up with, the earlier embossed glass logo had the seal carrying a large fish in his mouth. I jokingly presented it to a friend as evidence that for at least a century, seals had been feeding off our cod stocks and contributing to their decimation. The newer logo doesn't have a fish, just a seal basking in the sun.

Keep Kool aerated waters, what we now call soft drinks, were first manufactured in St. John's, in G.H. Gaden's factory on Water Street between Clifts-Bairds Cove and Prescott Street. Gaden had inherited the property from his parents, Olive and William Gadden, or Gaden, as their name was more commonly spelled.

I came across a surprising reference to the Gadens recently while reading Hans Rollmann's *Moravian Beginnings in Labrador: Papers from a Symposium Held in Makkovik and Hopedale*. I was intrigued to learn, from an essay by Garth Taylor, that when Jens Haven was en route to Labrador in 1764 to see if it would be possible to establish a Moravian mission here, he stayed in St. John's with the merchant "Mr. Gadden."

Unwilling to accept favours which might tie him to the government, Haven approached Gaden, whose premises and fish flakes were conveniently located near the harbour, and offered to work as a carpenter in exchange for lodging and "whatever payment the man wished to offer." Gaden was happy to have the services of a capable carpenter and agreed to take Haven on until his transportation north had been arranged.

According to Taylor, "The merchant and his wife seemed to have taken a kindly interest in their new lodger's welfare and were 'shocked' to learn that the purpose of his proposed Labrador trip was 'to look for the Eskimos.'" They insisted that he did not know what he was getting into and were convinced that the Inuit would try to kill him. Haven, who was reputed to be a fluent Inuktitut speaker and very familiar with Greenland, assured his well-meaning hosts that he was going ahead with the plan.

According to Haven, Olive and William Gaden thought him a most "peculiar person [who] doesn't ask for money but would like to find out whether the Eskimos will beat him to death." After his successful foray into Labrador, Haven again stayed and worked for the Gadens on his way back to Germany. He was something of a celebrity in St. John's on his return and was barely able to go about his business in town because "immediately throngs of people would gather around me to see the peculiar man who had made peace with the Eskimos and come away with his life."

The rest, as they say, is history. The Keep Kool bottle I found was manufactured by a company called Breffits in London, England, but someone must have told them to put that seal and that ice pan on the front. The happy seal with the enormous fish is a very positive image of the Labrador coast, and I'm betting it is another silent memento of Jens Haven's first sortie into Labrador, a reflection of the good impression he would have made on young George Hugh Gaden when the celebrated peacemaker lodged in his parent's house.

Sir Joseph Banks: the Chateau Bay Naturalist

The name Sir Joseph Banks is known throughout the world; an 18th-century botanist and natural philosopher, Banks had more than 80 plants named for him, served for 41 years as president of the Royal Society, was made a baronet and Privy Counsellor, and was inducted into the Order of the Bath. He was responsible for the settlement of Australia and New Zealand, the establishment of Kew Gardens in London as a world-class collection, and the preparation of the magnificent *Florilegium*, the record of his botanizing in the South Seas which was eventually published in 34 parts in the 1980s.

However, little was known of Banks's first voyage of exploration to Newfoundland and Labrador in 1766 until A.M. Lysaght located, annotated, and published Banks's diaries from that voyage in 1971. Banks himself never published an account of the trip.

Banks's initial interest in Labrador was probably prompted by his contact with the Moravian missionaries who lived in Lindsey House, the Moravian headquarters in England, near his mother's home in Chelsea. Sarah Banks was a deeply religious woman who admired them greatly, and according to Lysaght, Banks himself was greatly influenced by their teachings as "from them he learnt to practice goodness rather than to preach it." Many of the Moravians also took an interest in botany and other arms of science, so it was "no wonder that influenced by his Moravian neighbours' tales of Greenland, he should when opportunity rose have visited Newfoundland and Labrador."

By the time of Banks's trip on the *Niger*, the Moravians had not yet successfully established a mission in Labrador, but in 1765, the year before Banks set out on his first expedition, four of the Moravians had travelled on the *Niger* to Chateau Bay. Plants in Banks's herbarium are labelled "Labrador 1765, Soc. Unit. Frat."—Unitas Fratrum, or the United Brethren of the Moravians. Clearly, one of the four Moravians who preceded him to Chateau Bay had given these samples to Banks.

Thus, late in April of the following year, accompanied by his friend Constantine Phipps, the 23-year-old Joseph Banks set out on his first voyage. The *Niger* was under orders to provide protection to English fishing vessels off the coast of Newfoundland and Labrador, to make charts of the coast around the Great Northern Peninsula, and to take a party of marines into Chateau Bay to build York Fort, a small permanent fort where a garrison could overwinter.

The initial weeks of the voyage did not go particularly well for Banks. He suffered horribly from sea sickness on the way out, he was confined by 4 to 5 feet of snow at Petty Harbour at the end of May, St. John's in June was wet and foggy, and at Croque he was desperately ill for much of July. He was too weak to do any collecting, though his servant brought him some specimens.

Once the fever passed, Banks recovered his strength quickly and on August 9, the *Niger* arrived at Chateau Bay, where he was delighted to discover that, unlike the tangled tuckamore of Croque, there were open barrens that abounded with partridge, ducks, curlews, plovers, and other birds. He began collecting animals, plants, and insects, anything he could find on land or sea.

On September 2, the crew caught a halibut that Banks measured as 6 feet 11 inches in length, weighing 284 pounds. That same day, Banks and the ship's master set out on a 10-day cruise in an open shallop but turned back to Pitts Harbour when it began to blow hard. That night, the wind worked up into a severe gale and the French, who were fishing nearby in vessels that were smaller than those of the English, lost three ships and over 100 men. After this, the captain refused to allow Banks to go northward, so he was restricted to the environs nearby.

Toward the end of September, the Sergeant of Marines at York

Fort brought Banks a porcupine, which cheered the naturalist up considerably. After "sulking" for three or four days, the animal began to eat and Banks hoped to bring it back to England alive. Banks was disappointed not to have seen more of Labrador during his two-month stay, but it wasn't the water haul he'd experienced on the island.

As well as the porcupine, Banks collected specimens of hawk owl, short-eared owl, spruce grouse, willow ptarmigan, grey jay, yellow-shafted flicker, great auk, snow bunting, white-winged crossbill, peregrine falcon, golden eagle, red-breasted merganser, and many other birds, all from Chateau Bay. Mosses, lichens, grasses, sea life, and insects—nothing was too small or unimportant for Banks's attention.

Early in October, after just eight short weeks in Labrador, the *Niger* sailed for Croque and then went on to St. John's, which Banks called "[t]he most disagreeable town I ever met with." Shortly before the *Niger* departed Newfoundland at the end of the month, he attended a ball at Government House, where the food served was excellent but "the want of ladies was so great that my washerwoman and her sister were there by formal invitation." He summed up his opinion of the town by recording that "[f]or dirt and filth of all kinds, St. John's may, in my opinion, reign unrivalled."

A gale of wind off the Azores stove in one of the ship's quarters and filled his cabin with water, which resulted in his losing all the Newfoundland and Labrador seeds he had collected, as well as potted plants which had been carried on deck. However, according to his biographer Patrick O'Brian, Banks returned home with "specimens or exact records of at least 340 plants, 91 birds, many fishes and invertebrates, and a few mammals, including the porcupine that at least began the voyage alive."

On his return to England, Banks published "the first Linnean description of the plants and animals of Newfoundland and Labrador," thus establishing himself as a serious naturalist and paving the way to the presidency of the Royal Society. It was quite an accomplishment for such a young man.

Probably just as important for his career, that 1766 voyage brought Banks into contact with James Cook, whom he met at both

Chateau Bay and St. John's. It was this contact that laid the foundation for their later three-year circumnavigation of the globe aboard the *Endeavour* that made Banks famous as a scientist and Cook famous as a navigator.

In later years, the Moravian missionaries continued to collect plants from Nain, Hopedale, and Okak for Banks's herbarium, which can still be seen at the Natural History Museum in London. York Fort, where Mikak and other kidnapped Inuit were held the year after it was built, was eventually destroyed by the French. Today, the garden drills and the star-shaped stone foundations are still visible. There has been no formal excavation of the site, but archaeologists have visited it and are hoping to give it due attention in the future.

Strathcona: A North West River Love Story

Donald Alexander Smith, First Baron Strathcona and Mount Royal, was a fur trader, agriculturalist, financier, railroad baron, politician, and philanthropist. Best known to Canadians as the man who drove the last spike into the Canadian Pacific Railway line that opened up the western territories to settlement, Labradorians know Smith as the man who provided the Grenfell Mission with their famous medical ships *Sir Donald* and *Strathcona*.

According to D.W. Prowse's *History of Newfoundland*, Smith "in early life had spent several years in the Hudson's Bay Company's Service, at North West River, Hamilton Inlet." This is a curious understatement, for Smith had actually lived in Labrador for a total of 21 years and among other things spoke fluent Innu-aimun. The error is corrected in the *Encyclopedia of Newfoundland and Labrador*, published a century later, but another curious error creeps in, one that was deliberately injected into the official record by Smith himself, and it regards his marriage to Isabella Hardisty.

Born in the Rupert's River District in 1825, Isabella Hardisty was the daughter of a Scottish Hudson's Bay trader and a woman of mixed Scottish and Cree descent. At age 13, Isabella was sent to school in England, returning when she was 19 to join her family at Moose Factory. In 1848, the family moved to North West River, while Donald Smith, who was junior to Hardisty, spent the winter at Rigolet. Smith succeeded Hardisty as chief trader at North West River in 1852, and Isabella, who had stayed in Rigolet when her parents moved on, came up to stay at North West River the following year and married Smith.

By all accounts beautiful and clever, Isabella Hardisty adapted easily to life in the wilderness. Margaret Baikie records in *Labrador Memories: Reflections at Mulligan* that one Christmas she visited North West River and Margaret and her aunt were "the first womenkind she [Mrs. Smith] had seen that winter." According to Baikie, Mrs. Smith was a pretty effective doctor, for when Tom Baikie cut his foot with an axe, "Mrs. Smith sewed it up." She was comfortable in the woods and had a trap line down on North West Point where she once caught a particularly valuable silver fox, which she managed to take alive.

This little snapshot of the trader's capable wife is wrong in only one thing—Isabella wasn't Smith's wife. In 1852, Isabella had married a young post servant named James Grant in Rigolet, and within a year had given birth to his son. The boy was christened James Grant, after his father, by none other than Donald Smith. After her parents left Rigolet, Isabella had left her husband, declaring that she would never go back to him, and had promptly moved in with the chief trader in North West River.

Such informal marital arrangements, called by the traders *a la façon du pays*, or marriages made according to the custom of the country, were not unusual in isolated areas such as Labrador. However, Smith was a very formal and respectable Christian and to simply take another man's wife was out of character for him. It presented problems for Sir George Simpson, the governor of the Hudson's Bay Company, as well, and he ordered that Isabella be returned to the protection of her father in Lachine.

According to Donna MacDonald, author of *Lord Strathcona: A Biography of Donald Alexander Smith*, the affair took an interesting turn here. Once Simpson actually met Isabella in Montreal, and realized that her second child, Maggie, was Smith's daughter, he "approved of this intelligent and energetic young woman as a partner for his protégé and kept an eye out for her interests." When Isabella applied for permission to return to Labrador, Simpson approved the request and "the fact that he allowed it was his way of saying that she would henceforth be treated as Donald's wife."

While Governor Simpson might have been easy in his mind about Smith's marital arrangements, Smith himself was not. He wished to regularize the situation but did not see how he could do this when Isabella was already married to Grant. Here again, Simpson surprised him. According to the governor's letter to Smith, Hudson's Bay Company officers possessed the authority to solemnize marriages "within Company Territory," but Labrador was not Company territory—it was part of the colony of Newfoundland. The Company did not control the area, it merely traded under licence there and any marriages performed by their officers in Labrador had to be confirmed by a religious ceremony and reported to the registrar at St. John's.

Isabella's marriage to Grant, like most of the marriages that took place in Labrador at that time, was not legal, so she was free to marry whomever she chose, and she chose to marry Smith. Smith, being a justice of the peace and having the permission of the Anglican bishop of Newfoundland to perform marriages in the absence of clergy, lost no time in conducting his own wedding in the presence of some of the Orkneymen who were stationed at North West River. The wedding took place in June of 1859, six years after the date given in Debrett's *Peerages*.

Curiously enough, Smith did not register the marriage in Newfoundland but relied on the old Scottish law that allowed a couple to wed simply by making a formal statement that they were married. This failure was to haunt him in years to come. In MacDonald's words, "Donald was intensely embarrassed by questions about his marriage, Maggie's legitimacy and his relationship to Jamesie," Grant's son.

However awkward Smith's feelings were about his marriage, he had no doubts that Isabella was his mate for life. She played a large part in his progress upward through the ranks to become governor of the Hudson's Bay Company, president of the Bank of Montreal, a Member of the Canadian Parliament, chancellor of McGill University, rector of the University of Aberdeen, Canadian High Commissioner to the United Kingdom, and Knight Commander of Her Majesty Queen Victoria.

The legitimacy of his marriage did become an issue, though, when Charles Tupper began working behind the scenes to have Smith promoted from Knight Commander to Knight Grand Cross of the Order of St. Michael and St. George. Queen Victoria's England considered divorce to be more scandalous than infidelity, and the ambiguity surrounding Smith's marriage made it awkward for him to be presented at court. Furthermore, he was by this time a very wealthy man and he was concerned that questions about Maggie's legitimacy might interfere with her right to inherit that wealth. He also wished Maggie to inherit his title, a desire he thought "so unusual as to be all but impossible."

Smith's first hope was that he could claim that Scottish law applied to his marriage. In the Scotland Smith knew as a youth, it was sufficient for a man to be domiciled in the country or to demonstrate that he intended to return there in order for a declaration of marriage to be valid. Under that law, "children born before that declaration were considered to be as legitimate as those born after." Smith therefore purchased a large property called Glencoe on Loch Leven, a house that Donna MacDonald called "a grand love letter from Donald to Bella in celebration of their life together."

Unfortunately, Smith found that Scottish law had changed in 1847, and after that time, marriages by consent had to be registered in order to be valid. Therefore, on Monday, March 9, 1896, 43 years to the day after their North West River wedding, Isabella and Donald Smith were remarried in a private ceremony at the Windsor Hotel in New York in the presence of their lawyers. Finally, Donald Smith was able to face Queen Victoria and the House of Lords with a clear conscience. Isabella was 70 and Donald 75, but both were still active and alert, and continued so into 1913, when Isabella unexpectedly died.

Smith survived Isabella by a mere 10 weeks. "With Bella gone," writes his biographer, "there seemed little reason to carry on." He spent the last weeks of his life reworking his will to leave millions of dollars to charitable causes, including $3,000 to put new boilers into the Grenfell Mission ship *Strathcona*. His very last act was to make a deathbed statement regarding his marriage to Isabella. In that statement he backdated his civil marriage in North West River to 1852 (not 1859) and revealed for the first time their 1896 New York marriage.

Smith died on January 20, 1914, and was buried next to his

beloved Isabella in Highgate Cemetery, as he had requested. He had left orders that "any mausoleum to be erected should be simple, but not foolishly simple." His daughter, Maggie, inherited a modest $7.5 million, and became the second Baroness Strathcona and Mount Royal, the crown having ensured her succession in 1900 in recognition of her father having recruited and equipped a cavalry troop at his own expense for service in the Boer War.

Today, the title is held by Maggie's grandson Euen Howard, the Fourth Baron Strathcona. In Canada, England, and America, hospitals, libraries, streets, and districts are named Strathcona in memory of Donald Smith's contribution to business and charitable causes, and in Rigolet, his little house has been reconstructed as a cultural centre and museum in recognition of his place in Labrador's and Canada's history. His stepson, Jamesie, is buried in North West River.

The Follow-On Bartletts of Turnavik

Mention the name Bartlett anywhere in Newfoundland or Labrador and the response will almost always be "Captain Bob, the ice master." While it is true that Robert Bartlett is the best known of the family, a closer look at some of the historical sources reveals that "Captain Bartlett" might have been any one of a dozen men in the family who skippered ships around the north, including Captain Joseph, Captain John, Captain William J., Captain Henry B., Captain William A., Captain Will Jr., Captain Moses, and Captain Isaac Bartlett. As well, George, Harold, Isaac and Rupert Bartlett, and their cousins Jack Angel and Jim and Robert Dove, all crewed for Bartlett ships, and many worked in Arctic waters also.

The first Captain Bartlett to come to North America was William, known as "Follow-On" Bartlett. He settled at Brigus in the 1700s, and earned his name around 1800 when he went looking for seals at the mouth of Conception Bay in an open boat. Ice was scarce that year, and he found none so he went farther north to Cape Bonavista and then to the Funks, "following on" with each disappointment, until he came to a patch of seals off Hiscock Island in Labrador, where he bloodied his gunnels and sailed for home.

Follow-On Bartlett set the pattern for the family. In the early 1800s, Follow-On's nephew, Captain Abram Bartlett, established premises at Turnavik West, an island just north of Makkovik, and before long had established himself as a crew captain and supplier. Abram was also one of the leading sealing captains of Brigus and, in partnership with Baine, Johnston and Company, owned the 246-ton *Panther* and took her to the ice until 1884, when he turned her over to his son, William Abram Bartlett.

Young William first went to Labrador when he was 15 years old, around 1866. When in 1879 the Hudson's Bay Company closed its post in Kaipokok Bay, the Lyalls and McNeills of nearby Island Harbour went to the Bartletts for their supplies, and eventually built summer fishing premises in Turnavik East.

Bob Bartlett wrote that, in his youth, his father employed "about 150 men, women, boys, and girls, catching and curing cod" in Labrador. According to Rupert McNeill, William eventually had two crews on wages at Turnavik and supplied about 40 other crews. His station had a cooper shop, a blacksmith shop, and a huge coal shed with which to supply the northern boats. The fish they caught or bought was dried in Labrador and shipped directly to market in southern Europe. Unlike the McNeills and the Lyalls at Island Harbour, the Bartletts didn't overwinter; instead, William went back to Brigus in October to prepare for the spring seal hunt, leaving the premises in the hands of a caretaker, Tom Evans, who hunted and trapped there in the winter.

William and his wife, Mary, the parents of Captain Bob, were, according to Harold Horwood, "stern and chilly fundamentalists," which is consistent with granddaughter Ruperta Murphy's description of William as a "very strict, cold Methodist." There was no drinking or Sunday work on his ships, and he had a sarcastic tongue, but his crew called him "a good man" and "a nice man," who was very careful of those he employed. Wilfred Grenfell, in his autobiography, describes bringing a silver fox to William Bartlett to trade for an impoverished patient, and receiving a boat load of supplies from the Captain, "a man known for his generous sympathy for others."

Growing up, Bob and his brothers often went to Labrador with their father for the summers, and it was one of Bob's ironic boasts that as a boy on the Labrador he helped to exterminate the Eskimo curlew. But just when most of the other Bartlett boys were being prepared for a life as fishing and sealing captains, 15-year-old Bob was packed off to the Methodist College in St. John's to finish his education and—his mother's hope—become an ordained minister.

He stuck it out for two years, but realizing that he would never grow into the role, he gave it up and at the age of 17 took the *Osprey*, his first vessel, to the Labrador fishery, after which he signed on to earn his foreign-going master's ticket. In 1898, Bob's uncle, Captain John Bartlett, was master of Admiral Robert Peary's ship *Windward* and his uncle, Captain Sam Bartlett, was skippering her supply ship, *Hope*. Bob got his papers that year and was invited by Peary to be first mate on the *Windward* in its initial attempt on the North Pole. This was the beginning of a lifetime of Arctic exploration for Captain Bob.

On this expedition and many subsequent ones, Bob Bartlett would stop in at Labrador to resupply, catch up on the news, replace crew, and visit with family. For example, in 1896, Bob was in Turnavik when the *Hope* touched in, and he met US marshal Hugh J. Lee, who later helped him out in Alaska after the sinking of the *Karluk*. In 1906, when the *Roosevelt* ran out of coal on her voyage home from Greenland after her attempt at the Pole, Bartlett stopped in settlements along the coast of Labrador, acquiring "spruce, whale blubber, small amounts of coal and anything else that would burn," until they limped into Cape Breton, where they obtained enough coal to get them back to New York by Christmas Eve.

When Peary finally claimed to have reached the North Pole in 1909, he stopped at Turnavik before sending the famous victory telegram from Smokey. The following year Bob showed up in Battle Harbour on his way back from a hunting voyage with millionaires Harry Whitney and Paul Rainey. In 1921 he had engine trouble at L'Anse-au-Loup and got a tow from Les O'Brien and his father and brothers, and in 1926 he was in L'Anse-au-Loup again. In 1927 he was at Sculpin Island looking for archeological remains of the Vikings, and in 1929 he made a motion picture cruise to Labrador. A stop at Turnavik was generally included in all of his trips.

According to Horwood, Bob had an "immensely strong sense of family" and, when he could, he included his brothers and nephews in his crew. Family was understood to include the employees and friends at Turnavik West.

Bob's father, William, summered at Turnavik for 42 years with great success for much of that time, but as his crew aged and the Labrador fishery declined, returns fell off. According to Captain Bob, who described the situation in his book *Sails over Ice*, it became harder to get the right sort of men to carry on, and one summer, "owing to bad ice conditions," William got a water haul—94 quintals of fish instead of the usual 10,000 to 12,000 quintals. The Turnavik business never recovered from this loss, going deeper and deeper into debt until everything was mortgaged to Sir Edgar Bonny and his stepson, John Shannon Munn.

Captain Will Bartlett Jr., Bob's brother, was still going to Turnavik every summer when Bob purchased the schooner *Effie B. Morrissey* in 1925. Bob contacted him about buying the station and negotiated a generous deal from the Bonnys for the property and fishing gear. Turnavik West was once again in the hands of the Bartlett family. However, Bob Bartlett was never a successful fisherman or sealer, and his first season there was such a financial disaster that he realized he would have to find some other way to make a living. Turnavik became his stopping-off place for future expeditions in the *Morrissey*, a place where he could retreat to the peace and quiet he missed in New York.

Bartlett was already world famous by this time, so to finance his explorations, he took on some unique and unusual work. He signed endorsements (Wheaties breakfast cereal and Winchester firearms), gave lectures, made documentary films, wrote articles, captured and sold wild animals such as walrus and polar bears, and entertained working passengers and wealthy hunters on his ship. He also undertook hydrological work for the American navy, collected artifacts and biological samples, and was a scientific jack-of-all-trades. He transported archeologists, carried out work for museums, universities, and scientific institutes, made collections of marine life, did surveys, and starred in Varrick Frissell's feature movie, *The Viking*. During World War II, Bartlett helped establish supply bases and weather stations for the US military in Greenland and elsewhere.

None of this, of course, saved the Labrador fishery or Turnavik West, although it did extend its life for a time. The families at nearby Island Harbour used Turnavik West as a summer fishing station for a number of years until William Bartlett's death in 1931, and when Bob Bartlett died in 1946, there were still four families left in Island Harbour who continued to use the Bartletts' small sheltered harbour. By 1950, even that community was abandoned.

The Turnavik Islands are still visited by people fishing out of Makkovik, but the days when it was the stopping-off place for wealthy New York businessmen on holiday are long gone and all but forgotten. What is not forgotten, however, is the huge contribution to Arctic exploration that was made by Captain Bob Bartlett and his family. Their home in Brigus is now a National Historic Site, and visitors to Hawthorne Cottage can visit the "Ar'tic Room" and view memorabilia from Captain Bob's many voyages of exploration.

L.A. Learmonth: A Northern Man for Life

The settler history of Labrador is strongly rooted in the Orkney Islands, an archipelago of approximately 70 islands off the northeast coast of Scotland. The Orkney heritage of Labrador dates to the early 18th and 19th centuries, when the Hudson's Bay Company began hiring Orkneymen as labourers and fur trade apprentices, a practice that continued into the early 20th century. When Hudson's Bay supply ships heading out to North America stopped in Stromness for supplies, good Orkneymen were found to be available for hire.

By the end of the 18th century, fully 80 per cent of the employees of the Hudson's Bay Company fur trading posts in North America were Orkneymen. As one contemporary reported it, the Orkney Islanders were "more sober and tractable than the Irish, and they engage for lower wages."

Once their initial five-year contracted service was complete, many of these young Orkneymen headed home, but some stayed behind and married local women, just as they did in the Red River colony of Manitoba. John Goudie came to Labrador from Orkney in around 1839 and established a dynasty; Daniel Campbell arrived in 1844 and did likewise. The Olivers, Baikies, Montagues, and others, all Orkney Islanders, came as temporary Hudson's Bay Company servants but stayed on to make new lives in the country.

One of the last wave of Orkney Island men to come out to Labrador was Lorenz Alexander Learmonth, from Stronsay Island, who signed on at Stromness in 1911 at age 18. According to a CBC interview Learmonth gave for the radio program "The Days before

Yesterday," the Hudson's Bay Company vessel *Pelican* would came up to the Orkneys from London where they'd been wintering to "pick up fresh water, vegetables, chickens, pigs, and apprentices. You see, the apprentices came last. You had to be at least half way through high school before they'd accept you in the apprenticeship." It probably helped that Lorenz's older brother David was already a post manager with the company.

Cartwright, where Learmonth landed in Labrador, carried on a thriving salmon fishery at that time. "They made all their own casks on the post—regular coopers would make them, they got the material locally—and nets were made on the post. They'd ship beautiful salmon," Learmonth said. Most of that catch went out as salted salmon, which was eventually exported to Holland.

As an apprentice, Learmonth was assigned to "Sundry Posts" in the district of St. Lawrence-Labrador, which meant he went wherever he was needed, travelling with the supply vessels and staying until he was posted elsewhere. He worked at various posts, including Cartwright, Davis Inlet, Mud Lake, and probably North West River.

Not much about Learmonth's time as a young apprentice made its way into the official records of the Hudson's Bay Company, but the young man certainly made an impression on some of the Grenfell Mission people during his time at Mud Lake. Marjorie Wakefield, a welfare worker and wife of one of the mission doctors, described him in her 1913 diary as "a very shy and nice Scotch boy" who celebrated Christmas with the Grenfell staff and the Methodist minister, the only clergy within 100 miles.

Mrs. Wakefield reported that young Learmonth was also "a keen LF man," meaning that Learmonth belonged to the Legion of Frontiersmen, a paramilitary group that was preparing for the war with Germany that was so obviously looming. Anyone could qualify to join the Frontiersmen if they had previous military service, training at sea, or had "knocked about in the wilds." At Mud Lake, the Frontiersmen trained in elementary and single-stick drill, marksmanship, boxing, and first aid, and they participated in social programs such as concerts and "ward service."

Mrs. Wakefield recorded that Learmonth was "the doctor's

right hand man" there: "Last week when we were short of help for an operation he came and gave the anesthetic and gave it to the doctor's satisfaction although he had no previous experience." Learmonth also seems to have learned quite a lot about hunting and trapping as well as how to handle boats in Labrador, all of which came in very useful in his later life.

In 1914, when war broke out, many of the Frontiersmen, including Dr. Wakefield, signed on to the Newfoundland Regiment. Learmonth took leave from the Hudson's Bay Company, made his way down to St. John's where he got passage on the Furness Withy ship *Digby* to England, and joined the Essex Regiment of the British army. Building on his experience assisting the doctor at Mud Lake, as well as his Frontiersmen training, he went to Germany as a medical orderly, where in 1917 he was captured and spent a year as a prisoner of war in East Prussia. After the war was over, he went back to the Hudson's Bay Company and was posted to Port Harrison as post manager in 1919.

Although Learmonth spent the rest of his working years with the Hudson's Bay Company, he was never posted back to Labrador. However, it is clear that his initial introduction to northern life as a young man at Cartwright and Mud Lake had made him "a northern man for life." His only other St. Lawrence-Labrador district posting was in Chesterfield Inlet, on the western side of Hudson's Bay, and his subsequent postings were to the western Arctic district, although today these areas would be classified as central Arctic or Keewatin district.

Prior to air travel, Arctic voyagers could not pass from east to west or the reverse—Hudson's Bay could only be reached from the east via Labrador and the Queen Maud Gulf had to be approached from the west, around Alaska. Learmonth attempted to change all that when he established a post at Fort Ross in the Bellot Strait in 1937, becoming the first European to traverse the North West Passage from west to east, an accomplishment that received international publicity at the time.

Learmonth, a quiet man who valued his privacy, was known in the north simply as L.A. or *Mr. Learmonth*. Graham Rowley reports that, although the Inuit called him Eetungalik (Bright Eyes), he was "held in such well-deserved respect in the Company" that he was never addressed by his first name or given an English nickname.

Labradorian Ernie Lyall served as his assistant at Fort Ross and probably knew him better than most people. Lyall wrote that Learmonth "knew more about the north than anyone else. He was one of the best. He was very quiet spoken and very, very interesting, you'd never be bored while he was around." Lyall liked the freedom he experienced at Fort Ross, where he was allowed to go out hunting and trapping, because "Mr. Learmonth … liked to do that sort of thing himself": "Once we had our work done and the books up to date, and there was no great rush for trading, he and I used to take turns going out hunting."

When Learmonth wasn't trading or hunting Arctic animals, he was busy locating and collecting artifacts, stories, and information. An avid amateur archeologist and social historian, he "contributed nearly 2,000 ethnographic and archeological items to the Royal Ontario Museum." His documentation of Inuit oral history related to British explorers such as Orkneyman Dr. John Rae has contributed vastly to our knowledge of those expeditions.

Learmonth's greatest discoveries related to the fate of the Franklin Expedition, with which he had developed a strong fascination. With his apprentice, D.G. Sturrock, Learmonth located two sets of Franklin crew remains, along with identifying artifacts including buttons, coins, copper sheathing, and other items, all of which led to the eventual location of the wreck of the *Erebus* in 2014 and the *Terror* in 2016. Learmonth also collected stories about the British explorer John Ross, which perhaps explains why he chose the name Fort Ross for his post.

Richard Finney described Learmonth as "[o]ne of the most serious, most conscientious of the Hudson's Bay Company traders, and the fondest of the Eskimos." Henry Larsen, who encountered Learmonth numerous times in his travels, wrote that he was "greatly impressed with this man's profound understanding of the Eskimo way of life." Learmonth contributed ethnological and scientific notes to zoologists, archaeologists, linguists, meteorologists, and economists. He also helped to establish the DEW line sites for distant early warning radar. He was a capable photographer and had a darkroom at Coppermine where he taught Inuit friends how to print their own images, and he left almost 1,500 invaluable photographs to the Northwest Territories archives.

Although Learmonth wasn't one to go looking for honours or recognition, stories about his many exploits and accomplishments turn up in almost every book written about the Canadian Arctic in the first half of the 20th century. He was elected a Fellow of the Arctic Institute of North America when that honour was established in 1948, and he was one of three Hudson Bay fur traders honoured when Panarctic Oils named one of their steel barges after him. The 190-foot-long *L.A. Learmonth*, which was equipped with a prototype Axelbow that cut sea ice from below the surface and pushed it aside as it advanced into an icefield, was launched July 5, 1968.

Although Learmonth occasionally wrote articles for the history magazine *Beaver* and the Hudson's Bay Company staff newsletter *Moccasin Telegraph*, he never wrote a comprehensive account of his own diverse and adventurous career. However, in his 47 years with the Hudson's Bay Company, he was written up by such divergent reporters as Ralph Parsons, Farley Mowat, Peter Mansbridge, and even society columnist Zena Cherry. The staff at the Mud Lake hospital would probably have been surprised at just how big an impact their "very shy and nice Scotch boy" had on the opening up of the Canadian Arctic.

Richard White: Trader and Ethnographer

Labrador can boast of many unusual and eccentric citizens, but one of the most colourful is Richard White Jr., a famous trader whose house at White Harbour, just south of Nain, was declared a registered heritage structure in 1993.

White was born in 1878 into an upper-middle-class merchant family in St. John's and trained in law at the London School of Economics. However, when he returned to Newfoundland to take up legal practice, he was told he had consumption and advised that "if he wanted to live he should move to the north."

He did just that, moving first to the Northwest Territories as a gold prospector and then into Labrador with a survey party, with odd jobs in between as the proprietor of a boxing academy and some time as a private investigator.

In Labrador, he found what he had been looking for—a home and a job that suited him. He set up as a trader first in Hebron, where he met and married Inuk Ruth Townley in 1912. The following year he moved his business to Nain. However, the Moravian missionaries didn't welcome the competition and used their land grant to force him out. He tore down his house, moved it to Kauk, just outside the Nain boundaries, and also built a seasonal house at Voisey's Bay.

Although White initially found it hard to break into the fur trade, he persisted and instead of waiting for the trappers to come to him, he went to the trappers. Travelling by dog team as far south as Frenchman's Island and Battle Harbour, White intercepted the fur trappers on their way to more sedentary traders and got the pick of their catch.

According to Roy Hammond, who worked for White, one of White's canniest moves was to become a shareholder in the Hudson's Bay Company so that he could access "invaluable news of fur sales results and other helpful data" that was withheld from the general public. He would also give a prime skin to a compliant friend and send him to get an evaluation from his rival, thus allowing him to set an appropriately competitive price at his own post.

Flexibility was always one of Richard White's strengths, and he exercised good judgment when he established a seasonal post at Voisey's Bay. Other traders considered Innu trappers to be unreliable or unpredictable, but White learned their patterns of movement and accommodated them. He usually spent the month of August at Voisey's Bay and the Innu would come out to the coast at that time, bringing with them whatever they had to trade.

Although the Moravians and some of the Hudson's Bay traders spoke Inuktitut, they did not speak Innu-aimun, which gave White an advantage. According to a member of the Pasteen family, "Mishti Uait's Innu-aimun was not the best; he sounded like a child when he spoke, but at least one could make sense of what he said."

When World War I began, family responsibilities and his age prevented White from volunteering, but Joseph Smallwood claimed that the trader recruited a dozen Labrador sharpshooters for the Newfoundland Regiment. In 1918, with the war still dragging on, White's specific skills were called for, so he was actively recruited and signed up as a sled-dog handler with the Canadian Siberian Expeditionary Force. Leaving his wife and child with his Townley in-laws in Hebron, White went to war.

Along with 4,000 other Canadian soldiers, White was sent to Vladivostok during the Russian Revolution to support the allied presence there. Hammond said White later complained of "an enforced immobility ... as a prisoner of war," but this was probably just White employing a metaphor for wasted time. Possibly his health was affected by conditions in Siberia because, according to his war record, he was "[e]vacuated to Canada on compassionate grounds (health)" in March of 1919 and discharged in June of that year.

White returned to Labrador to find his wife, Ruth, dead and his child being cared for by her grandparents. Contradictory sources say Ruth died of measles or the Spanish influenza epidemic which decimated the Labrador coast, but White's relatives in St. John's believe she died of tuberculosis. Once little Ruth was old enough, she went to boarding school in St. John's, where she was a frequent visitor with her cousins, spending her summers back home in Labrador with her father.

In 1921, White married Judy Pauline Hunter and started another family, which eventually grew to an even dozen. However, the period between the two wars was a difficult time in Labrador. The population was decimated, the caribou were scarce, and fur prices were down, but Richard White was a true entrepreneur. A gifted intellectual with a large library and an insatiable curiosity, White became the middle man for anthropologists who were scrambling to document what they thought were dying cultures.

White began collecting artifacts and crafts from the Inuit and Innu in his area as a way of carrying these families on his books even when they didn't have any furs to trade. In Stephen Loring's words, he was "seeking to recoup advances paid to the Naskapi who traded at his posts during periods of poor fur returns." This was something that the Hudson's Bay traders occasionally did also, but in White's case, he wasn't satisfied with just obtaining the objects. He also wanted the information that made the objects valuable to museums and collectors.

According to noted anthropologist Frank Speck, White collected over 1,000 Aboriginal artifacts for the Museum of American Indians, the National Museum of Denmark, and other institutions, all of which were accompanied by valuable notes on the social structure and economic life of the people who made them. Many of the Labrador clothes, toys, and hunting implements currently held at The Rooms and the Labrador Interpretation Centre were also collected and documented by Richard White.

Dr. W.H. Drover described White as "a tall, lean, learned man ... widely read with a large library and a profound knowledge of current world events, an interesting character." Roy Hammond said he had "a habitually theatrical, sometimes almost flamboyant appearance and manner." When he made his annual business trip to St. John's, he was likely to dress in a bright green blanket jacket, yellow deerskin breeches, and Indian moccasins, with a bag full of cash clutched in each hand. He was a gifted storyteller and didn't mind being noticed.

White had a reputation in Labrador for having a hard, unbending character, yet he was also widely admired for his dealings with the Innu, who were often in difficulty in those years. At one point, in the late 1930s, he led a party 100 miles into the interior to bring food and supplies to the Mushua Innu who were starving to death. In the words of Roy Hammond, "He was not a philanthropist; he was a man of business who didn't need legal coercion to keep him kindly."

The Innu Nation website includes a story about how Richard White once traded a package of gum for a *tapaikan*, a pin and bough game that had no commercial value. Some interpreted such trading as evidence of White's avaricious nature—he would not give a child so much as a pack of gum without being paid for it. However, the story could also be interpreted to suggest that White saw cultural value in even a worthless, disposable toy and was prepared to pay for it. The Innu youth he traded with clearly thought he got the best of the deal when he got a good "chaw" for a worthless "fire starter."

The death of Winston White, Richard White's youngest child, resurrected a story that Harold Horwood used to tell. Apparently when Horwood, a journalist-turned-politician, was travelling around Labrador, stirring up votes for the first post-confederation election, he made his way on snowshoes to Richard White's house outside of Nain. Letting himself in, he found himself face to face with a small boy, who was pushing a lit candle across the floor. "And who would you be?" he asked the child. "I am Diogenes in search of an honest man," answered Winston. Clearly, that apple didn't fall far from the tree.

The book based on Richard White's anthropological notes that Frank Speck claimed was "being prepared for publication" in 1931 never appeared, and Winston White's biography of his father was incomplete when he passed away a few years ago, so the whole story of Richard White may never be known. However, he does appear, thinly disguised, as the trader Hugh Richardson in Harold Horwood's novel *White Eskimo*, and he is still spoken of as "Misti Uait" by the Mushuau Innu.

One conclusion that can be drawn from the life of Richard White is that if you have a good library and insatiable curiosity, the wilds of Labrador can provide even an educated man with plenty of intellectual stimulation and entrepreneurial opportunity for a rich and fulfilling life. He left a wonderful legacy, not just in the artifacts and information he collected but in the family he raised to love Labrador as much as he did.

Frank Banikhin: The Matjes Herring Man

Every tourist longs to find a deserted island, a pristine getaway untrodden by human foot. When I stepped out of a boat onto an obscure island near Cape Charles one summer, I couldn't see anything to suggest it was ever inhabited. However, Nelson Smith, my guide from Battle Harbour, has a sharper eye than mine and within minutes he had scoured the landwash and come up with an assortment of old square nails, chainies (pieces of sea glass and broken china), and bits of brick from a forge. The final proof—a large clump of rhubarb gone to seed—convinced me we had found the elusive Banikhin Island, a place that turns up in books and stories but appears on no map.

A hundred years ago, an itinerant Jewish trader named Froim (Frank) Banikhin fled the pogroms of the Ukraine for the goldfields of the Yukon, and from there headed east to work the fur trade of the Northwest Territories until he landed on the coast of Newfoundland and Labrador in 1917. Banikhin's interest in Labrador was considerable. He had three steamers, and he traded in scrap metal, hides, pit props, and anything else that could turn a dollar. He was also interested in the iron ore deposits near Churchill Falls, but the location was considered too remote and nobody would touch it.

In the 1930s, however, Banikhin finally struck gold of a sort. This gold was silver—silver and wet with a slight reddish tinge to the skin. Matjes herring, the highest quality of mature, fat herring, were being used throughout Newfoundland and Labrador as bait fish.

For Banikhin, watching schmaltz or matjes herring being used as bait was akin to using $100 bills to start a fire. Always the entrepreneur, Frank didn't give up on his trading business but he quickly set up shore factories that could process and pack Scotch cured herring for export to the United States and Europe. Before long, Banikhin has no fewer than 18 herring factories around the island of Newfoundland and on the coast of Labrador.

One of the first factories he set up was on the Seal Islands, about 2 kilometres northwest of Cape Charles. He sent in a couple of men, Noel and Richard Taylor from Carbonear, and according to Pearl Pye, speaking to *Them Days* magazine, Banikhin "had barrels come down and men come down to cooper the barrels. Every Fall he'd be down there buying herring, packing them and having a boat come down. He'd be shipping them out and taking them away to other countries."

During this time, Banikhin taught the people of Cape Charles not only to pickle and pack herring but to dress them with bread crumbs, the way they dressed codfish, and bake them in young cabbage leaves in the oven for their own consumption. "It was delicious," said Mrs. Pye.

The Banikhin Island herring factory was a thriving business, drawing workers from all around the district, including 25 men from L'Anse-au-Loup. The island on which it was built was small, and close enough to the mainland that you could reach it by way of a wooden bridge, but the water was deep enough to allow boats to get in close for loading and unloading. Robert H. Davies, who took shelter there one night aboard the *Glad Tidings III* in a thick fog, called it "a nice little harbour."

According to John C. Kennedy, Cape Charles people were very glad to work at the herring. Local fishermen "often worked for Banikhin part-time, during the afternoons, leaving them the morning to fish or work at other jobs. Pay was 15 cents per hour in 1938." Some men only caught and sold herring, while others actually did the pickling. Those working at readying the herring for export removed the gills and entrails, "gibbing" the fish.

For those who wished to catch herring, Banikhin provided nets similar to gillnets, with a 2.5-inch-mesh size, though sometimes they also used seines. These men were employed on shares, $2.50 per tub in 1941. By 1945, Banikhin had raised the price to $5 a tub, compared with the $3 fishers got using their own nets in the Red Bay area. Herring prices during the war were particularly good because herring oil was used to make explosives.

Banikhin always had an eye to the future, and prior to the war he had proposed a scheme to open up Labrador for immigration to German Jewish refugees. Sir John Hope Simpson and the Commission of Government backed the plan, but the Zionists—not realizing the Holocaust that was about to engulf them—did not approve, and the proposal died. Sadly, Banikhin's son, Flight Sergeant Lawrence Banikhin, was shot down and killed over India in 1942. After that, "the good went out of the old man." Family members say he never fully recovered from the blow.

Eventually, when the herring runs diminished and the market dried up, Banikhin moved his factory building to nearby Matty's Cove on Great Caribou Island and switched to packing salt fish. Retired pilot Ralph Bradley recalls that Banikhin left two big boats on the beach at Indian Cove—he and his friends used to play in them when they were boys.

The Matty's Cove salt fish factory continued into the 1950s with Harry Sampson as overseer and caretaker. As a young teen, Ralph Bradley worked there, walking across the island from Indian Cove. Banikhin's son Wilfred oversaw the on-site management of the business. The plant burned down in 1957, at which time Banikhin and Sons moved their operation to Assizes Harbour, where they purchased an old herring facility from Curling Fisheries.

Harry Sampson, who was left in charge of the house and outbuildings at Matty's Cove, remembers Frank Banikhin fondly. When he decided to get married, Mr. Banikhin offered him the company house, but Harry wasn't comfortable accepting it, thinking Wilfred might want it one day, so he asked if he could build a new house on the site of the old factory. Banikhin wired permission back to him via the Marconi Station at Battle Harbour, wishing him all the best, and Harry still has the transcript, which serves as a deed to his property.

Harry continued to spend summers at Matty's Cove with his wife, Emma, and it was Emma who told me one of the better known local stories of "the old man." According to Emma, Mr. Banikhin used to dye his hair, and when the dyed hair grew out, he'd send the youngsters to collect blackberries as a substitute. One day, it began to rain unexpectedly, and the blackberry juice came trickling down the old man's face and into his collar, much to the amusement of everyone.

Not much remains of the old operation at Banikhin Island. Ralph Bradley says there is a home on the point in Mary's Harbour that was built from the beams of the factory, and one of the sheds at Indian Cove was floated over from Banikhin Island and is still in use today. The story of Mr. Banikhin's hair dye still circulates among the older people of the area, and his recipe for herring wrapped in cabbage leaves can be found in the *Caribou Cakes* cookbook.

Froim Banikhin died in St. John's in 1970, at the age of 82, and today there's only a few scraps of iron and china, and a clump of rhubarb, on an officially unnamed island, to mark the site of one of Labrador's most successful businesses. But on a sunny day, it is a veritable paradise, a fitting place for the memory of a fine man to rest.

LABRADORIANS
AT HOME AND AWAY

Victor Croucher: The Boy with the Giant Cod

The image is iconic—a little boy in a sailor suit standing between two gigantic codfish. Sometimes the photo is titled "Boy with Giant Cod," and more recently, it has been labelled "In Cod We Trust[ed]." Visitors to Battle Harbour know that the boy is five-year-old Victor Croucher, but when the photo appeared at the Interpretation Centre at North West River, it simply carried the number VA 21-18, and the tag "Big cod fish from the trap, Battle Harbour, Labrador 1901," identifying it as the work of Robert Edwards Holloway, a gifted teacher, scientist, and hobby photographer.

Photohistorian Manfred Buchheit, who curated the exhibition "The Holloways: Newfoundland and Labrador's First Family of Photography" explained to the staff that the archivists at The Rooms didn't consider the identification of Victor Croucher to be verified, so for the purposes of the exhibition, the child remained anonymous. It was staff member Audrey McLean who noticed that photo G 6-11, Battle Harbour, Labrador 1901, contained another picture of the same child, this time with a man, presumably his father.

G 6-11 is a shot of the Baine Johnston canneries and the Deep Sea Mission at Battle Harbour, taken from across the tickle on Great Caribou Island, and perched on the hillside nearest the photographer, in what Buchheit says is typical Holloway fashion, are two small figures. The man, with a white collar and tweed cap, has his arm wrapped protectively around the little boy, who is wearing the same adorable sailor suit as in the photo with the cod. Originally, the catalogue tells us, the photo was "published in cropped, panoramic format as plate 102 in *Through Newfoundland with the Camera*, eliminating the two figures in the foreground. Buchheit's print, taken from the original glass negative, gives us the whole picture.

A visit to the offices of *Them Days* on the day of Buchheit's departure from Goose Bay led to a lively discussion of the identity of the child and what constitutes adequate identification. Artist Mavis Penney decided to solve the problem in typical Labrador fashion—she phoned up Sharon Rideout, Croucher's great-granddaughter, who was busy at work in her hair salon around the corner on Grand Street. Twenty minutes later, Sharon was in the office, carrying a photo of her nan, Margaret White, an article about the famous photo with the cod, and a Xerox copy of a previously unknown photo of Victor taken by Holloway at the same time.

The article, by Ron Young, describes how Ron noticed an original copy of the cod photo on the wall of Jim and Margaret White's home in Chamberlains and asked about it. Margaret explained that her grandfather, John Thomas Croucher, worked for fish merchants Baine Johnston, and spent every summer on the Labrador employed by the company at Battle Harbour. "Young Victor would accompany him on these occasions [and] it was on one of these trips, when Victor was about five, that the picture was taken."

When Victor grew up, he married Elsie Bradbury and settled at Battle Harbour year round. Sadly, when he was just 21, he died in a hunting accident. On May 1, 1918, Victor was turr hunting off Battle Harbour, but when he reached for his muzzleloader, seizing it by the barrel, it accidentally went off, killing him instantly. He left a baby son, John Edwin—known as Jack—and a pregnant wife. Margaret was born 10 weeks later. The white marble monument to Victor, in the lower graveyard at Battle, was erected by Elsie and John Thomas Croucher.

Victor's widow later married Mark Penney, and had five more boys, Victor, George, Graham, Adolphus, and Keith and a girl, Mabel. Jack married Hazel Stone in 1937 and had seven children, 17 grandchildren, and 24 great-grandchildren. Margaret Croucher married Arch Lunnen and then, after Arch's death,

James White. When she passed away in March 2010, she left two sons, seven grandchildren, 13 great-grandchildren, and eight great-great-grandchildren. Jack, who died in April of 1997, lived to be 80; Margaret was 89 when she died.

By the time Manfred Buchheit caught his plane to St. John's (with a stop en route to pick up some smoked char at the Torngat Fish Co-op) he was well armed with the verified documentation of the subject of one of the most famous photographs in Newfoundland and Labrador's history. He also had information about a previously unknown Holloway photo. Sharon went back to work, knowing the whereabouts of a photo of her great-great-grandfather, John Thomas Croucher, and Mavis Penney could congratulate herself on another Labrador mystery solved.

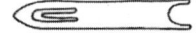

Anauta: Labrador's Grey Owl

Throughout the early decades of the 20th century, there was a big demand for lecturers in North America, people who today would be called motivational speakers. In particular demand were speakers from exotic places or with unusual topics. Captain Bob Bartlett, with his "Ar'tic" exploits, Dr. Wilfred Grenfell with his muscular Christian medical mission, and Admiral Peary with his assaults on the North Pole, were for years staples of the Chautauqua clubs and church groups. Aboriginal people were so in demand that, even without the lectures, they gave demonstrations of dog-team driving and igloo building.

Women speakers were in short supply, and women who could claim any affiliation with Aboriginal people were particularly hard to come by. Pauline Johnson, the Mohawk poet, was a huge star in her day. Mina Hubbard, of course, could claim any stage she cared to step onto, but having conquered the Naskaupi River, she was content to marry and settle in England. Ready and willing to fill the demand for Aboriginal women speakers was Sarah Elizabeth Ford Blackmore, otherwise known as Anauta.

The Ford family of Kingsbridge, Devonshire, England, first came to Labrador in 1857, when John Ford was brought out by the Hudson's Bay Company to make wooden barrels for shipping furs. John had 14 children, many of whom also worked for the Hudson's Bay Company throughout Labrador and Arctic Canada. John's son George, with his Labradorian wife, Harriett Merryfield, followed in his father's footsteps and went into service with the Hudson's Bay Company.

George and Harriett Ford were posted by the Hudson's Bay Company to Chekettalluk on the northern tip of Baffin Island, where they had two sons, Solomon and Henry, and a daughter, Sarah Elizabeth. They later went to Rigolet, where Lizzie met and married William Richard Ford, her father's half-brother's son.

Once married, Lizzie and Willie lived first in George River but then went to Cape Wolstenholme, where Willie was assistant to the Hudson's Bay Company manager, a Scotsman named Sheppard. The Fords had two daughters at Wolstenholme, and a third was on the way when Willie and Sheppard were drowned in a hunting accident in 1913. Sheppard's wife had already died, leaving a baby to be cared for by Lizzie, so the Hudson's Bay Company gave the widow a small allowance, and she brought the baby to its grandparents in St. John's. She then moved to Twillingate, where she ran a hotel. In 1920, she emigrated to Indiana and there she married again, had three more daughters, and divorced.

In Illinois, Sarah Elizabeth Blackmore began her transformation from Lizzie to Anauta. When she was first interviewed by Mildred Shoen for an Indiana paper, "Mrs. Blackmere," as she was called, "claimed the distinction of having been further north than any other living white woman." Lizzie explained, quite truthfully, that she was born in Baffin Land, and grew up speaking Eskimo as fluently as English. "I never had seen a town, city, church or school until I was taken to St. John's, Newfoundland, when I was ten," she said. Her mother had taught her to read and write prior to her schooling in St. John's.

In Illinois, two of the Blackmore children died, and during the Depression, Lizzie had rather a hard time making ends meet. For a number of years, she ran a boarding house with her mother-in-law, and after Mrs. Blackmore died, she went to work in a factory, making batteries. During her last two years at the factory, she began to give talks to schools and temperance groups, volunteering her time in exchange for "the social life which she enjoyed and for which she had been starved." It was a chance meeting with Chick Jackson, a noted American cartoonist, that led to Lizzie launching her career as a lecturer. Jackson helped her shape a program and acted as her first manager, and she soon became a professional speaker.

By the time Lizzie, now known as Anauta, was established on the lecture circuit, she was claiming to be a full-blooded Inuk. For her performances, she dressed in caribou clothing, told stories, and sang hymns in Inuktitut. She said she grew up speaking only Inuktitut, was unaccustomed to wearing European clothes, and did not know when she had been born. She insisted she only found out that her beloved grandmother was only half Inuit while she was writing her first book. It was a great shock to her to discover that she was one-eighth white. She closed each talk by playing sentimental American favourites such as "Home Sweet Home" and "Sweet Bye and Bye" on her accordion.

Anauta's book, *Land of the Good Shadows*, co-written with children's book author Heloise Chandler Washburn, was not a money-maker but her stage presentations were a huge success. She spoke to schools, church groups, university audiences, temperance groups, women's clubs, Kiwanis clubs, and Masonic lodges. She spoke to anybody and everybody who would pay her a small fee, and often worked for little or nothing. She had a booking agent, Will J. McEwan of Columbus, Ohio, who billed her as "The Only Eskimo Woman on the American Platform," and she apparently supported her family through her appearances.

Some of Anauta's recollections of Arctic life would have come as a bit of a surprise to Inuit themselves. She said they did not eat fats or raw meat, nor did they rub noses as a sign of affection, and they were modest, never got colds or other illnesses, and abhorred murder and theft. She also claimed that her husband had been eaten by a shark.

As she became better known, Anauta's skill at speaking Inuktitut was sometimes called upon. The Icelandic-Canadian anthropologist Vilhjalmur Stefansson used her as a translator, and so did the Church of England missionary Rev. E.J. Peck. Anauta, over the course of two years, translated many of the Anglican hymns into Inuktitut and transcribed them in Roman orthography and Inuit syllabics for eventual publication in England. Her adherence to Christian values seems to have been genuine, and she told one newspaper, "The story of Jesus is the one thing I would like to take back to my people. Otherwise they are far better off without 'civilization.'"

Labrador scholar Dale Blake, writing about Anauta in her doctoral thesis, "Inuit Autobiography: Challenging the Stereotypes," posits the theory that the Inuit Anauta was describing—the ones who didn't eat blubber and who loved Jesus—may have been "her own close-knit group of mixed-bloods, seen as superior to other full-blood Inuit." Blake advises that Anauta and her co-author "catered to the tastes of the American public of the 1940s" and suggests that Anauta "wished to portray herself as naïve with respect to the unpleasant aspects of civilization, but as wiser with respect to the simple, sensible life." Anauta had, in effect, invented an "ideal society" that she called Eskimo but which was really what she considered the best of both worlds.

It is evident from the numerous newspaper articles about Anauta that she was a natural performer. Will J. McEwen's Chautauqua pamphlet, produced by an advertising agency, quotes from numerous newspaper reviews which describe her as amusing, delightful, compelling, and uplifting, captivating her audiences and holding their attention "with the charm of her personality and with quick, descriptive gestures that added much to her words."

Anauta's daughter Mary Buckner, in a letter to Blake, asserted that her mother was happiest in front of an audience: "She seemed to know just what to say whether it was a room full of male Elks or small children. She never disappointed the program chairmen responsible for her appearance."

Was Anauta even a little bit Inuit? The genealogy of the Ford family indicates that Harriet Merryfield's mother was Elizabeth Lane from Zoar. Mary Buckner said this made Anauta's mother half Inuit, which would have made Anauta exactly one-quarter Inuit. If so, Anauta carried as much Aboriginal blood as poet Pauline Johnson, and certainly more than Grey Owl—Archie Bellamy—who was of 100 per cent English stock.

Another way to consider whether Anauta was Inuit is to view her as she would have initially been viewed in the early days of the Labrador Inuit Association, the precursor of the Nunatsiavut government. When the LIA was first formed, and the rules for membership were being developed, a person would be considered Inuit if he or she fulfilled two of three criteria: self-identified as Inuit, were identified as Inuit by others, and spoke the Inuit language. By this reckoning, Anauta probably would have been accepted into the LIA and today would be a Nunatsiavut beneficiary.

Anauta died as she had lived—happily working the lecture circuit. She succumbed suddenly at age 77 to a heart attack in Ashland, Kansas, January 13, 1965. She was buried in Indianapolis, and according to her daughter, she would have made an amusing story of the event. There was a sudden storm which dumped 12 inches of snow on the area, so the funeral party couldn't get to the cemetery. "We needed a dog sled," wrote Mary Buckner. "We all thought Mother was playing a joke on us in heaven."

Ernie Lyall: The White Man Who Wasn't

Although most people think of the old Hudson's Bay Company men as having come out from Scotland, particularly the Orkney Islands, quite a few Labradorians made their careers with the Hudson's Bay as traders in the high Arctic. One of the best known of these men was Ernest Wilson Lyall, who was born at Island Harbour, between Makkovik and Hopedale, in 1910.

Ernie Lyall signed on to work for the Company when he was a 16-year-old attending school in St. John's, and his first posting was at Port Burwell. From there he went to Wolstenholme, Lake Harbour, Pond Inlet, and Arctic Bay. He then took over the new post at Fort Ross before going on to found the community of Spence Bay, now called Taloyoak, on the Boothia Peninsula. He also became a justice of the peace, a game officer, and a coroner.

What made Ernie different from all the other Labrador traders who went farther north was that he spoke fluent Inuktitut, married a woman from Cape Dorset, and never went south again for more than a brief visit, but stayed in the North his whole life. Ernie became the father of some of Nunavut's most valued citizens, including policemen, interpreters, and Members of the Legislature.

Ernie acted as guide and interpreter for government workers, policemen, judges, doctors, and all manner of people, but it was writers who first brought him to the attention of the rest of the world. Douglas Leechman, Farley Mowat, G.J. Tranter, and Kenneth C. Butler all wrote about Ernie, who was so appalled by the errors they perpetrated about him and about Inuit in general that he decided the only recourse was to write his own book.

Ernie's autobiography, *An Arctic Man*, was published by Mel Hurtig in 1979 and was described as "sixty-five years in Canada's North by a man who chose the Inuit way of life." The book begins: "The main reason I decided to do a book about my life in the north is that I finally got fed up with all the baloney in so many books written about the north." That was typical of Ernie—a blunt, no-nonsense man who told it like it was.

One of Ernie's claims to fame was that in 1940 he was classified as an "Eskimo" by the Canadian government and issued an E disc the following year. The E discs were modelled on the leather dog tags issued to soldiers during World War I and they allowed RCMP officers to list people who did not have surnames for the purposes of issuing hunting permits, welfare payments, and inoculations. E stood for eastern Arctic (there were also W discs in the west), and Ernie wrote that he "became E-5-1, an Eskimo, and as far as I know, I'm the only white like this in the Arctic."

The reason Ernie lobbied for and received an E disc was because the Hudson's Bay Company tried to transfer him from Fort Ross to a new post without his wife, Nipisha, who was expecting their second child. He resigned rather than leave her behind even for a short time and chose instead to support his family as a hunter and trapper. The RCMP knew that if they refused Ernie an E disc, he could not trap and would have to go on relief.

Ernie, who believed his mother "came from Ireland" and his father was "of Scottish descent," always got a big kick out of being a white Eskimo, but after his book came out, it turned out that the joke was on him. Relatives from his enormous extended family in Labrador contacted him and he learned that, in fact, his mother was at least half Inuit.

Ernie's mother, called Aunt Stana by the community, was Christiana Bright, a widow who had been married to Henry Ford. When Ford died, she married John Lyall. Stana and John both brought children to the new marriage, and they also had children of their own. The last of them was Ernie, who had 18 brothers and half-brothers, and sisters and half-sisters. In fact, Ernie had so many siblings that he didn't even know all their names. Aunt Stana's mother was Inuit and it is thought her father was a Norwegian whaler.

Amos Lyall, Ernie's nephew, once admitted that he would never understand why Uncle Ernie didn't know his heritage, but a look at Ernie's history from the Labrador perspective gives a few clues.

First of all, Ernie grew up in a very isolated place in Island Harbour. There were only two houses anywhere near where he was born, both Lyall family homes. Ernie recalled that his father spoke only English, but his mother "could speak very good Eskimo." Being the youngest, Ernie's closest playing companions other than his older brothers were the children of the Moravian missionary, so Ernie grew up speaking German as well as English and Inuktitut. Ernie said that by the time he was 15, he had "picked up a very little Eskimo, but it was more than anyone else around." Most likely Ernie had a flair for languages, so he would not have found it unusual for his mother to be similarly blessed.

Secondly, like many Inuit and settler children in Labrador, Ernie went to residential school. His first teacher was the RCMP officer in Port Burwell, where his father was the Hudson's Bay Company manager, but eventually the officer was transferred and Ernie was sent to Makkovik, where he was enrolled in the Grade 4 class. Clara Broomfield Dickers, who attended school with Ernie, recalls that he was "very forward and he didn't like his teacher," Miss Alsop. Once, Ernie slammed the door just as she was walking through and the blow stunned her so that the other children were "wonderful upset," thinking he'd killed her.

To get to school in Makkovik, Ernie and three of his siblings boarded the Moravian supply ship *Harmony*, which stopped in at all the settlements on the coast. The trip took about three weeks each way. The children never heard from their parents while they were at school, and they had no contact with them from when they left on the ship until they got home the following year. According to Ernie, "When summer came the ship would pick us up at the school on its way north, and we'd spend about a week at home with our parents while supplies were being unloaded. Then we'd go right back to school on the ship's return south."

Residential school was probably a miserable time for a rather spoiled little boy who sincerely believed that, of 19 children, he was his mother's favourite. "We were very close," he wrote in *An Arctic Man*, and each Sunday of his adult life, he wrote his mother a letter, even though it took two full years for the letters to arrive in Labrador. "Each summer, when the ship came in, something like 50 letters would go out to her." At the same time, Ernie would receive the letters she wrote to him. He occasionally heard from his father, but his brothers and sisters rarely wrote.

Ernie estimated that he was 10 years old when he went to school in Makkovik, and at 16 he went out to St. John's to go to high school, which is where he signed on with the Hudson's Bay Company. Ernie made only two trips home after that, once when he was recovering from appendicitis shortly after he left home, and once in 1934 when he was 24. Despite his fondness for his parents, his time with them from the age of 10 onward can be counted in weeks rather than months or years, so it is understandable that he did not know much about his family history or heritage.

The third reason Ernie Lyall didn't know his mother was Inuit probably relates to simple, old-fashioned racism. It's been said that Ernie's McNeill grandmother didn't hold with intermarriage and objected to Christiana's marriage to her son John. Since the in-laws were their only near neighbours, Aunt Stana might have decided that it would be best to say little or nothing that might be difficult for a child to understand.

This view of things is supported by Ernie's discussion of what he thought about Inuit before he went to live with them in the north. As a child in residential school, he knew that about one-third of his schoolmates were Inuit, but he wrote that "[he] didn't notice any difference at all." Inuit near Makkovik lived in houses as the non-native families did, and most spoke English.

However, he thought the Inuit farther north would be different, that "they would be dirty, greasy, hair all matted with grease, and this sort of thing ... It was in [his] mind that the Labrador Eskimos, like those at Burwell, were probably a much more civilized people." This stereotype was one that Ernie's cousin, Anauta Ford Blackmore—Labrador's Grey Owl—went to some pains to correct, so much so that when she spoke at Chautauqua Fairs and such, she insisted that the Inuit ate no blubber or raw meat at all.

The fact was that the many non-native people who came in contact with Ernie and saw how comfortably he lived an Inuit lifestyle with an Inuit family couldn't believe that a non-native could do that. This belief was fairly harmless, but in many ways it was as racist as the belief that the Inuit were an inferior race. Ernie was, in his own mind at least, walking proof that if you worked hard and lived cooperatively, anyone could make a life in the north.

RCMP Constable Kenneth C. Butler wrote of Ernie's parents that John Lyall "spoke English and Eskimo and liked to think of himself as a white man," while Christiana "looked to be a full blooded Eskimo." Neither statement was correct as John didn't speak a word of Inuktitut and had no Inuit blood, while Christiana was only half Inuit. Ernie said that Farley Mowat's claim he had "Eskimo blood" was "baloney, of course, though [he]'d be proud if [he] did."

It was with no sense of pride that Ernie Lyall wrote, "I think that my own parents figured they were better than Eskimos, though they were always friendly and did what they could for them." It's a great pity that Ernie didn't know the truth about his heritage and that it was probably to keep peace in the family that his mother kept such things to herself. A century after Ernie was born, his 11 children and his numerous grandchildren and great-grandchildren live and work as cultural Inuit. Ernie would have loved to be a citizen of Nunavut like them, just as proud as he was to be E-5-1, an Eskimo.

Labradorians in the Great War

Over 100 years ago, on August 4, 1914, the British Secretary of State for the Colonies sent a telegram to the governor of Newfoundland advising him that Great Britain had formally declared war against Germany. With that telegram, Newfoundland and Labrador automatically entered World War I as part of the British Empire.

Although the colony had no standing army, war had been anticipated for some time and quite a number of paramilitary organizations had been recruiting and training young men to take part in the conflict. The Church Lad's Brigade, the Catholic Cadet Corps, the Methodist Guards, and the Newfoundland Highlanders, mostly centred in St. John's, were the primary sectarian groups providing military training and discipline in Newfoundland.

The only non-denominational military organization in the colony was the Legion of Frontiersmen, an Empire-wide commando-type group, founded during the Boer War. The Legion was established in Labrador in 1911, when Dr. A.W. Wakefield, who was serving with the Grenfell Mission in Battle Harbour, started up an active corps. The following year, a branch was established at St. Anthony, and very soon after, Mud Lake, Red Bay, and Nain could boast their own units.

When war broke out, approximately 150 Frontiersmen joined the Newfoundland Regiment and guarded posts in various areas of Labrador and St. John's. Many of these men went on to fight and die overseas, yet the public perception is that few Labradorians participated as active combatants in the Great War.

A list compiled by *Them Days* in 1991 named 20 Labrador volunteers, while the Newfoundland and Labrador Heritage website post in 2007 estimated 15 Inuit and Métis volunteers. As of 2018, the Labrador War Memorial lists 73 servicemen, but the list is considered, at best, a "draft of the nominal rolls," full of "errors, omissions and duplications."

Probably the only Labradorian really known for his war service was the Inuit sniper, Lance Corporal John Shiwak of Rigolet. Shiwak had expressed a desire to be a soldier and when war broke out, he volunteered for the army at the urging of Dr. Harry Paddon, for whom he had worked in previous years and who identified him as one of the "first little local detachment of the Legion of Frontiersmen ... going to join up." Shiwak enlisted on July 24, 1915, and following training in Scotland, he landed in France in July of 1916, shortly after the decimation of the Newfoundland Regiment at Beaumont Hamel.

For the next 15 months, Shiwak acted as a sharpshooter in the trenches. He told a friend in the Regiment that "sniping was like swatching seals." As time passed, though, Shiwak became more and more despondent over the slaughter in which he was participating. Nevertheless, he wrote that he was determined "to stick it till it's over."

On November 20, 1917, Shiwak and six other men died when a shell exploded near them during the battle of Cambrai. Shiwak received the British War Medal and the Victory Medal, but his primary claim to fame was the result of an article journalist William Lacy Amy wrote about him for *Canadian Magazine* the following year, titled "An Eskimo Patriot."

Shiwak had developed a friendship with Amy in the years leading up to the outbreak of war and had maintained correspondence with him. The numerous letters and diaries that John Shiwak regularly mailed to Amy have never been located, but researchers, including Wally McLean, Kenn Harper, and John C. Kennedy, all seem to hope they will eventually come to light.

The various photographs of Shiwak in uniform that have survived have also ensured that his service in the Great War has been remembered. Of particular note is a photo of him in what appears to be the uniform of the Newfoundland Highlanders. It had long been assumed this photo was taken during his training in Scotland, but it may have been taken when he was in St. John's on his way overseas. The Newfoundland Regiment adopted the caribou-head insignia of the Highlanders.

While Shiwak's fame is certainly well deserved, it is unfortunate that many other Labrador volunteers have been forgotten. Frederick Freida of Hopedale went overseas and returned unscathed; decades later, his continued interest in the military led him to join the Canadian Rangers in 1951.

One of the soldiers who doesn't appear on the Labrador War Memorial is Edward Seaward, who died August 12, 1916, and who is buried at the Menin Road South Cemetery in Belgium. Edward, the son of Thomas and Rosely Seaward of Red Bay, was one of over 200 "boy soldiers" who signed up, fought, and died while still in their teens.

According to regulations, volunteers had to be 19 years old to sign up, but could sign up at the age of 18 if they had their parents' permission, although they could not be sent to the front lines until they had turned 19. However, no proof of age was required—"apparent age" was the term used on the enlistment form—and many boys lied about their age in order to sign up.

Little is known about Edward Seaward except that he was 18 when he died and may have been as young as 16 when he entered the military. The death rates for boy soldiers were considerably higher than those of older soldiers, probably because the boys believed they were invulnerable.

Howard Morry, who was about 30 years old at the time, became something of a surrogate father to many of these teenaged soldiers and recorded in his diary their reaction when they arrived on the front lines, which Morry said was "like a butcher-shop in hell."

"What a sight it was for these poor devils of kids fresh from home. When we came to the first dead lying around and then the field hospital, with hundreds lying around, and the doctors and the Red Cross guys with their white suits blood all over, some of the kids got sick, others began to sweat and one kid turned and ran away. We let him go and never reported him, except to say he was missing. He came back three days afterwards, and was a real good soldier. Poor kid."

Another of the Labrador soldiers who died at the front was Daniel Groves, sometimes incorrectly listed as David Groves. Daniel, the son of Fredrick Malcolm and Mary Ann Groves, was a trapper with a line on the Goose River, between what was known as the Fourth Tilt and the Sixth Tilt, approximately half of Goose River. When he left for the war, he gave the trapline to his brother to work for him until he got back.

Dan Groves was killed in action or died of wounds fighting at Monchy-le-Preux on April 17, 1917. One hundred and sixty-six members of the Newfoundland Regiment died or were missing and presumed dead after that action, another 141 wounded, and 153 made prisoners of war. Twenty-eight of the prisoners died in captivity. Dan, who was 24 years old, is remembered as the trapper who tried to tackle Labrador's legendary Travespine sasquatch.

Other men killed in action were Edward Gear of Rigolet, John Blake of North West River, John Anley James of Forteau, who was lost at sea while serving in the Newfoundland Royal Naval Reserve, Harry Hedderson of Battle Harbour, William McKenzie of Sand Banks, Archibald Ash of Red Bay, and George Toumishey of Fox Harbour. Virtually every small community in Labrador suffered a loss during the war.

A great many of the soldiers who died in the Great War perished as a result of illness rather than battle. An estimated 50 per cent of Newfoundland and Labrador recruits were found medically unfit for service, a figure that was no better or worse than the comparative figure for Britain. However, the Labrador men seemed to have less resistance to some diseases due to the isolation of their previous lives. James Ford, son of Henry and Christiana Ford of Port Burwell, died of measles on February 26, 1916, and is buried at Paisley, Scotland. His brother Abe served also but survived the war.

Despite being medically unfit, many Labrador men went to great lengths to enter the military. Robert George Brown of Cartwright went to St. John's and then England to enlist in the Navy but was turned down because he had poor eyesight. He returned to St. John's and worked at the post office for a month, but then went back to England and managed to get into the Army.

Many of the soldiers who made it home after their service were in pretty poor shape. John Curl emerged from the war with shell shock. The military at that time were not allowed to mention shell shock, and military doctors were forbidden from diagnosing it, but most people recognized the severity of post-traumatic stress disorder, even if it didn't officially exist. Thomas Curl recalls that his family had a very hard time when he was growing up because of his father's illness. To add to their misery, his father went blind when Thomas was 12, leaving him and his older brother to care for their parents and siblings.

Dr. Harry Paddon gave potential recruits their medical examinations and, when he examined Manuel Pardy in the spring of 1915, prior to his volunteering for the war, he declared Pardy "as fit a young man as was ever on the Labrador ... strong and healthy." When he got home, Pardy's fiancée said he was "just skin over bone. All broke up from the war."

Levi Pottle of Rigolet, who joined up in Newfoundland, told *Them Days*: "There was lots of men joined up in Newfoundland when I did, but a lot of them didn't pass, wasn't strong enough, but I was. They told me I was an A-1 man." However, he claimed he was gassed while in the trenches, and either as a result of the gas or the stress, he remembered few details of the war.

Getting home even after being demobilized was not easy. Anne Budgell has written about the difficulty James Goudie and Charles Michelin had making their way back to North West River from Newfoundland. The two returned to Battle Harbour aboard the schooner *Ethie*, and from there they travelled overland, passing through the small communities such as Cartwright that had been devastated by the Spanish influenza epidemic. James Goudie arrived January 6, 1919, with the "glorious news that Peace had been declared."

Although most of the Labrador men who served in World War I went and returned as foot soldiers, some acted as officers. Richard White, a lawyer and trader from Voisey's Bay, joined the Canadian Expeditionary Force and saw action in Siberia. Wilfred Grenfell served as an Army doctor in France. Captain Connors of the *Kyle* was an officer in the British Navy. Job Michelin, Robert's brother, attained the rank of Sergeant and gave instruction in machine gunnery. Harry Paddon acted as a recruiting agent for the Regiment.

Many others associated with Labrador were affected by the war, either directly or indirectly. Hudson's Bay Company clerks Peter Smith, Heath, Learmonth, and Blackhall all joined up. Marjorie Pye's brother Hayward was a war vet, and she married veteran William George, who was discharged after being gassed. Marjorie lived to be 100 and became the last of the Regiment's widows. Duncan Collins, who survived the July Drive, was born in Spaniard's Bay but spent 62 years fishing on the Labrador.

Although it has taken a full century for the sacrifices made by the people of Labrador to be recognized, the Great War roll of honour is slowly being filled in. Whether these men were motivated by patriotism, community pressure, a desire for adventure, or simply a dollar a day and rations, they paid the price of that brutal conflict with their health, their peace of mind, and, in many cases, their lives. They will be remembered.

ON LAND AND SEA

Labrador Snow Slides

It generally comes as a surprise to people that Newfoundland and Labrador had, until recently, the highest death rate from avalanches in the country. Over 60 people have died from snow slides in recorded accounts, and many of those deaths happened in Labrador.

According to David Liverman, a geologist at Memorial University, the earliest recorded avalanche in Canada happened at Nain in the winter of 1781. The Moravian missionaries reported that about 12 miles from Nain, probably at West Red Island, a group of 32 Inuit gathered in a winter house at the base of a hill were crushed when "a monstrous body of snow ... shot all at once down" and pressed the house even with the ground. Twenty-two of the inhabitants were killed. Probably the only comparable Canadian avalanche was the 1999 slide at Kangiqsualijjuaq, Quebec, that killed nine adults and children and seriously injured 12 people celebrating the New Year at the local school gym.

Snow slides of various degrees turn up in a number of oral histories published in *Them Days*. Suzannah Igloliorte described how her father was caught in a slide while checking his traps south of Hopedale in the 1920s. He was buried except for his head and one hand, and as he was wearing snowshoes, it took him a long time to dig himself out.

Frank Davis reported three deaths at Goose Cove near Cartwright in 1893 when Tom Davis, Andrew Reeves, and Solomon Morgan were buried by an overhang. John Davis, Tom's brother, was saved because he had hung back when he got a sudden nosebleed. John was able to dig his father out but could not save the others. According to Frank Davis, one of the victims "had his back broken across a birch tree."

Doris Peacock, the wife of the Moravian missionary in Nain, recalled that when she was on her way back by dog team from a visit to Makkovik in 1950, her driver pointed out "the place where the avalanche had descended on the house of old William Barbour many years ago." Barbour, an Inuk who fished out of Nain, died at an advanced age around 1925 at Okak.

Leonard Budgell, who was posted with the Hudson's Bay Company at Hebron from 1938 to 1942, was familiar with several avalanche areas in Hebron Fjord. On one hunting trip he saw "the remains of a large snow slide" where two young men had escaped burial by running uphill. They lost their dog teams and equipment but walked away from the site. On another occasion, while out hunting, he visited a family in an old sod hut. Later, he saw that the house had been abandoned because "a huge cornice hung menacingly several hundred feet above the little house. There was no one there, they had seen the signs and had moved to safer quarters."

When Budgell and his hunting partner Bill Metcalfe visited the area later, he saw that hundreds of tons of wet, compressed snow had swept the house away. "Every vestige had been swept out on the ice of the fiord and disappeared at break up." When they landed on the shore to have a look, "there was only a jumbled mass of broken stone." Among the few scraps of evidence to show that people had ever lived there was a tiny toy kayak covered with membrane from seal intestine. Bill put a small stone in the hunter's seat to give it balance and set it adrift in the sea to mark the end of a way of life for the Inuit family who had lived there.

The Moravian records describe other avalanches, including one at Ramah in 1886 which damaged their mission powder house and graveyard. The area around Okak, however, seems to have been the worst hit by avalanches over the years.

Retired Inuit fisherman Alex Saunders recalled that his mother used to talk about a snow slide that had happened in the bottom of the harbour in Okak, which has high, sloping mountains in the south and southwest corners. "A snowslide or snowball she called it, went right through the house. The old woman was sitting in her rocking chair knitting when the ball hit. When they found the bodies, hers was stuck full of knitting needles."

Bob Lyall recalls hearing about a snow slide at Ulliak, which is north of the Kiglapait Mountains before you get to Okak Bay. Members of the Zarpa family were staying at a place belonging to Joe Millik when they were caught in an avalanche. An old lady called Caroline was killed. It's possible that this is the same slide in which Karoline Uvloriak died, though except for the first name, most of the details are different.

Moravian missionary George Harp reported from Hebron in 1935: "A very distressing accident happened among some of our Okak brethren during the winter. On March 26 Ida Kohlmeister and Karoline Uvloriak were killed and eleven others injured by an avalanche at Udlik. A great mass of snow rolled down a slope, went through one end of a house, and out at the other, carrying everybody and everything before it. One little child had a broken leg, and was very badly scalded on the head. Other people were almost smothered. One old woman, sitting sewing at a treadle-machine, escaped unhurt, though the machine was smashed to pieces, and carried about fifty yards away from the house."

Another slide, reported in the Okak areas in 1935, was described by Hudson's Bay trader Ernie Lyall in his book *An Arctic Man*. Lyall was on leave after having his appendix out and was staying with his parents at Okak. The older folk had gone to visit his brothers at Nutak and Ernie was going down with his brothers' dogs to bring them back. The weather turned, and he stopped at a camp near quite a big hill, about halfway between Okak and Nutak, where an Inuit family was living. They gave him a meal and suggested that he stay the night to wait out the storm, but he was anxious to join his parents.

The next morning, as the Lyalls were preparing to leave Nutak, they saw a team coming into the post. "It was the man whose camp I'd stopped at the evening before," Ernie wrote, "and he had his boy with him. We knew there must be something really wrong." During the night, an avalanche had buried the house and killed the wife and daughter.

Given that in both avalanches a woman and girl died, avalanche expert David Liverman initially thought that the two tragedies might have been the same one, but examination of a map shows that Udlik, though in the general area, is well south of Nutak and not on the way from Okak to Nutak. "When snow conditions are such that avalanches are possible, they will affect a wide area, not one single site," Liverman explains. "Thus it is possible that numerous avalanches might occur in a narrow time period."

Six years later Ernie Lyall had an even more tragic encounter with an avalanche after he moved farther north to Fort Ross. An Inuk named Josie came to his camp to report that a month before, his entire family except for one child had been buried by a snow slide at Cresswell Bay. He had built a large double igloo at the bottom of a steep hill, and during a storm one night the snow came "over the top of the hill so fast it was like a river." He managed to get out with one of the boys, but lost his mother, his wife, and four other children. When the Mounties went in the spring to check it out, bringing Ernie along to interpret for them, they found that the women and children had survived the avalanche but, in attempting to free themselves, had dug along the base of the cliff instead of out away from it. They had tunnelled for about half a mile before dying of exposure and starvation. Lyall was haunted by the knowledge that if Josie had gone for help immediately, he might have saved them.

Currently, the threat of avalanches to Labradorians is more likely to be related to recreational sports rather than to domestic or harvesting practices. Snowmobilers are particularly vulnerable. In the winter of 2003/4, at least four avalanches were triggered by humans in the Nain area, one of which buried two snowmobilers and another which narrowly missed killing two young snowboarders. In that same winter, the road to Capstan Island was cut off by slides and children in L'Anse-au-Loup could not go to school because of 10-metre-high snowdrifts overhanging the road.

Two years previous, a party of teenagers in Forteau had taken their snowmobiles to Richard's Brook Pond, where two of them climbed up to take shelter under a snow cornice. They were buried when the overhang broke off. One of the teens was found within five minutes but 14-year-old Meagan Buckle was under the snow for half an hour before being located and rescued.

In Labrador City in 1985, five teenaged skiers were buried on Smokey Mountain while training for a race. All were rescued without injury due to quick action by the others in the team and the ski patrol and lift operators. In 2006, in the same area, snowmobiler Andrew Milley was doing a bit of hill-climbing on his machine. Liverman says that after Milley made a loop at the top of a slope, he "looked over his shoulder and saw 'a wall of snow' chasing him down the hill." He was unable to outrace it, and was torn from his snowmobile. Friends found his pack and used the shovel he had been carrying to dig him out.

Across the Quebec border at Blanc-Sablon, 17-year-old Jamie Lavallee and his father were killed in 1995 when a snow slide struck their house. Rescuers were able to dig out Jamie's mother but two dozen houses had to be evacuated and the Army was called in to dynamite the slopes and dislodge the unstable snow.

Snow slides or avalanches are not the first thing you might worry about in the Labrador wilderness, but they are a real and present danger, and being aware of that is the first step in taking measures to avoid being caught and possibly killed by one.

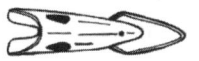

Sea Stacks, Cairns, and American Men

When one thinks of the north, visions of igloos, polar bears, and Arctic owls come to mind, but one of the most prevalent images of northern Canada is the inukshuk, or *inutsuk* as it is called in Labrador. The word *inutsuk* is usually said to mean "like a man," but it is really an ancient word that predates the modern translation.

In Labrador, as elsewhere, *inutsuk* are everywhere, but visitors often get them mixed up with cairns and sea stacks, and all three formations are often referred to there as "American men."

It isn't always easy to distinguish the difference between the various terms applied to stone pillars, but a cairn is man-made—a stack of stones set up as a marker—and, as such, an *inutsuk* is a type of cairn, just as a cairn is a type of *inutsuk*. Generally, though, English speakers use the term "inukshuk" to mean a cairn that is shaped like a person.

Unlike cairns, sea stacks are natural occurrences, pillars of rock that have been formed by the sea. Steep, shelving beaches produce plunging breakers that create sea caves, which eventually become arches. When an arch collapses, it becomes a sea stack or stone pillar. Some sea stacks that formed thousands of years ago now appear to have emerged on dry land because when the ice age ended, the land rebounded, leaving the shore features high inland.

Elder Alex Saunders says he saw rock columns in lots of different places in his fishing days, but reports that "Port Manvers Run seems to be an ideal place for them to occur, just because of the way the land is."

The term "American man" is usually applied to sea stacks but can also refer to piles of rocks used to guide coastal navigation. Linguists have speculated that the term American man comes from "marker man" or "marking man." Such a marker can also be referred to as a "naked man" or as a "Nascopi," possibly because the Mushuau Innu, formerly called Naskapi Indians, were thought to have left them along the coast.

Alex Saunders has another explanation for the term American man: "I've seen them from the Straits to Nachvak Fjord ... the south coast of Labrador is full of them. The local people call them American men, probably because the Yanks made them at all those radar sites."

Stone men have an ancient lineage. In the Old Testament, the Creator was said to have kneaded Adam from mud, and in the Psalms, we get the first golem, "curiously wrought in the lowest parts of the earth." In Greek mythology, the gorgon Medusa could turn anyone to stone who looked at her, and in fairy tales, people are turned to stone in tales such as "The Giant Who Had No Heart in His Body" and "The Water of Life." King Midas is a variation on the theme.

Stories about people who turned to stone are particularly prevalent in Inuit legends. In Hudson's Bay, an old lady who was abandoned on Marble Island was turned to quartz; in Smith Sound, a little orphan boy named Qituazssung was swallowed by a rock; among the Ammassalik Inuit, a man was turned into a blubber stone, while in Hudson's Bay, a girl who pretended a stone was her husband was turned into a stone also. In Point Barrow, there is a story of a stone baby who killed anyone who looked at it.

One of the earliest Labrador legends about stone beings was collected by E.W. Hawkes and published in 1916. It concerned a curiously formed stone found about half a mile from the old Hudson's Bay post at Nachvak. This stone looks like a woman, thinking, with her hand on her chin.

According to local legend, an outcast woman who was abused and badly treated by everyone wished to be turned into a rock like the one she was sitting on, and when a crow came and flew in three circles around her, she gradually turned into stone. Hawkes writes that the Inuit "make offerings to her of needles, tobacco, and matches whenever they pass. Some of the women have put a string of beads around her neck."

Alex Saunders reports that he often saw rock cairns made inland, mostly near rivers, where the old people would cache their meat and fish for the winter. "Inuit visiting cairns or graves would always leave a little present to appease the spirits of the place," he says. "I've seen the people leave little pieces of yarn, pieces of match sticks, etc." One stone marker boasted two large, brass gun shells.

Inuit place names, which are generally descriptive rather than honorific, can indicate the presence of sea stacks and cairns. The Pillar Islands are called Inuksutoguluk, meaning "small *inutsuk*." Directly east of Hopedale, on the outer Kingitok islands, is a place called Annatalik, "place where there is a woman," and on the port side as you are going into Kanairiktok Bay is Ukkusitsalik, "made into soapstone."

Once when John Terriak of Nain was out berry picking with his father, he heard a story about an old woman who was abandoned on the island where they were. Terriak says that "when her family was leaving, the old woman sat on a rock and started crying and at that moment she turned to stone. You can still see her."

Stone animals as well as people appear in some of the legends. Rose Pamak and other Nain elders tell the story of the polar bear in the rock, which was published as a book by the Labrador Institute in 2012. The rock is near a brook called Annanak, just across the harbour from the town. In the Hopedale area there is Okaliak Island, so called because it looks like an *okalik*, an Arctic hare. Fin Island is called *Tikkavuklik* in Inuttut because it looks like a stone fin from the south side.

Bruno Bettelheim, in his analysis of fairy tales in *The Uses of Enchantment*, equates deathlike sleep such as that experienced by Snow White with having been turned to stone. He argues that being turned to stone does not symbolize death; "rather it stands for a true lack of humanity, an inability to respond to higher values, so that the person, being dead to what life is all about in the best sense, might as well be made of stone."

In other words, a person who is not valued (in most cases, a woman or child) is treated like an object and eventually is unable to respond as a human being. Alice Miller, the famed child psychiatrist, described unloved children as "abused, exploited and turned to stone."

Clearly, the cairns, sea stacks, and *inutsuk* have practical functions as markers for food caches, fishing spots, and camps, but they also serve to remind people of man's inhumanity to man. Each sea stack and cairn has a story that helps people to remember that even the weakest individuals need to be cared for and helped through this life if we are all to be alive in the best sense of the word.

Fata Morgana: A Looming Phenomenon

In January of 2017, the sea ice off North West River was the site of a rather unusual public event. Artist Kay Burns, founder/curator of the Museum of the Flat Earth in Fogo Island, set out to re-enact a century-old experiment that had been done with boats on the Bedford Canal in England, based on Zetetic philosophy and rooted in the idea of "observable phenomena" as the impetus for skeptical inquiry.

While Scott Hudson drove a team of dogs 9.65 kilometres out onto the ice, Burns watched and photographed him though a powerful viewing scope to see if he would disappear below the horizon, thus affirming the curvature of the earth, or if he remained in view, supporting the belief in a flat earth. Hudson and his dogs did not disappear below the horizon, nor did he fall off the edge of the earth, prompting skeptics to posit that this Canadian winter re-creation of a 19th-century experiment proved once again that the earth is flat.

Some of the more scientific of the spectators that day pointed out that Burns was ignoring the possibility of light refraction, a phenomenon with which Labradorians are particularly familiar.

Depending on the light, temperature, and moisture in the air, various weather phenomena are observable at different times of the year. Rainbows, sun dogs, St. Elmo's fire, auroras, and mirages all fall into this category of atmospheric antics. *Fata morgana*, or what in Labrador is called "looming," is a particularly fascinating example of the tricks nature can play on rational people.

In its simplest form, looming is just the embodiment of the

old sailor's adage that distant shores loom up nearer before rain because of thinning of the air. Anyone driving from Goose Bay down into Happy Valley will have observed that, on some days, the Mealy Mountains appear to be very distant and on others they crowd the sky. A true *fata morgana*, named for the sorceress Morgan le Fay, takes this illusion one step further and can actually trick viewers into believing that what they see is an actual reflection of reality.

In 1818, British admiral Sir John Ross went in search of the Northwest Passage, but at the foot of Lancaster Sound all he saw was a wall of mountains that halted further exploration. He drew them onto his charts, named them the Croker Mountains, and went home, despite the urging of William Parry and other of his officers that he take a closer look. Subsequent exploration by Parry led to the discovery that the Croker Mountains did not exist, ruining Ross's reputation.

Any of the many Newfoundlanders and Labradorians who had sailed the Strait of Belle Isle could have warned Ross that, under certain conditions, he was not to trust his eyes. Newfoundlanders looking for seals on the ice, or Inuit looking for caribou on the tundra, were well aware of an effect called "sky mapping," where dark animals are reflected on the underside of clouds. If they could not see over the curvature of the earth, they would try looking upward. The Cape Dorset artist Pudlo Pudlat drew a complex and highly specific sky map of his community titled "The Settlement from a Distance," depicting this phenomenon. Similarly, the heightening effect of the *fata morgana* allows people to see ships, mountains, or animals that would normally be out of sight.

Henry Youle Hind, travelling the Labrador coast in the 1860s, commented on the frequency of mirages in the Strait of Belle Isle, where "a telescope generally enables the observer to detect in the confused and highly distorted image of a ship or boat high above the horizon, as many as three and sometimes five, images of the object, blended together and overlapping one another."

Dr. Eliot Curwen, who came to Labrador in 1893 to work with Wilfred Grenfell, wrote that the expression "I'll believe it when I see it" had ceased to have any meaning for him after an afternoon spent in "wonder and confusion" watching icebergs: "I look at an iceberg on the horizon; it looks quite small and square; in a moment like a jack-in-the-box it is 4 or 6 times taller than it was. Then after a few minutes it is divided into two, and by carefully examining it with my glasses I find I am looking at a berg in the sea with another one just like it but upside down immediately over it, but this one is in the air and not in the sea at all, then while I am looking it is all small again, to alter in appearance again by & by."

R.E. Holloway, who took the famous photo of little Victor Croucher between two giant cod at Battle Harbour, was fascinated by the *fata morgana* effect he saw in his travels on the coast. A man of science, Holloway explained in *Through Newfoundland with a Camera* that the variety of mirage known as looming is "due to the existence of layers of air of different density and humidity lying one over the other and produced partly by the direct heat of the sun and partly by its radiation from the surface of the water." He goes on to assert that it is produced by exactly the same causes as desert mirages, but on the ocean the hot and cold layers are reversed so that the upper layers are hottest and lightest. A church on the island (or a dog team in Labrador), "though hidden by the curvature of the earth or sea, may be distinctly visible in Nature's copy."

Anthropologist Frank Speck, writing in his 1935 book *Naskapi*, lists *fata morgana* as one of a number of natural phenomena recognized and named by the Innu: "The weather conditions in summer often produce very beautiful minor mirages causing the distant shores and island to appear elevated to magnificent heights," which his Innu informants said were "the sign of good weather."

One of the most extreme cases of *fata morgana* to be documented by a scientist was experienced by the famous ice navigator Captain Bob Bartlett. In midsummer 1939, Bartlett was halfway between South Greenland and Iceland on board his schooner the *Effie M. Morrissey*. According to William Hobbs, the schooner was calculated to be in latitude 63°38′N and longitude 33°42′W. "The ship's three chronometers had been checked daily by the Naval Observatory signal, and the air was calm and the sea smooth." At 4 p.m., there appeared in the direction of southwestern Iceland the Snarfells Jökull, which is 4,715 feet high, and other landmarks known to the captain and the mate. They appeared "as if they were at a distance of about twenty-five or thirty nautical miles, though the position of the schooner showed that these features were actually at a distance of 335 to 350 statute miles."

In more recent times, the *fata morgana* effect has been observed and documented by travel writers and sailors, including John Bockstoce, who spent the summer of 1996 sailing on the Labrador Coast. On a run between Black Tickle and Cartwright, he explains, he was in the midst of "twelve good-sized icebergs, one of them with two large vertically-elongated spires. The mirage, too, distorted the outlines of the islands nearby into tall, narrow objects, and occasionally produced an upside-down image that hovered above the horizontally distorted lower one. At the same time the horizon seemed to swim upward, as if made of jelly."

Bockstoce's work references naturalist E.C. Pielou, who explains *fata morgana* as follows: "Light travels slightly faster through warm air than through cold, causing a light ray, as it passes from cooler to warmer air, to curve back towards the cooler air. This means that to somebody observing a distant object, say an ice floe through air that is warmer above than below, the floe will seem higher than it really is; it will also be elongated vertically, making it seem taller than it really is, because single points are drawn out into vertical lines."

Kay Burns and the Flat Earthers want to make the point that you should not believe things unless you have seen them with your own eyes, but *fata morgana* mirages remind us that we cannot always trust our eyes. As Pielou puts it, "The curvature of the light rays compensates for the curvature of the earth, causing distant scenes that 'should' be below the horizon to rise into view." In Labrador, what you see is not always what you get.

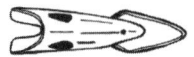

The Greatest Light Show on Earth: Auroras in Labrador

Each year, tourism increases in Labrador. The Department of Tourism has worked hard to make Labrador attractive to visitors by paving roads, establishing parks, improving accommodations, and providing information on historic sites. The really exciting things that draw people to Labrador, however, are often out of government control.

Natural phenomenon such as mirages, comets, icebergs, and animal migrations are not subject to the will of even the most determined officials. Still, people come from far and wide in the hopes of being lucky enough to see some of these unusual events. They rarely see all that they hope to, but they usually leave satisfied anyway.

Chief among the attractions that Mother Nature offers irregularly to the eager visitors to northern regions are displays of the aurora borealis, or northern lights. Auroras, which occur at times in the regions near both the north and south geomagnetic poles, are visible fairly regularly in Iceland, Norway, and Sweden, where you can book a guided tour for the purpose of viewing them, but the presence of the northern lights in Labrador is not something you can count on.

Accounts by early travellers to Labrador almost always contain some description of the northern lights, or "merry dancers" as they are whimsically called in this region. Justice of the peace George Simms, on August 23, 1830, while travelling as clerk of the Supreme Court aboard the schooner *Belinda*, wrote, "The Aurora Borealis appeared last evening more beautifully than I ever beheld in my life." When he reported more displays in September of 1830, July of 1831, and September of 1833, each time it was judged better than the last.

Henry Youle Hind reported that one night in the summer of 1863, when he and his companions were camped in a deep and narrow gorge, they could only see the sky by glancing directly upward. Toward the north they saw brilliant stars, a comet, and an aurora that turned their thoughts "from the gloom of a narrow crack in the earth to the fields of space."

Exposure to the northern lights was also one of the drawing cards for medical people coming out from England to work with Wilfred Grenfell. Dr. Eliot Curwen, who accompanied Grenfell on his second "expedition" to Labrador, reported that on July 8, 1893, they were treated to a brilliant display of the aurora.

Jessie Luther wrote that in August of 1910, when she and some of her Grenfell Mission colleagues went out one night to view a full moon, they were surprised to find a glorious aurora streaming above them: "The colours danced and swirled like living things, green, pink, crimson, yellow and violet in great waves, constantly changing and darting from one part of the heavens to another. From a crown overhead, long fingers of light fell like a fringed curtain, then suddenly changed, and a swirl of wonderful colour intensified in another place."

Labrador's Aboriginal people have thousands of years of familiarity with the aurora, and their legends and beliefs reflect the awe that a display of them evoked from more recent settlers. The Innu of the Labrador Peninsula, like most Native American communities, associate the aurora with "fire, death, blood and omens." The Aboriginal people of Australia have similar beliefs.

Anthropologist Frank Speck, writing in 1935, reports that the aurora is "remarked by all the bands and much commented upon." Among Labrador Innu, northern lights are called *uashtuashkuan*, although among Lake St. John's Innu it is called *wawaectockwao*—night lighting illumination—and *wawactockwun*—shining clouds. The traditional belief is that the aurora is caused by the spirits of the dead, dancing in the northern sky where they abide.

Accounts from the Inuit tend to be more complex. Inuit, like

Innu, believed that the lights, which they call *atsanik* in the Labrador dialect, were torches held to light those who have died to the afterlife that waits them, but according to Lucien Turner, it involves a complex cosmology in which there is a narrow bridge between the world of the living and that of the dead. Turner and E.W. Hawkes agree that the only being besides the dead who can pass that bridge is the raven. When the aurora is particularly active, it is because the dead are in the afterworld, feasting and playing football with a walrus skull.

It is tradition right across the circumpolar world that the sounds of the northern lights, crackling and whistling, are the voices of the spirits trying to communicate with the living. One has to answer them in a whispering voice, and one must never whistle at them, although this can make them swoop down to hear better. Some powerful shamans are able to "call the aurora and converse with it." Lawrence Millman claims that the belief that northern lights are the spirits of stillborn children is held throughout the Arctic from Alaska to Greenland.

According to Emilia Merkuratsuk of Nain, the northern lights predicted the Spanish influenza epidemic of 1918. She said there was a display of bright red northern lights, the reflection of which coloured even the snow, and that the doctor in Okak warned people there was going to be a flu: "We knew there was going to be something happening [but] we never thought it would be anything so bad."

Northern lights are also used to explain the origins of the colourful feldspar called Labradorite. The colours that can be seen in the stone are usually green, gold, or blue (the famous local "blue eye" stone), but all colours of the rainbow can sometimes be found when the microscopic plates of different metals catch the light. It is said that the northern light spirits once became imprisoned in the earth until a powerful shaman struck the ground with his harpoon and freed them. Some of the spirits hid away in the rocks until they were discovered by the sun and the water, which is why we have Labradorite today.

The origins of the northern lights, according to modern geophysicists, are rather more complex, though perhaps just as magical. In early times, scientists thought perhaps the lights originated in the northern seas or were from a reflection of the sun on polar ice, but in the 1880s, the suspicion arose that sunspots had something to do with their occurrence. The suspicions about sunspots became a certainty in the 1950s when research for International Geophysical Year confirmed the connection.

A sunspot is a "temporary concentration in the magnetic field of the sun," when the "convection of hot matter from the sun's interior is inhibited." Eventually, the blockage breaks, resulting in something like a volcanic eruption that sends an explosion of electrified particles racing toward the earth. Considering that the average sunspot is approximately the diameter of the Earth itself, this is quite a powerful event.

When the electrified particles strike the Earth's atmosphere, they become magnetized and flow toward the north and the south magnetic poles, producing the aurora borealis and the aurora australis. The light displays are the result of "collisions between gaseous particles in the Earth's atmosphere with charged particles released from the sun's atmosphere."

The various colours produced by the northern lights depend upon the type of gas particles that are colliding. The most common colour, pale green, is produced by the oxygen that can be found about 100 kilometres above the Earth's surface. Nitrogen produces a blue or purple aurora. The rare all-red aurora that Emilia Merkuratsuk described as predicting the Spanish influenza outbreak comes from high-altitude oxygen from almost 300 kilometres away.

Although the aurora borealis is usually associated with cold winter nights, auroras can occur at any time of the year. Consider the dates of sightings recorded by sojourners such as Luther, Curwen, and Simms. They were only travelling in Labrador in the summer months, so that is when they saw them. However, the auroras are concentrated at the north and south magnetic poles, and since the poles have extended periods of light and dark in winter and summer, in Labrador, your chances of seeing northern lights are more than doubled in the winter, when there is only eight hours of sunlight.

Auroras also have a cycle of frequent activity, approximately every 11 years—the next cycle is predicted to be around 2024. That doesn't mean you cannot see northern lights in other years, but by being aware of the cycle, tourists can increase their chances by timing their visits to coincide with those periods. Clear nights, which are more common in winter, provide ideal conditions, and midnight usually provides the best display.

Although visitors to Labrador often enthuse about the northern lights, they do not go unappreciated by Labradorians themselves. The lights are an important theme in the art and written literature of the region. *The Songs of Labrador*, compiled by Tim Borlase, contains seven works that refer to the northern lights, including songs written by such respected lyricists as Leslie Pardy of Cartwright and Shirley Montague of North West River.

Labrador art embroiderers often use textiles and beads to depict the aurora. The first major exhibition of Aboriginal artists in the province, organized by the St. John's Native Friendship Centre in 1996, included tapestries featuring the northern lights by Doris Saunders, Barb Wood, and Shirley Moorhouse. Betty Learning depicts the aurora in her quilts, while her daughter Lisa does digital "paintings" of them and works them into her caribou hair sculptures.

In 2017, an exhibition of Labrador art in Nova Scotia featured northern lights in paintings and prints by a young Natuashish artist, Scott Rich, and Postville's Lester Burry. Photographers such as Chris Sampson, working in the Torngats, and Larry Jenkins, in Labrador City, have also managed to capture what Birches[*] gallerist Herb Brown calls "the greatest light show on earth."

The northern lights might be elusive, but the journey in search of them is often as satisfying as the destination. Tourists who luck out in their desire to see northern lights in the skies of Labrador might be surprised to find them in a Labradorite sculpture by Gilbert Hay, in Kimberly McKinnon's contribution to the "Uncommon

---

* Herb Brown ran Birches Gallery in Happy Valley-Goose Bay from 1990 to 2014, when he relocated to Nova Scotia, taking the gallery with him. Birches Gallery has been open in Kempt Shore, Nova Scotia, since June 2014.

Clay" mural at the O'Brien Theatre in Happy Valley-Goose Bay, in a photographic display in Labrador West, or in the words to a song or poem at a concert.

If all else fails, anyone can find or buy a bit of Labradorite, wet it with a little water or hold it up to the sun, and the northern lights will dance for a privileged audience of one.

The Voice of the Iceberg

When curious travellers go in search of natural wonders, they often bring field guides to help them find and identify flowers, birds, trees, animals, geological features, and even whales. In Newfoundland and Labrador, travellers from within and outside the province often carry a much rarer book, the field guide *Icebergs of Newfoundland and Labrador* by Memorial University's Dr. Stephen E. Bruneau. Now in its fifth edition, this fascinating little book answers every question you didn't know enough to ask about icebergs.

Icebergs, which originate in glaciers, proliferate in both the north and south regions of the planet, but as the author reminds us, they are "rare or absent in all populated places in the world except Newfoundland and Labrador." Each year, approximately 40,000 of these beautiful behemoths come floating down our coasts, and each one is ancient and unique. Dr. Bruneau's handbook enriches the experience of seeing an iceberg, whether it is for the first time or the hundredth.

Labrador has long been associated with icebergs, but the reality is that, although icebergs travel along the coast, they do not originate in Labrador. Ice from Ungava Bay arrives in the form of large, flat pans of drifting sea ice, but most of the icebergs that travel the area from Baffin Bay to the coast of Newfoundland and Labrador known as Iceberg Alley come from the glaciers of Greenland and are composed of fresh water. There are freshwater ice masses in northern Labrador, but as none of the 195 small Torngat glaciers flow to the sea, they do not produce icebergs. Furthermore, due to climate change, summer temperatures in northern Labrador have increased by 2 or 3 degrees in recent years, enough to make the glaciers shrink.

One of the things that makes icebergs so attractive to artists, photographers, and people in general is their variety. No two icebergs are the same, yet unlike snowflakes, their shapes are all different. Scientists have identified general categories such as domed (rounded), tabular (flat and wide), blocky (flat-topped with steep sides), pinnacle (pointed), and drydocked (eroded with a U-shaped slot at water level), but in truth many are so irregular that they are almost impossible to categorize. And just when you think you have them pinned down, they turn or split or melt or find some way to change shape, so a viewer can't even be sure that the iceberg they were looking at yesterday is the same one they are seeing today.

The other tricky thing about any individual iceberg's appearance is that what you are seeing is only one-tenth of what it looks like. Think of the old parable of the blind men and the elephant—one feels the tail and thinks the elephant resembles a rope, another feels the leg and thinks it is like the trunk of a tree. An iceberg may look tall and thin like the spire of a church, but under water it may reach out three times or more its length in vicious horizontal spurs that can rip the bottom out of a boat.

Generally, icebergs are white due to the air trapped inside, but occasionally you will see icebergs with coloured streaks or seams. Black streaks in an iceberg may be the result of an ancient volcanic eruption, while red streaks come from contact with dust containing iron oxide. If an iceberg has grounded and then turned over, the sea bottom that adheres to the ice may cast a variety of hues. Brilliant blue bands come from meltwater which has refrozen after releasing its air bubbles.

Labrador Innu are familiar with icebergs because of their travels out to the coast, but because they do not hunt near or on the ice, icebergs are not featured in their mythology. In fact, the word "iceberg" does not appear in the print version of the Innu-aimun dictionary, although they do have a word for it. The Innu-aimun for iceberg is *mista-mishkumi*, meaning both iceberg and ice floe. Icebergs are fresh water while ice floes are salt, a fact almost certainly known to Innu but apparently of no particular significance to them.

The ancestors of the Inuit were the world's first ice experts, although Newfoundlanders probably ran a close second. Newfoundlanders and English-speaking Labradorians have dozens of words for ice and icebergs, including sish, growler, conker bell, bergy bit, bally catter, glitter, pummy, and slob. A lot of the ice terminology adopted internationally for describing ice comes from Inuktitut and the Newfoundland dialect.

In Labrador Inuttut, the word for iceberg is *piKalujak*. Traditionally, Inuit used ice for a variety of things; ice provided windows for igloos and shelters for fishing, it was a healing agent for treating wounds and fevers, it was a preservative for food, it was adapted as bridges and rafts for hunting, it made shoeing for komatiks, and much more. Ice was a tool, an aid, and a comfort in traditional times.

In myths and stories, ice is associated with the feminine and with sexuality. Sea ice is traditionally thought to have been created when a cannibal woman threw her ulu—her half-circle woman's knife—after a hunter who was escaping from her in his kayak. It skipped over the water like a flat stone and, where the knife touched the surface, the water froze.

Marble Island in Hudson's Bay was said to have been transformed from an iceberg when an old lady was abandoned there—tourists today are still instructed to crawl up the beach on their hands and knees when they land, out of respect for the suffering of this old woman. Cape Dorset historian Pete Pitseolak's prenatal memories included sliding down between two clapping mountains of white ice that were his mother's thighs as he was being born.

In Labrador, the name *piKalujak* is attached to an island near Nain, because, according to F.W. Peacock, PiKalujak Island was once an iceberg. The legend is that in the old times, there was a famous *angakok* living in the area who, in order to show off his powers, changed an iceberg which had drifted into the channel into an island. Titus Joshua, one of the Nain elders, said he didn't initially believe this story because an iceberg as big as that island would have grounded while floating into the bay.

Inuit also explain the presence of red-stained icebergs by telling a story of a girl standing on the peak of a mountain who, seeing her lover drown in the sea below her, impaled herself on the peak, which was subsequently transformed into an iceberg.

Although icebergs are frequently compared to ships or floating cathedrals, they often act more like islands. When an iceberg grounds for any length of time, it quickly develops its own ecosystem. Plankton clings to its underside, attracting fish, which attract birds, whales, and seals. The seals in particular attract polar bears, and the polar bears attract human hunters. Icebergs become a link in the food chain.

Grounded icebergs are also seen as refuges for hunters and travellers. Any seal hunter will tell you that if you are caught on sea ice that is breaking up, head for the highest iceberg in the area as it is almost certain to be grounded and unlikely to float farther from shore. Ice is not just inert, frozen water—it has the power to heal, nurture, feed, and accommodate life.

In early times, fishermen harvested ice from icebergs as a source of fresh water for ships, and before the introduction of refrigeration, they used iceberg ice as a way to preserve bait such as caplin and squid. They often climbed onto icebergs to harvest ice for "pinnacle tea," which was appreciated for its freshness and purity. In the 19th century, fishing vessels off the Labrador coast were known to hitch rides by attaching cables to icebergs, a dangerous manoeuvre, as icebergs are so unstable and unpredictable. Today, messing around with icebergs by anyone but an expert is discouraged.

Icebergs have good qualities but they can also create problems, not least of which was made known to the world when the *Titanic* sank. Fishermen in Newfoundland and Labrador learned to handle ice in a defensive way, towing bergs away from cod traps and wharves and using sturdy metal-tipped poles to push small icebergs away from boats and gear. In recent years, much progress has been made in developing forms of radar that can detect icebergs, but ice impact against ships and oil rigs are still issues in northern waters.

Labrador-born Denny Christian, now retired, probably knows

more about towing icebergs than anyone on earth. While working as a logistics expert at Memorial University's Centre for Cold Ocean Resources Engineering (C-CORE), Christian oversaw a series of ice-impact studies at Pack's Harbour off the Labrador coast in the 1980s and 1990s. His team attached sensors to a cliff emerging from deep water, then lassoed small icebergs and, using a pulley system, towed the bergs into the cliff, thereby measuring the force an iceberg might have when it hits an oil rig or a bridge footing.

It is estimated that, on average, 11 icebergs a year could collide with a platform situated in the Hibernia oil field, and since icebergs can range in weight from 100 tons to 10 million tons, an encounter between the two is a serious threat to both lives and the environment. According to Stephen Bruneau, deflecting icebergs away from rigs by towing them is now "a common practice in the management of icebergs for the offshore oil industry." C-CORE's technicians have developed a towing net that reduces the chances of an iceberg rolling as it is being moved.

Icebergs can create local tidal waves as they roll, and they can also explode from the compressed air trapped in them, tossing the fragments for hundreds of metres. They are also a menace to underwater pipelines. Scientists at C-CORE have located and studied fossilized iceberg scours in the Winnipeg area that show that ancient iceberg ruts of 1 to 2 metres' depth also have cracking and faults a farther 5 metres or more beneath them. Researchers concluded that North Atlantic pipelines have to be buried a good deal deeper into the ocean floor than originally estimated.

Iceberg spotting is generally over by early summer in Newfoundland but icebergs continue to proliferate later in the season in Labrador. According to Dr. Bruneau, the coastal communities of Point Amour, Battle Harbour, and Cartwright, all of which are accessible by road, are well situated for iceberg viewing. On a clear day, large icebergs are visible from as much as 30 kilometres away, although icebergs become virtually invisible in fog.

A good local guide is highly recommended for iceberg hunting offshore. The depth of water, currents, wind, and a dozen other factors have to be assessed to ensure safety when in the vicinity of ice and icebergs. Guides will listen for the "voice" of the iceberg, which manifests as a high pitched hiss or whistle, warning that air is escaping from disintegrating ice and that the iceberg might roll. If seabirds leave their iceberg perches, it is often an indication that the iceberg is unstable. Local boaters are also aware of what is unseen under the water, as well as the magnificent spectacle above the surface.

As with most natural phenomenon, iceberg spotting depends a good deal on luck, but on the coast of Labrador, you generally need less luck in your search than you do farther south. If the weather, the season, or even the ferry schedule prevents visitors from spotting icebergs in Iceberg Alley, they can console themselves with Iceberg Vodka at the nearest watering hole. Failing that, keep an eye out for homemade signs offering iceberg ice for sale, and boil up a soothing cup of pinnacle tea. Better still, pop a chunk of the ice into a glass of water to make "bergy seltzer." The air that comes sputtering and crackling from the surface of the glass—the voice of the iceberg—is 15,000 years old.

PEOPLE OF THE INTERIOR

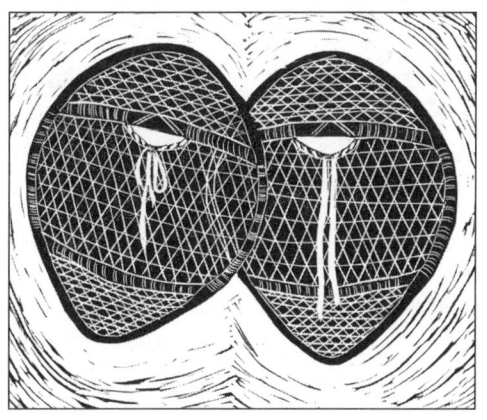

Playing for Keeps: Innu Checkers as Spiritual Struggles

Checkers, or draughts as it is known in Britain, is one of the most popular games in the world. Archeologists date the existence of checkerboards to 3000 BC in Iraq, but the game is known in various forms around the globe and it is probably even more ancient than that. People have been playing checkers for more than 2,000 years longer than they have been playing chess.

On the Labrador Peninsula, checkers or *atinakan* was particularly popular among the Innu, whose checkerboards sometimes showed much of the craftsmanship that went into traditional toboggans and skin coats. The game was marked out on a piece of skin that could be rolled up for travel or on a board that could be folded. The pieces, which in a commercial set are usually simple red and black discs, were more often square or circular counters painted with intersecting blue and red lines. The Rooms Museum in St. John's has several Innu checker games collected by the trader Richard White, and there are probably examples in other collections as well.

We think of checkers as being a very simple game—each player has 12 pieces and must clear the board of his opponents' pieces by jumping them diagonally to capture them—but, in actuality, the rules for the game can vary from one culture to another. Players may have five, 12, or 20 pieces, and the method of "crowning" or capturing an opponent's pieces varies widely.

Like most games, however, checkers can take on a secondary level of importance and meaning. Consider the patriotism that adheres to the Olympics games, the riots that follow victories at football or hockey, the bloodied noses or stabbings that end some card games. The notion that the hidden opponent in any game is not the human opposition but the devil himself is almost universal.

Anthony Jenkinson points to the game of chess played between Death and the medieval knight Antonius Bloch, in Ingmar Bergman's celebrated film *The Seventh Seal*, as the most famous board game with a supernatural dimension to be found in art and literature. The chess game with the Red Queen in *Alice through the Looking Glass* ("Off with her head!") must run a close second.

The notion that you can lose your life in a game of chess or checkers is parallel to the tradition in European thought that if you play cards with the devil, you can lose your soul. The same supernatural element can be found in dozens, if not hundreds, of songs, from Mick Jagger's "Sympathy for the Devil" to Von Bonneville's "Cards with the Devil." The songs have variations—in "The Devil Went down to Georgia" (or "Texas," depending on who is singing it), the narrator plays in a fiddle contest to win a gold violin or lose his soul. The story of the stranger who has cloven hoofs instead of feet is so common that folklorists have identified it as "type ML 3015."

While most anthropologists who worked in the Labrador Peninsula were aware of the popularity of checkers among Innu, many early researchers missed out on the use of the game as part of a spiritual struggle. Lucien Turner, writing in 1894, identified checkers as the "principal source of amusement with the men," a game to employ their idle moments when they were awaiting the approach of herds of caribou, or "to while away the tedium of the long winter evenings with only the light of the flickering fire of the dry limbs of spruce."

Turner does concede that there are "slight differences" in the way the game is played in what he calls "civilization," and admits that "some of the men are so expert that they would rank as skillful players in any part of the world." However, he missed out on the significance of the game.

Frank Speck, writing 40 years later, comes closer to the mark when he admits that game pieces can act as magical devices which "would be regarded as existing purely for amusement were it not for a native attitude that, even though they can hardly be called religious, they nevertheless involve the exertion of magic influences over animals." He compares the function of games as "comparable to that of decorative art, since the emotional pleasures of the arts stand forth as nourishment to the soul."

When Georg Henriksen published *Hunters in the Barrens* in 1973, he, too, saw the game of checkers as simply a pastime or entertainment that the Innu played with skill and enthusiasm. "All the hunters usually follow one game at a time," he wrote, "hanging over each other's shoulders and shouting advice to the two players, every now and then moving the bricks for them."

By 2009, when *I Dreamed the Animals,* Henriksen's biography of John Poker (Kaniuekutat) was released, it was clear that he finally understood the complex nature of Innu checkers. Like Turner and Speck, Henriksen recognized that Innu were passionate and extremely clever players, but he was also aware that the checkerboard was sometimes used for divination and as part of a spiritual fight. The loser of the game was also the loser of the spiritual contest.

In fact, Poker asserted that, like many others, he used checker games to "find out what's going on in other Innu communities." For example, it could tell you who the community's shaman was, what animals they were catching, and other sorts of information.

One of the stories Poker told Henriksen, which involved a shaman who transformed himself into a fox in order to kill a man, centred around a game of checkers between an old man from George River and a younger hunter from Davis Inlet. The younger man realized he was playing for his life, but by winning he also enraged his opponent. After the game was over, the transformed loser tried to block the barrel of the victor's gun so that it would explode when he fired. The victor, possibly because of his win at the game, was able to shoot the fox, and back in his tent the old man died.

Poker himself was at one time a master player, though the only opponent he chose to take on was a man named Meshkana, whom he suspected of having murdered his mother. Anthony Jenkinson identifies Meshkana as the powerful Mushuau Innu shaman and shaking-tent practitioner known in English as Sam Riche. Poker's anger at Meshkana was such that he would play to win, saying to himself each time, "I wish you were dead." One night he and Meshkana played checkers in their sleep, and the next day Meshkana died. Poker himself was never entirely sure if he had killed the man. When Henriksen asked if they were playing about life and death, Poker could only answer, "Maybe ... I always thought, 'I wish you dead by beating you at checkers.'"

The ability to kill through checkers seemed to be channelled by anger at the opponent. In his interviews with Henriksen, Poker admitted that "[p]eople thought that Meshkana became sick because he got something that had to do with the checkerboard." After Meshkana's death, Poker lost his ability with the checkers, and as an old man, he just played for the fun of it.

The use of the checkerboard to facilitate spiritual battles is not confined to Labrador. In the Irish tradition, fairies will sometimes battle for a man's soul by playing out the fight in a game of checkers, and this tradition came to the island portion of the province with the Roman Catholic settlers. Patrick Kavanagh, in his iconic novel *Gaff Topsails*, has one character recall that his grandfather once stumbled upon a band of fairies playing checkers on a tree stump, and thinking fast, he sat down and joined in, consequently winning the game and saving his soul.

Checkers is recognized everywhere as good training in logic and thought, so that even those who do not see it as a source of spiritual domination admire the skill of those who are good at the game. It is not clear that the game as it is played in non-Innu cultures is the same game the Innu played. When the late Francis Penashue was asked about the rules, he explained that they were too complicated for non-Innu to understand.

There seems to be a gender bias also. All the anthropological references to players specify that it was a game for hunters, for men only. Elizabeth Penashue said that, in Sheshatshiu, women do not play checkers, but she had heard that Mushuau Innu women in Natuashish do. Elder Agathe Piwas is said to be an enthusiastic player.

Jean Pierre Ashini didn't play checkers when he was a boy because he was usually out in the bush with his grandfather. However, he said the game required remarkable concentration, because the elders could often think four moves ahead of younger players. Jenkinson believes the Innu concept of *tshemetentshian*, or the accomplishment of superhuman or even supernatural tasks through intense concentration, may be relevant when considering the association of checkers with spiritual struggles.

Although Frank Speck does not specifically discuss checkers in his work on divination devices, he does remind his readers that just because a game is fun to play does not mean it can't have other functions as well. Among Innu, string games of cat's cradle were played by both old and young. The concentration required to form the shapes, the physical control needed to do it quickly and well, and the patience to learn the figures would all have been good training for a hunter. Under certain circumstances, however, there were spiritual aspects that the Innu directly identified as being effective in helping to snare animals.

As Speck saw it, games like checkers were spiritually strengthening because they "satisfy the soul-spirit of the individual who indulges in them." Today, checkers may have lost its spiritual significance for many of the younger generation of Innu, but it is possible that young Innu, like children all over the world, are finding spiritual sustenance in some apparently simple computer games that their elders are not even aware of. After all, the very existence of computer games would have seemed nothing short of magical just 50 years ago.

Elizabeth Penashue's Labrador Walkabout

Each spring for the past 12 years, Elizabeth Penashue has gone for a walk in the bush, a walk that can last up to a month, just as, each fall, she puts her canoe in the river below Churchill Falls and heads for Goose Bay, 170 kilometres away. Every time, she is accompanied by friends, strangers, and relatives of all ages, and each time a few more people are won over to her side in the battle to save the Innu way of life, a battle that has consumed her attention and occasionally landed her on the docket.

Throughout the year, Elizabeth Penashue lobbies government and Aboriginal politicians on a variety of issues—to stop the Lower Churchill development, to clean up the environment, to increase Innu cultural content in the schools, the list is endless—but twice a year, she leaves the lecture circuit behind and just travels in the country. In the old days, the migration went in the other direction—to the coast in spring and to the interior in fall—but times have changed and the Innu have changed with them.

Each fall and again in the spring, Elizabeth and her supporters pack up her huge tent and stove, sort through her paddles or snowshoes, fill the grub boxes with flour, tea, butter, and jam, and gather around them a dozen or more companions. Some are grown children or small grandchildren, some are journalists or educators, others are friends from countries far away who have been caught in the spell of Elizabeth's dream of a worldwide movement to save the Innu way of life.

Except for the *akenashau*—the non-Innu—who have to negotiate airline tickets and annual leave to make the trip, the composition of the group is a matter of negotiation up until the last minute. Who will go, when they will leave, and how far they will travel is a matter of speculation up until the final moments. However, an hour or two before they depart, the Innu participants turn up, or follow behind, quickly catching up with the main group.

The first day or two is generally chaotic as everyone tries to find his or her place in the disparate group, but it soon settles into a routine. The men take charge of getting the tent up each evening, locating old lodgepoles or cutting new ones, preparing wood for the stove, and hauling water. The women gather spruce boughs for the floor, start supper, and air and arrange bedding. The older boys usually range free, hunting porcupine or beaver, trying for a fish or two, while the girls supervise the younger ones.

In a traditional camp, such as Elizabeth's, the old ways of dividing labour are soon re-established. By the third day, even the neophytes are starting to get the hang of bush life. Elizabeth is a tireless teacher, and it's not long before even the shyest child or adult is searing a beaver tail preparatory to skinning it, or mixing bannock dough for Innu donuts. The bush is where the old practices are maintained, where the land becomes familiar again.

"If there is no land," Elizabeth warns, "the children will have lots of problems in a couple of years' time. That's why I always include some *akenashau*, so they can know my concerns, where I come from. I want to make them understand. They shouldn't just see me in jail, they should see me in the country too, where I walk."

Elizabeth's late husband, Francis, who was the silent partner in this ongoing process for many years, was less political in his reasoning. "Living in a house, you just sit, watch TV, drink tea, but in the country you have something to do," he explained. "I find stress in the community, not in the country." Francis felt Innu bodies needed to walk or work hard to be in condition. Resting for a few days was okay, he said, but then he started to feel unhealthy.

"It's all a circle," Elizabeth explains, "culture, school, canoe, protecting the animals, *akenashau*, the government, it's all a circle. That's why I walk." Francis may have had different reasons for travelling, she says, but they were both on the same *meshkanau*, the same path.

That *meshkanau* is a curious mix of quite ancient Innu practices and modern technology. Elizabeth travels the traditional way, hauling her toboggan. The previous generation of Innu had adopted the use of sled dogs and komatiks from the Inuit, but Elizabeth's dog is only along to help with hunting porcupine and partridge. Francis, who had had quadruple bypass heart surgery, ran visitors back and forth from the community on his Ski-Doo, and helped to beat down the trail they followed, a chore that today is done by younger recruits to Elizabeth's service.

According to Elizabeth, the word *meshkanau* has a philosophical and spiritual meaning as well as a literal one. For European explorers, and even for today's adventure tourists, half the lure of the Labrador wilderness is the sense that nobody has set foot there before. Innu are the opposite—they want to walk where their ancestors have walked for a thousand years. "We follow the paths our parents took," she adds. The Churchill Falls development flooded the travel route her maternal grandparents and her mother took, but her father used to hunt at the headwaters of the Eagle River.

Francis may not have agreed with his wife's politics, but he fully agreed with the need to walk in his ancestors' footsteps. "So many Innu want to be drinking alcohol like white men," he explained, "and so many white men want to be like Innu, hunting and that. But they don't really understand." Elizabeth adds that sometimes when she sees Innu people on the other side of a river or lake, the white people with her don't see them and she knows they are her dead relatives, walking on the same *meshkanau*.

"In my heart, I don't tell the *akenashau* everything when we're out there," Elizabeth explains with some hesitation. Sometimes in the bush, she sees her family who have passed on, and she goes expecting to meet them. She's afraid the *akenashau* will not believe her, so she says nothing of this to the non-Innu supporters who accompany her on her journeys.

Over the years, Elizabeth's peaceful protest has shifted emphasis. First, it was to protest low-level flying by NATO military, then it was to stop the Voisey's Bay mine, and now it is to demonstrate against the development of the Lower Churchill. So far, her efforts have not been effective, but she continues. "We walk and canoe to protect the earth," Elizabeth says. "One day the children will understand what I am doing."

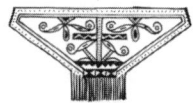

Francis Penashue: the Man Behind the Activist

Innu activist Elizabeth Penashue is known throughout the province and across the country for her impassioned work to preserve Innu culture and save the environment, but those who know her are well aware that she does not work alone. Behind Elizabeth, working to support her, are numerous friends and relatives, but for many years, the person doing all the heavy lifting was an equally extraordinary person, her husband, the late Francis Penashue.

In the 1980s, it was Elizabeth who protested low-level flying and Francis who stayed home and held the family together, Elizabeth who went to jail and Francis who worked behind the scenes to get her released, Elizabeth who gave impassioned speeches and Francis who translated for her. Elizabeth led walks into the Mealy Mountains each spring and organized canoe trips down the Churchill River late each summer. But it was Francis who collected the walkers and canoeists at the airport, drove the truck up the highway with the canoes, put up the huge tent to house the travellers, chopped wood, hunted game, ran the rapids, drove the snowmobile, hauled water, and did a thousand other things to make the trips work.

For her unceasing efforts to save Innu land and Innu culture, Elizabeth has received an honorary doctorate from Memorial University, a national Aboriginal Achievement Award, and a Queen's Diamond Jubilee Medal, while Francis sat in the background and applauded along with everyone else. Francis told journalist Marie Wadden that in the past, before he stopped drinking, "he'd have been consumed by jealousy to see her in this role." The story of Francis Penashue's transformation into the man behind the woman is as compelling as Elizabeth's own story.

Francis was born to Kanani and Matshiu Penashue up in the Mealy Mountains some time during World War II. His mother died when he was a baby, and as an only child, he was often handed over to relatives for long periods of time while his father was in the bush hunting. The records are unreliable, as he was known by five different names before he appears consistently in the records as Francis Penashue. Among the Innu, he was known as Kanatuakueshis, which means "little porcupine hunter," after his father's Innu name.

His childhood was that of the son of a nomadic hunter. For a time in the summers, Francis attended a little Roman Catholic school on the Innu side of North West River (known today as Sheshatshiu), where a priest identified him as a good candidate for further education. At the age of 12, he was sent to the notorious Mount Cashel Orphanage in St. John's to be groomed for leadership. His experience there was one of beatings, abuse, humiliation, and loneliness.

After two years, Francis went back to Sheshatshiu and refused to return to Mount Cashel. He finished Grade 8 at Peenamin Mackenzie School and began to look for employment. In 1963 he married Elizabeth, but the traditional skills he had learned from his grandparents in the bush were not in demand in the village. Through the 1960s he alternated trapping and hunting with a variety of more conventional jobs such as running the cable car across North West River, maintaining the airstrip, and guiding sports fishermen for the Cooper fishing camps. It was around this time that he began drinking. Elizabeth joined him and life became a nightmare for the whole family.

Ironically, when things got bad in the community, it was Francis who wanted to retreat into the bush and Elizabeth who insisted they stay in Sheshatshiu. She believed that the children had to have an English education, while Francis, who had been to school in the south, knew that education was of no use if it came with poor self-esteem, addictions, and despair.

Despite the drinking and an increasingly long record for domestic assault and other alcohol-related offences, Francis began to work his way into a position of leadership in Sheshatshiu. For three years he worked for Labrador Legal Services, acting as an interpreter, getting people to court on time, explaining the justice system to Innu for whom the court was a foreign concept. He later worked as the recreation director for Sheshatshiu. In 1982, he became chief of the Sheshatshiu Council, the first of two terms he served. If anything, the stress of the position made his depression worse.

By this time, Elizabeth and Francis's eldest son, Peter, had developed his own drinking problem, but in 1991, when Peter sobered up, Francis took a long, hard look at what he was doing to himself, his family, and his community. Sobriety took several tries, but three months at Brentwood Treatment Centre in Ontario miraculously brought Francis out of the slough of self-loathing and bitterness that he had immersed himself in, and he never looked back.

In 1993, Francis found his true calling and went to work at the Sheshatshiu Group Home, doing for other people's children what he had failed to do for his own. For the next 11 years, he provided counselling to youth in open custody, cleaning and cooking for them, taking them into the country, teaching them the Innu way of life, and helping them develop respect for themselves, the animals, and the land.

At home, he learned to bring that patience, passion, and commitment to his wife and children. While Elizabeth became the public face of Innu protest, she relied heavily on Francis to make her work possible. Everything he did, from reading newspaper reports to Elizabeth (who did not read English) to fishing and hunting for country food for his large extended family, was intended to help his people on the road to wellness.

In 2011, when the Truth and Reconciliation Commission held a hearing in Goose Bay as part of the Indian Residential Schools settlement agreement, Francis was one of a dozen Labradorians who came forward to give public testimony of the abuse they had suffered. Francis was calm and factual when he described getting a brutal beating at Mont Cashel for taking his 15-minute break at the wrong time. It's clear that the anger and rage he once felt at his own suffering was now channelled to a positive end.

It's hard to reconcile the wild man Francis was one-quarter of a century ago with the humble, unobtrusive, kind elder of his later years. Dr. Elizabeth Yeoman of Memorial University's Faculty of Education travelled with the Penashues on their spring walk to the Mealy Mountains and she summed up the qualities that made Francis such a valuable member of the community. "His keen intellect and reflective nature, combined with inexhaustible patience and a high degree of competence in almost any kind of practical matter, made him a true leader," she writes. He neither asked for nor seemed to expect recognition.

Early in 2013, Francis Penashue suffered a debilitating stroke which greatly limited his physical activity, yet he still found the time to help others. When Supreme Court Justice William Goodridge visited him at his tent in Sheshatshiu, Francis responded to a problem the judge was having with his canvas tent by drawing him a diagram of the proper way to rig it. When his speech became laborious, he somehow found the energy to answer the endless questions visitors and young relatives bombarded him with. Like his father and his uncle Pien before him, Francis Penashue embodied the strength, grace, and quiet confidence of the traditional Innu hunter.

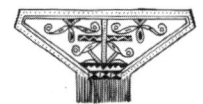

St. Anne's Green Cathedral

On July 26 each year, Aboriginal people across Canada gather together to honour their elders and to celebrate the feast of St. Anne, grandmother of Jesus.

In Quebec, Sainte Anne de Beaupré has been the gathering place since 1658, now attracting over 1 million visitors a year. In Alberta, native people began making pilgrimages to Lac St. Anne in 1887, and today up to 30,000 pilgrims attend, with 4,000 of them camping on the site. In Newfoundland, Qalipu people come together at Flat Bay. Many Labrador Innu go on pilgrimage with their relatives in Quebec, but for those who cannot make the trip, a gathering is organized just outside Sheshatshiu on Radar Hill.

While St. Anne is honoured throughout Canada and the world with churches, paintings, and relics, in Labrador the St. Anne's mass is celebrated under the open skies. A table is set up for an altar, wild flowers are gathered, food is prepared, a statue is carried up the hill, and a priest welcomed. The service and the feast are both simple, but participation is heartfelt and honest and the view out over Lake Melville is magnificent.

One question that often arises is whether it is appropriate to have a Catholic mass in the open air. Prior to Catholic emancipation in 1832, when the practice of Roman Catholicism was still illegal in Newfoundland and Labrador, Roman Catholics in communities such as Renews and Torbay gathered on high hills usually known as Pulpit Rocks, to celebrate weddings and to say the rosary. It was thought at the time that mass should only be said in a church or another "respectable" shelter. Anyone allowing their premises to be used for Catholic observance risked having their houses and fishing stages forfeited or burned.

Interpretation of canon law is more liberal now, as is evident in the open-air masses said by Roman Catholic popes in recent years. Missionaries, military priests, and other clergy regularly celebrate masses under the open sky. The St. Anne's Day mass near Sheshatshiu is organized by Elizabeth Penashue with help from the Sheshatshiu Band Council, so it is almost inevitable that this environmental activist would opt for the "Green Cathedral" as a suitably magnificent site for this spiritually important service.

Although best known as the patron saint of Canada and of the Mi'kmaq people in particular, Anne is also the patron saint of childless women, expectant mothers, women in labour, homemakers, and even cemeteries. Very little is known about the actual woman, who is not even named in the New Testament, but legend has it that Anne and her husband, Joachim, were wealthy, elderly, and childless when an angel visited to tell them that they would conceive a child who would be famous around the world.

Devotion to St. Anne first began in the sixth century when the emperor Justinius raised a basilica in her honour at Constantinople. From there, the cult spread to Jerusalem, Rome, Britain, Ireland, and, in particular, to Brittany and Canada. Pictures and statues of St. Anne often show her teaching the Virgin Mary to read.

The practice of using St. Anne's oil to anoint people began more than a century ago. If someone was too ill to make the pilgrimage to a St. Anne's shrine, the oil that was burning in the sanctuary lamp, in front of the relic of St. Anne, was brought back to strengthen the patient physically and spiritually. The oil is blessed with "a formula from the Roman Ritual which includes exorcism, or asking God to protect those who use it from the influence of the devil." At Radar Hill, the elders and others who feel a spiritual need are anointed on the forehead with the sign of the cross and the blessing of St. Anne.

When the feast day falls on a Sunday, baptisms, too, are a part of the St. Anne's celebrations in Labrador. During a baptism, a child is welcomed into the Catholic faith. Two godparents or sponsors, usually one of each gender from both sides of the family, promise to act as models for the child, who is draped in white, anointed with holy oil, and then doused with water three times. Given St. Anne's association with childbirth and the education of children, a St. Anne's Day baptism is seen as particularly propitious.

Unlike Lac St. Anne or Sainte Anne de Beaupré, which have both been made National Historic Sites, Radar Hill cannot claim any miracles to date, but it is slowly acquiring the aura of a sacred site for the Innu and their friends. What started out as a small gathering of a few devout elders has swelled to close to 100 people, there to acknowledge the role of prior generations in the education of the next.

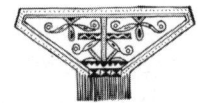

LIFE AND DEATH

Layman's Language: Medical Terminology in Labrador

Newfoundland and Labrador is famous for fierce adherence to its many dialects and accents, and 30 years after the publication of the *Dictionary of Newfoundland English*, certain words that were thought to be dying out have come back into fashion. Women window-shopping will now declare that they are "twacking," T-shirts proudly ask "What are you @?," and arguments get ignited in the bars of St. John's and Goose Bay if someone calls another a "streel" or a "skeet."

One of the most widely cited sources for dialect in the Newfoundland dictionary is Wilfred Grenfell, the founder of the International Grenfell Association. Grenfell wrote prodigiously and he added colour and even a patina of exoticism to his books by using—and explaining—dialect words he encountered in the course of his work. Many of the British and American nurses and doctors he brought to coastal Labrador were as entertained by the dialect as he was and wrote at length about their attempts to break the language barriers they encountered with their English-speaking patients.

Medical historian Dr. John Crellin, in his book *Home Medicine*, has observed that communication difficulties between physicians and patients are widespread in many countries, particularly in rural areas. A few of the many issues that cause patients and medical professionals to misunderstand one another include the popular use of medical terms that have disappeared from professional medicine, changes in the meaning of medical terms, and the use of euphemisms for sensitive or embarrassing conditions.

Many of the nurses who came to Labrador were midwives, trained in England or Scotland, and they all had trouble adjusting to the evasive way Newfoundlanders and Labradorians alluded to pregnancy. When Ruth Trees Sampson, who was working in Port Hope Simpson, got a call to come because "Suzy's sick," she didn't realize that it meant the patient was having a baby. "They would say so-and-so is due to be sick on a certain date, which was the delivery date." Relatives would call at the nursing station asking if the patient was "well yet," meaning had she had the baby.

Until relatively recently, the word *pregnancy* was simply not used by many Labrador women. One patient, when asked if she was pregnant, replied, no, she was Church of England. As a woman came closer to term, she "improved," meaning she got bigger. When her time finally came, a baby wasn't delivered, it was "borned," and it might even be "borned on her mother's floor," meaning not literally on a floor but at the grandmother's home.

Millicent Loder of Double Mer, the first Labradorian registered nurse, had no trouble with the dialect. Loder strongly believed that Labradorians were quite capable of learning the basics of home treatment "if the importance of these matters was explained in layman's language, rather than medical terms." Loder's mother was a "granny" midwife, and as a child Loder often awoke to discover her mother was "gone to find a baby." She developed a great desire to "find babies and care for the sick and injured, as [her mother] always did," and despite excellent obstetrical training in the US, she took pride not in delivering babies but in "finding" them.

Maggie Arkell Linstead, a nurse who worked in Cartwright, encountered the dialect problem when a woman brought her young son in because "he had a problem with his bird." When the mother pulled up the child's shirt, the nurse thought his "bird" was his belly button, but when she pulled down his pants, Linstead realized what the problem was. In Labrador, that part of the male anatomy is sometimes also referred to as the "bud."

Like many rural people, Labradorians were and are extremely modest and tend to use indirect expressions when discussing the private parts of the body. If a man became impotent, he might say to the nurse, "I've lost my nature." His potency was known as his "pride," and rather than go to the nursing station, he might even treat himself with the scent glands of the beaver that he would normally save to bait his fur traps. A woman's pelvic area would be called a "spraddle," her pubic hair was referred to as "king hair" (the same phrase used for guard hairs on a fox pelt), and if it were absolutely necessary to speak about female specifics, the word "mussel" might be employed.

Sometimes it was the most common words that confused the visiting or immigrant medical workers. The Newfoundland and Labrador intensifier "wonderful," according to Dr. Robert Ecke, "demands special treatment." In his memoir *Snowshoe and Lancet*, Ecke explained that "[i]t means a strong 'very'—to be wondered at. It has no connotation of good ... If you simply say something is wonderful, chances are it is horrible." A wonderful pain might be terrible, cruel agony, and a wonderful temperature in a patient might be 104 degrees.

Similarly, the word "find," meaning to experience or feel a sensation, gives no hint that there is pain involved. "I finds me back" or "I finds me knee" seems like a pretty benign observation to the come-from-away nurse or doctor, but to the Labradorian it can suggest intense, cruel torment. "Shocking," like "wonderful," means "very," but it is frequently a positive intensifier, as in a shocking fine day or a shocking good meal.

One intensifier that is unique to Labrador, and which doesn't show up in the Newfoundland dictionary, is the word "ugly." If someone is ugly, it means he or she is angry, aggressive, or dangerous, but you can also have an "ugly fine day" or an "ugly bad day." One nurse recalls that there was a daily domestic from Makkovik at the Happy Valley nursing station who was "some proud of her ugly old diapers on the washing line!"

Often, confusion would arise from a common word being applied in a way that was uncommon for the medical person from outside. To the medical practitioner, a doctor is a physician, but to a fisherman it is a small fish or a water spider. A nurse speaking of a needle would probably envision a hypodermic syringe, but a lay person might picture a flat wooden implement used to knot meshes in a net. A stretcher might be a framework of poles and canvas for carrying a patient or an upholstered couch in the parlour.

Similarly, the Labradorian thinking of a "splinter" might have in mind a cast made from small strips of wood and bandages, and if he's in need of a "banger," he wants an overcoat, not a sausage. "Tow" is what passes for cotton wool elsewhere, and a cot or finger stall is a "nipper" in the Straits area. Stethoscopes were known as "sounders," and if a doctor "sounded" a patient, she listened to the lungs and heart.

Medical treatment provided room for further misunderstanding. The story about the constipated man who, complaining of the suppositories he had swallowed, said that he "might as well have stuck 'em up [his] back passage," may be apocryphal, but confusion did often happen. Back in the UK, a teaspoon of dill water was often given to babies with colic, but on this side of the Atlantic, dill water is pumped from the bilge of a boat and not many mothers would consent to dosing a baby with that. "Medicine" in Labrador was liquid—pills were never called medicine.

Grenfell doctors and nurses often came from the UK. Over here, a "hurt" is a blueberry, an "ear" is the forked part of a claw hammer, and an "earache" is a centipede. A "one-lunger" is a boat with a single cylinder engine, a "dieter" is someone boarding in your house against the promise of service in the next fishing season, and "the one-eyed captain" is a bottle of rum. Over the water, to "knock a girl up" is to wake her up, not to put a bun in her oven.

Specific diseases had local names, but they did not always coincide with the same name used elsewhere. Shingles (herpes zoster) in Labrador is often called St. Anthony's Fire, a term employed elsewhere for the disease erysipelas. Tuberculosis was often called simply a "cough," while deadly pneumonia was just "inflammation." An American doctor might refer to a gastrointestinal upset as crud, which was also American slang for venereal disease, but in Labrador, "crud" is milk curds. The local name for influenza was "Eskimo cold," not to denigrate the Inuit but to stress the danger of the infection, which was often lethal in the northern communities.

When a patient didn't wish to refer directly to a disease such as tuberculosis, or a private body part, he or she substituted another word. Crellin gives as an example of this a woman who claimed to have a "wonderful pain" in her stomach. The pain was actually in her breast, but she didn't want to say this and the stomach was "a respectable area nearby." Such substitutions are called "codings." A louse might be referred to as a "boo" or a "traveller," a mark that appears without any apparent cause is "a dead man' pinch," and to "urge" or "yuck" is to vomit.

Grenfell loved all these dialect differences, and even as he tried to eliminate folk beliefs in the Labrador population, he documented them for his fundraising speeches. He amused his American and British audiences with stories such as the one about the old man who, when asked about a charm he wore around his neck, said it was a "toothache string" to prevent toothache. Grenfell also described his bafflement when a patient reported having a "kink in her glutch," which any Labradorian would have known meant she had trouble swallowing.

Many of the dialect words Grenfell encountered came directly from the trapping or fishing life of the Labradorians he was treating. Squid hand or seal finger was infection and swelling caused by handling these animals, while a man with a big appetite might be called a "gulvin," after the cod's alimentary canal. A small child or a very thin person would have been called a "skiver" because they were as thin as a fish prong, or "slinky," after the slink, a salmon in poor condition after it has spawned. A person with diarrhea would be said to have the "scutters" from the word meaning to sail swiftly before the wind. A "cruddy" was a bed for a small child, after the little cabins on a ship.

A greater exposure to standard English on television and radio in Labrador has caused most of the old dialect terminology to fall into disuse in recent years. As Dr. Crellin points out, when patients today talk with physicians and other health care professionals, "they tend to switch from vernacular speech to what they perceive as medical language." However, he warns, although the words and phrases have disappeared, "the concepts behind them remain a living force." Health care workers need to be sensitive to the feelings and concerns, as well as the cultural attitudes, that were once embedded in the old terminology and to ensure the patient fully understands and is understood when seeking treatment and counselling in hospitals and nursing stations today.

Labrador's Granny Midwives

On September 30, 2016, a series of regulations came into effect in Newfoundland and Labrador that outlined the necessary training and qualifications for midwives in this province. The implementation of these regulations means that midwives will once again be legally allowed to practice the art and science of catching babies both in Labrador and on the Island.

Professional midwives had been introduced into Newfoundland and Labrador by Wilfred Grenfell after 1892, when he staffed his hospitals and nursing stations with British nurses who had also trained as midwives. These midwife nurses and some doctors, with Grenfell's encouragement, trained hospital staff and other interested women to assist at births, and in 1920, midwifery legislation was passed in the House of Assembly and various programs established to train midwives who were not nurses.

By the mid-1960s, however, most women were choosing or obliged to give birth in publicly funded hospitals, with their babies delivered by obstetricians, rather than pay midwives privately to deliver babies at home. The result was not just unnecessary expense to the health care system but it also resulted in Newfoundland and Labrador having the highest rate of Caesarean sections in Canada and the lowest rate of breastfeeding. The reintroduction of professional midwives into the birthing practice is intended to bring balance back into the system and to improve the delivery and post-delivery experience of parents and babies.

Absent from this brief history of midwives, however, are the women who were known as granny midwives, informally trained or self-educated women who for little or no payment took on the responsibility of birthing babies in small and isolated communities. At a time when childbirth was often a life-threatening process, the burden accepted by these women was emotionally stressful and physically exhausting. The midwives not only caught the babies but they cared for them and their mothers and for the other children in the household for 10 full days, until the mother was considered out of danger and able to get up and resume her duties.

In Labrador, which has four distinct cultural groups, birthing practices varied in some ways, but physiology being physiology, there was also a remarkable consistency to the process. In times of difficulty, women of all cultures turned to one another for help and it was never refused.

Remarkably little is known about traditional Innu, Inuit, or Southern Inuit (NunatuKavummiut) birthing practices, largely because until well into the contact era, most missionaries and anthropologists were men, and men were rarely involved in childbirth. Lucien Turner, writing in the late 1890s, records that the Innu women "appear to be exempted from the curse of Eve" (pain and sorrow during childbirth) and William Duncan Strong, writing in the winter of 1927, noted that "[w]hen a woman is in labour, all the men except the husband leave, and the other women come in to help."

We know from accounts of settler women that the Innu were highly experienced midwives. When Annie Blake went into labour up on the Naskapi River, her husband, Gilbert, went to a nearby Innu camp and brought two midwives back to tend to her. Mabel Manak had a miscarriage one spring, when loose ice prevented midwife Lizzie Adams from travelling from Adlatok to help her. A group of Innu was camping nearby, on their way to the coast for the summer, and two of their women came to help out as she had not expelled the afterbirth. The Innu midwives heated rocks by boiling them and placed them against her abdomen, to draw out the placenta. The settler men were convinced the Innu did not know what they were doing, and the Innu men went in a frantic search for a white midwife for fear they would be accused of killing the patient.

Olive Lane intervened and insisted that the Innu women were "doing the same as the doctor would," only using hot rocks instead of hot water bottles. The intervention was successful, Mrs. Manak lived, and throughout the following months of her recovery the Innu midwives continued to visit and help her out. Of the two old Innu ladies, she said, "They were the only ones that helped me, the only ones that were able to do it." Mrs. Manak had no money and the only payment she could give them was an old worsted wool coat, out of which they made leggings for themselves.

A little more is known about Inuit birthing practices, although most of that information comes from farther north. E.W. Hawkes, writing in 1916, recorded that when a Labrador woman went into labour, the midwife would have her kneel down and would slip a sealskin thong around her waist before taking up a position behind her. With her hands locked around the woman's abdomen, the midwife exerted pressure downward until the baby was expelled.

According to Hawkes, when occasionally a shaman attempted to act as midwife, his efforts usually ended in disaster: "Hence cases are usually left to the old women [midwives], who seem to have a good understanding of their work and are uniformly successful."

As very few European women settled in Labrador in the early days, the Southern Inuit birthing practices tended to be rooted in their Inuit heritage rather than their European culture.

No history of midwifery in Labrador has ever been written but the back issues of *Them Days* magazine contain the names of many of the granny midwives and the communities they served in during the first half of the 20th century. Emma Kaujuatsiak's mother was a midwife in the Aulatsivik area. Her paternal grandmother delivered her own babies because there was no other woman around. An Inuit woman known as Mrs. Keith was "curer" and midwife at Black Tickle. Midwives Alex Poole and Gertrude Chubbs delivered children around Fox Harbour. Sally Goudie was midwife in North West River, on what is now the Sheshatshiu side. Alice Anderson was midwife at Makkovik for many years. The midwives at Nain were known simply as Old Paulina and Old Frederika. Natalia Fry also delivered babies there. Spotted Islands had three midwives: Sarah Webber, Minnie Turnbull, and Mary Ann Elson.

Because of the isolation, midwives often had to deliver one another's children or even their own grandchildren. As Mary Dumaresque put it, "That's a different feeling altogether, borning your own grandchild." Will Coombs's mother, Jane, delivered three of her grandchildren at Longstretch in the 1920s and Sam Lyall's mother delivered three of his children at Tasiuyak Bay in the 1930s. Margaret McNeill Lyall's children were delivered by her mother, Wealtheness. In turn, Margaret delivered Susan McNeill's children and Susan assisted with Elizabeth Lyall's. Conflict of interest was not an issue back then.

Often the midwife was called on to do more than just birth babies. Alex Poole delivered a baby that apparently had a club foot and was forced to devise a splint for his leg. Twice a day she removed the splint and manipulated his leg before bandaging it back up, successfully treating the child, who survived without a disability. A little girl who had been delivered by Mary Ann Elson of Spotted Islands fell and broke her wrist, and the midwife straightened the arm, splinted it, and followed up with soaking and exercise until it healed as good as new. Sarah Webber used maggots to clean up seal finger infections. Midwives often had to pull teeth also, and some became very good at it. In later years, medicine chests and dental pliers were supplied to them by the International Grenfell Association.

Most midwives learned from older midwives how to deliver babies safely. During the 1930s, Margaret Saunders of Davis Inlet learned from Augusta Ford because "Aunt Augusta" had a crippled hand that made it difficult for her to handle the babies. Augusta would deliver the babies and Margaret would bath them, until eventually Margaret took over her work. Generally, if a woman didn't come forward with an interest in midwifery, the community would figure out who they thought would make a suitable "doctor," and coax her into learning by including her in group consultations.

The number of babies delivered by these women was considerable. Most midwives didn't keep count, but Lou Cabot delivered as many as 12 children in one family. As Stella Fowler of Capstan Island put it, "Aunt Lou Cabot born three parts of what was here on the coast." Susan Andersen delivered 50 babies on her own at

Makkovik. Samuel Chard's child was Bertha Andersen's 80th delivery; she was 76 at the time.

For those who could read, books such as *Brookes's Practice of Physic* were a helpful guide, but many of the granny midwives were illiterate. Although the granny midwives didn't have professional training, some of them learned from professional sources. The Moravian missionaries generally got some medical training before being sent out to Labrador, and they handed on what they had learned to anyone who showed an aptitude for healing. However, when their own wives were in labour, they sent for a granny midwife from a nearby community to come and deliver their babies.

Once the Grenfell Mission was established, doctors and nurses taught midwifery and health practices on the job. Alice Rumbolt, in the late 1930s, learned midwifery from the nurse midwives when she was working at the local nursing station. Nurses who were not midwives frequently asked granny midwives to assist them at births, so it was an exchange of knowledge. Mary Dumaresque's mother was taught by Dr. Curtis over at St. Anthony.

What motivated these women to become midwives? For some it might simply have been love of the whole miraculous process of new life, but many were simply responding to the needs of their community. For Mary Dumaresque of L'Anse-au-Clair, it was "not a sunshine job"; she found the work difficult due to the shortage of medical supplies, the long hours, and the stress of "fighting for a life." However, she learned midwifery from her mother and accepted that with knowledge came responsibility.

Alex Poole, when asked why she became a midwife, said, "You get strapped up, there's no doctor, no nurse, and if somebody don't take care of the situation, the mother and baby might die. You do what you got to do." Augusta Ford was the midwife in Davis Inlet because the other women "were too young or too afraid to tackle it." Mary Dumaresque admitted that her "hardest dread" was the afterbirth because, "if it don't come at the right time, you don't know what to expect."

Although the granny midwives considered birthing babies and doctoring the ill and injured to be an obligation, they often refused payment for their work. Lou Cabot, who covered the coast from Red Bay to Long Point, charged 50 cents a day for her services, which included cooking and laundering as well as delivery of the child. Samuel Chard, writing about Makkovik midwife Bertha Anderson, claimed that "[t]o offer Aunt Bertha money for her services was an insult to God and herself." Often the midwives were paid, if at all, "in kind," with fish, firewood, or homemade vamps and mitts.

Although men were usually exempted from participating in births, not all men managed to evade the duties of the delivery room. Captain George Cartwright was that rare species, a male midwife. On February 12, 1771, he wrote in his journal, "At six o'clock this evening, my maid was taken in labour: and for want of better assistance, I was obliged to officiate as midwife myself. She had a severe time; but at half eleven I delivered her of a stout boy: and she did me the honour to say that ... she never met with a person who performed the part better."

Cartwright went on to write that he had no wish to repeat the experience, but he subsequently delivered at least five other babies, including two to his Inuit servant Tweegok, and one to his housekeeper and unfaithful mistress, Mrs. Selby. In 1776, he was called to the lying in of an older Indian (probably Inuit) woman called Nooquashock, where his skills as a midwife were put to the test: "She had both a cross birth and twins, but at two in the afternoon I delivered her of a brace of daughters."

When Mrs. Manak ran into trouble with that miscarriage, it was Joe Rich who located the Innu midwives and acted as interpreter for them. Some Labrador-born men, like Gilbert Blake, delivered their own children simply because, due to isolation, they were the only adults available. Men also assisted midwives like Bertha Andersen, who didn't let storms stop her when she was needed; during bad weather, she goaded men into transporting her by boat or dog team to women in labour. Gar Lethbridge, coming back from a summer of fishing, stopped in Cartwright so that his wife could deliver a baby for Isaac LeMare's wife—they both caught the Spanish flu and died there on the floor of LeMare's house.

Although midwifery is now once again legal in Labrador, and the regulations are about to come into effect, it will take some time for midwifery to become available throughout the province. The regulations have been identified but now need to be implemented. Although the Minister of Health has expressed the hope that implementation won't take too long, it will be at least several years before midwives have been integrated back into the health care system. It can't come too soon for many Labrador mothers-to-be.

Miles Frankel: The Travelling Doctor

In late 1969, Englishman Miles Frankel came across a notice in the *British Medical Journal* advertising for a travelling doctor for the International Grenfell Mission with "interesting work in the Sub-arctic." Two years out of medical school and unsure about whether he wanted to specialize like his father or work as a general practitioner, Frankel longed to be free of "the millstone of hospitals"; so with very little knowledge about what he was getting into, he signed on.

The position he took was unusual for the time—he was to look after approximately 20,000 people in northern Newfoundland and Labrador, spread out from Roddickton on the northeast coast of the island, around Cape Norman to Castors River in the west, and across the Strait of Belle Isle from Blanc-Sablon north to Pinsent's Arm.

Depending on the season and the location, Frankel travelled by road, water, airplane, or dogsled. During his two and a half years with the Mission, he spent two summers aboard the hospital ship MV *Strathcona III*; when weather permitted, he climbed aboard the Mission's De Havilland Beaver aircraft, and where there were roads, he drove in the Land Rover he'd had shipped out from England. But when everybody else was zipping around on Ski-Doos, Frankel and the local nurse would send for the men from Rexons Cove to come to Mary's Harbour with their dogs to "haul the Doctor."

In his memoir, *I Want to Know if I Got to Get Married: A Doctor on the Grenfell Mission*, Frankel claims he was "possibly the last person ever to have gone on a medical emergency by dog team" and admits that if he had been more cold-blooded he would have "shot the dogs and pushed their anachronistic carcasses through a hole in the ice." Instead, he argued intensely and successfully for the continuation of the dogsled trips with a passion that overcame even the counterarguments of his more practical boss back at base in St. Anthony.

At heart, Frankel wasn't convinced that his presence on the coast was really necessary. He judged the staff at the nursing stations to be highly competent, and if anything came up that they could not deal with, they called for help from St. Anthony. He visited each of the seven nursing stations only once every four to six weeks, so most of the patients he saw were fairly routine cases. However, he did feel that knowing there was a doctor available, however intermittently, was a comfort to the people in these relatively isolated places, and that was justification enough.

Frankel was an unusual doctor in that he had never liked school and was frequently truant. He found his early days at medical school "brutalizing, disgusting and Victorian" and was unsure how he managed to pass his medical exams. In his first two years as a house doctor in London's Docklands, he estimated that advice from his father saved the lives of 20 or 30 of his patients. What he did learn, though, was that medicine was an art composed of fact and kindness, and that of the two, kindness was perhaps the more important.

Dogsled travel, like travel on the *Strathcona*, got Frankel out of the hospital and away from the English colonial life and parochial atmosphere of the Mission headquarters and into the homes of real Newfoundlanders and Labradorians. As a visitor and sometimes a guest in the homes of his patients, he was better able to connect to ordinary people. He was the stranger, the one who needed care and feeding, and he was at the mercy of their kindness. When he was travelling, he saw people at their natural best, surrounded by their families, their work, and their possessions. In such circumstances, the social barriers between the doctor and his patients broke down and they began to trust him as he was forced to trust them.

Frankel's close relationship with people in Labrador came at a price. Aside from the tragedies any medical practitioner has to deal with, Frankel knew 10 people who died unexpectedly during his short time with the Mission. Probably the most personal loss he suffered was the death of Bob Russell, who had been his dog-team driver during his first sled trip on the coast. Ironically, Russell died when a Ski-Doo he was riding went through thin ice, an accident that probably wouldn't have happened if he had been out with his dogs instead.

The style of medicine Frankel was able to practice in the 1970s settlements probably wouldn't be possible today, when everyone expects to receive the most up-to-date technological treatment, no matter how hopeless or painful it might be. Frankel felt it was counterproductive to send dying people away from their families to an antiseptic atmosphere of impersonal purpose. Instead, he tried to offer them the comfort and the security of their own homes. If silver nitrate didn't cure a child's warts, he sent her to a wart charmer in the next settlement. He was happy to spend the down time on his dogsled trips learning to make a bread poultice from an old woman.

For recreation, he went fishing—not the salmon fishing of most of the other Mission doctors, but hauling herring nets and gutting cod. He even did a little illegal sealing and saw first-hand why no sensible man would want to go out on the ice without a gaff. He concluded that the ethics of good sportsmanship had been "forcefully introduced into an arena where they had no natural place." Hunting and fishing were activities Frankel could fit in between his clinics, and he recorded that even if it was taxing or exhausting or repetitive or occasionally frightening, it put a charge into his batteries and also made him glad he "was not a fisherman, nor had to be."

Just as he learned to like the landscape, Frankel learned to like country food as he ate his way "into becoming a Newfoundlander." He consumed not only cod tongues, caribou, moose, flipper pie, and "salmon, and yet more bloody salmon" but he also ate porcupine, muskrat, owl, turrs, and anything else the local people ate, including illegally killed Canada goose. These foods, he reported, were often "spiced by the blessing of the meal and the talk of the table, the children playing about my stockinged feet with a gin trap and a razor sharp hatchet."

Whether tending to a man with a serious chainsaw wound in Port Hope Simpson, holding a clinic at George Poole's house in Fox Harbour, working with nurse Margaret Harris in Mary's Harbour, or counting icebergs in Alexis Bay, Frankel saw a world that was foreign to him, but he viewed it with compassion, admiration, curiosity, and plain common sense. He considered the troubles of his patients, whether real or imagined, as important, and did his best to bring solace and reassurance, alleviating their anxiety as much as their pain.

After Frankel returned to Europe, the medical dog-team trips came to an end and he was told that the last dog was drowned in 1973. Frankel eventually settled as a doctor in rural Ireland, where he raised a family and took up breeding Percheron horses. He died in November 2014 at the age of 70 from a previously undiagnosed brain tumour, but he would have been delighted to know that, like his Percherons, the sled dogs of Labrador's South Coast are making a comeback.

Marvelous Moss: The Patriot's Renewable Resource

During the various centennials of World War I marked throughout Newfoundland and Labrador, much was made of the long-neglected work of the WPA, the Women's Patriotic Association. The 15,000 members of the WPA raised money for hospitals, made quilts, knit socks, prepared bandages from old linen, gathered medical supplies, and sent cakes, cigarettes, and other treats over to the men who were living and dying in the trenches.

One area in which the WPA made a significant contribution, but which is seldom mentioned in the media, was the dirty and difficult but vital work done by the women and children of what was then a very patriotic country: collecting moss from the peat bogs of the Dominion of Newfoundland.

Moss, sphagnum moss in particular, was an important part of the dressings used on wounded soldiers both on the battlefield and in hospitals behind the front lines. Cotton for bandages was in short supply as it was needed for nitrocellulose explosives, clean water for washing bed linens and clothes was scarce, and in emergency situations, body fluids had to be drained off as quickly as possible under difficult circumstances. Moss, which can absorb up to 22 times its weight in fluid at three times the rate of cotton, was cheap, effective, and efficient at absorbing blood, urine, and "corruption" and was in high demand throughout the war.

Moss not only did the job of efficiently removing bodily fluids from wound sites but it also had significant antibiotic properties due to its natural acidity. In the days prior to the discovery of penicillin, moss was the closest thing people had to a magic bullet for treating infection. It was not only used to bandage injuries but it was literally stuffed into wounds to clean them out.

Today, the chief commercial value of moss is as an element of peat, which is used for gardening and fuel, with secondary uses as a decorative item in wreaths and floral arrangements, but moss has a long history of practical significance in both Newfoundland and Labrador. Labrador Inuit, like their relatives in other parts of the Arctic, used *uruq* or stringy moss (*Rhacomitrium lanuginosum*) to line the bottom of meat caches because it never froze solid, allowing the meat to be easily removed when needed. *Manniq*, or lamp moss (*Dicranum elongatum*), was used to carry embers for lighting stone lamps and was also worn as an amulet to ensure good health.

Aboriginal people used various mosses for diapering babies and absorbing menstrual blood, for shoeing sled runners with mud, and for insulating socks. Five-thousand-year-old Otzi the Iceman, the world's oldest known human mummy, was found wearing moss-packed boots. In times of starvation, plant material which is normally toxic to humans becomes eatable once it has been fermented, so Aboriginal people also learned to eat—and enjoy—the stomach contents of the caribou. Moss was used to protect and warm babies when they were tied into toboggans, to cushion broken limbs, and to insulate tents, lean-tos, and underground huts. It was also used to pack fresh fish as it lowers the pH of the package, inhibiting the growth of bacteria and slowing the onset of putrefaction.

Over 12,000 varieties of moss have been identified worldwide so far, and one of the first scientists to try to sort them out was Sir Joseph Banks. During his voyage to the New World in 1766, Banks reported collecting mosses in the neighbourhood of St. John's, as well as Petty Harbour, Croque, and Labrador, and made notes as to how they could best be collected and preserved "in the same kind of [canvas] bags in which they may be put while a little damp as they are then pliable but when dry become quite brittle."

George Cartwright, too, was alert to the value of moss. His diaries reveal that each fall in the 1770s and 1780s, he set his men to collecting large quantities of moss to "chinse" his houses and stores against the fresh gales of winter.

Henry Youle Hind, while exploring the interior of the Labrador Peninsula in 1861, was most impressed by the geographical effect of mosses "silently destroying the surface rock and preparing it for the disintegrating action of atmospheric agents." He marvelled at the "rich undergrowth of Labrador tea plant, and mosses or lichens of every hue and depth of colour ... over which the well-worn Montagnais portage path runs." Hind's brother William painted images of their Innu guides resting on the portages in moss beds which were as much as 2 feet deep.

Newfoundland and Labrador settlers were among the first Europeans to learn to use moss from Aboriginal people. From the earliest contact era, they too began using moss to treat wounds, preserve fish, transport fire, and insulate their houses. They also added a new use, which they probably learned from Aboriginal people farther south—they used it as a substitute for tobacco. The old Newfoundland "Tobacco Song," which lists withrod (wild raisin), wood shavings, and tea as things you can smoke when you run out of the noxious weed, also warns against wasting moss: "Them that smokes moss, the worst robbers of all, / Going off with their bags picking that in the fall, / Just leave it alone, it will keep your house tight / And you'll only be making a fool of the pipe."

Moss as a medical aid was used from earliest times and is reported as having been employed by the ancient Gaelic-Irish after the battle of Cantarf in 1014 and by the Highlanders after the battle of Flodden in 1513. It was also used by native and settler people of Newfoundland and Labrador from early in the contact era. However, it only came to popular notice in the western world in the late 19th century. Dr. Eliot Curwen, who came to Labrador with Wilfred Grenfell on his second voyage in 1893, collected moss at Hopedale. The gifts of two stone lamps, one from the Moravian missionary Mr. Kästner and one from an Inuk named Josiah, prompted Curwen to collect samples of lamp moss, but by the time he donated the samples to the British Museum 40 years later, he would have been well aware of the medical importance of the material.

Ironically, it was the Germans who brought moss to the attention of the modern medical world. In 1880, a German workman with a badly injured arm took several days to reach a hospital, where doctors noticed that the peat-wrapped wound had started to heal when they would have expected it to deteriorate. German scientists publicized their subsequent findings regarding the healing properties of sphagnum moss, and the idea spread. In 1895, moss dressings were used in the French War Department and moss was subsequently employed during the Russian-Japanese war of 1904. By the time World War I had begun, English botanists were promoting the use of sphagnum, which was soon widely accepted. Collecting began in the British Isles and soon appeals went out to Newfoundland and Canada for more of the material.

In the early years of the war, collectors frequently had difficulty identifying the ideal types of moss needed for bandages. Lichens, which often grow in conjunction with moss, often look like moss. Reindeer moss and Icelandic moss, both lichens, even have moss in their common names. Irish moss, used as a thickener in commercial foods under the name carrageen, is actually a seaweed. Most Newfoundland and Labrador moss collectors were already familiar with the various types of moss and those that weren't very soon learned.

Little has been written about the collection of sphagnum moss in Newfoundland and Labrador, although The Rooms' "Great War Database" does say that volunteers "squelched into boggy areas to collect the moss, then dried it," after which it "was packed in barrels and sent to hospitals throughout Europe to dress war wounds." In October of 1916, Fanny Cluett travelled to St. John's for training to go overseas with the Voluntary Aid Detachment, and on her first day in town, helped pack five barrels of bandages in the grounds of Government House.

Memorial University historian Terry Bishop Stirling, who has written about the Women's Patriotic Association, says that very little is known about the collecting process, but nevertheless she was quickly able to produce a dozen newspaper clippings reporting on the collecting, shipping, and reception of local mosses which were sent out to England by the WPA. In England, Girl Guides and Boy Scouts volunteered to work in moss-collecting parties, while in Newfoundland, groups of Sunday school children were led by their teachers on moss forays.

One clipping that particularly caught Bishop Stirling's attention was a 1917 article in the *Daily Star* which gave brief, specific direction on how to make up sphagnum moss bandages, including exact measurements for the recycled cotton sheeting to be used and the way the packed bandages were to be labelled for shipping. The moss bandages were so important to the war effort that, after hostilities ended, Newfoundlander Mrs. Henrietta Palfrey Holloway was honoured with an Order of the British Empire for her work with the WPA's Moss Committee. Mrs. Holloway had lost her only son, photographer Robert Palfrey Holloway, in the war.

There are no known personal accounts of Newfoundlanders and Labradorians collecting sphagnum moss, although they certainly did it, but a Derbyshire historian has speculated on the collecting conditions in England and no doubt they were similar or worse in the New World. He writes that the moss collectors "would have been cold, absolutely sodden, the women would have been trailing long skirts in the wet. It would have been back-breaking work and can't have been much fun, but they felt it was their patriotic duty." The work, probably no worse than making fish or picking bakeapples, was one of the few contributions, other than cannon fodder, that poorer families could make to the war effort.

Once gathered, the moss had to be wetted down and cleaned of twigs, grasses, and lichens, then squeezed by hand or put through a laundry mangle before being air-dried and packed into barrels for shipping to an overseas depot. When it reached England, the moss was put into small, flat muslin bags and sterilized before being forwarded to hospitals and field stations.

Once the war was over, the demand for moss bandages continued but without a volunteer labour force of women and children who were prepared to do the work for patriotic reasons, the cost of sphagnum moss rose so dramatically that it become commercially unviable.

Today, sphagnum moss is not considered suitably efficacious for modern medical practice, so it has once again been relegated to the sphere of alternative medicine. However, if antibiotic resistant strains of bacteria continue to proliferate at the rate they have been, moss may once again become the go-to treatment for minor infections, in which case Labrador will be well positioned to become the source of small, artisanal medical products. There are plenty of bogs in Labrador, and where there are bogs there are mosses, a proven and reliable renewable resource.

Healing Sweat

"When you go into the sweat lodge, you have to bring your heart." That's the advice Max Penashue has for anyone thinking of trying out the traditional Aboriginal steam tent. In Labrador, sweating is serious business, but it is a business with a spiritual side.

Each sweat lodge operates differently, and rituals vary from one sweat to another, but participants generally enter a small, dark enclosure where the steam from water on hot rocks encourages their pores to open. There might be singing, drumming, praying, or smudging with herbs. People are often encouraged to express what is on their minds.

My first opportunity to attend a sweat came about by chance. After several months of sleeping poorly, being plagued by bad dreams, and suffering fatigue that defied exercise and improved diet, I had a choice between waiting four weeks for an appointment with a family doctor or six hours at the local emergency room. So, when Penashue invited me to participate in a sweat lodge ceremony, I jumped at the chance.

Penashue has been studying sweating rituals for many years and has himself completed the sun dance ceremony, a lengthy and arduous vision quest. It was all part of his decision to abstain from alcohol and return to a more traditional Innu lifestyle. To lead a sweat lodge is a serious commitment and it was only in August of 2006 that Penashue experienced the required visions and received permission from his mentors to perform these rituals.

Penashue's sweat lodge, set up near Route 520, a few miles outside of Sheshatshiu, was a large lodge covered in an orange tarp, with a smaller tent inside swathed in black cloth. Both lodges were made of young birch saplings, bent and tied with strips of coloured cloth that hung down in ribbons like Tibetan prayer flags.

The lodge that enclosed the steam tent was heated with an oil-drum stove and had a traditional spruce-bough floor. There was a simple wooden bench, boxes of water and juice, and a scattering of spare towels and shorts hung against the walls. The overall effect was rough, cheerful, and welcoming.

Although many sweat lodges accommodate only one gender, Penashue welcomes women as well as men; the son of environmental activist Elizabeth Penashue, he is well aware of the importance of women. In keeping with Innu practice, most of the men modestly leave their T-shirts on during sweats, and the women wear long dresses or wrap lengths of cloth around their waists over their exercise clothes.

There was little conversation as we prepared to enter the steam tent and the first session began quietly. We crawled into the tiny space, cautiously avoiding the central hearth with its red-hot rocks. The gatekeeper, who watched over us during the sweat, lowered and tucked down the flap. The dark was impenetrable except for the eerie, glowing stones at our feet. The smoke of a sage smudge was in the air.

After a few minutes of silence, Penashue invited the participants to introduce themselves and say a few words. Most of them spoke in Innu-aimun—some prayed, some sang, a few wept. Apenam Pone, a family friend, was at my right hand and his benign presence gave me the courage to shakily admit that I was homesick and not sleeping well. Somehow, it seemed unnecessary to go into detail about the terrifying dreams I'd been having.

When everyone had had a turn, Penashue threw water on the rocks and a mighty cloud of searing steam pulsed up and pulled my breath from my mouth. Before it became really uncomfortable, Penashue was drumming and singing Innu songs that had been coming to him since he began to lead the sweats. Before I knew it, the gatekeeper released us and we all tumbled out into the outer lodge to share water and cool off.

Three more sessions followed, each hotter and shorter than the first. With each sweat the camaraderie grew, the tension decreased, the sense of rightness swelled. By the end of the evening, there was no more need for talk. I stumbled through the dark woods to the main road and drove home on a wave of euphoria. Once home, I scarfed down a bowl of soup and fell into bed, where I slept for nine blissful, uninterrupted hours.

Sweat lodges or steam tents are not new to Labrador. When archaeologists were surveying the Voisey's Bay area prior to the development of the mine, they found the cobbled hearths and fire-cracked rocks of old sweat lodges in many of the Innu sites. Ethnographers such as Lucien Turner and travellers like William Brookes Cabot reported that steam tents were a habitual part of Innu life well into the 20th century.

According to Turner, steam baths, or sudatories (steam rooms) as they are more properly called, were commonly found along the paths where Innu had travelled for many years, and sweats were often undertaken not just when the people were camping for a period but also when they were on their journeys overland.

It's unclear exactly when the practice of sweating was forced underground in Labrador, but by the 1920s, Christian priests were forbidding Innu to engage in practices that might be deemed pagan. According to anthropologist Georg Henriksen, a sharp decline in the caribou population resulted in a need for both the shamanistic shaking tent and the steam tent as a way to call back the animals. Because the Catholic church forbade the old Innu practices, people tended to remove themselves into the bush to build their lodges and carry out their sweats in seclusion.

Ask Innu who are 60 years or older today and they will tell you that ritual sweating was common in their youth. However, sweating at that time was presented as merely medicinal, undertaken when someone was seriously ill or injured. Furthermore, it was a fairly solitary practice, with individuals assisted by others who would erect the lodge and heat the stones.

Communal sweating is known around the world in many cultures, but in recent years it has taken particular hold among the First Nations of North America. Plagued by alcoholism, drug abuse, suicide, and other calamities, North American native groups have encouraged the use of sweat lodges in prisons, rehabilitation centres, longhouses, and youth camps. The results have been so successful that even groups that did not traditionally use sweating have taken up the practice.

Labrador's Innu, of course, have had more than their share of trouble adjusting to 20th-century technology and the incursion on their lands of non-Aboriginal people. In the 1990s, the entire country watched in horror as children in Davis Inlet acted out their gas-fuelled, suicidal rage on nightly news broadcasts. They paid less attention when, in 1993, Innu leader Katie Rich reported that elders and youth in Davis Inlet were building a sweat lodge for the purposes of healing.

"The heat and steam cleanses the body and the spirit of the person who enters the sweat lodge," explained Rich. This simple statement belies what anthropologists and Innu agree is the complex dynamic of communication with the animal spirits that comes with the sweat. The steam of the sweat lodge opens the channels between the human and the spirit world, according to Max Penashue, who said it is a very powerful force.

Apenam Pone, an addictions counsellor in Sheshatshiu, established a sweat lodge for healing and treatment in his home community 25 years ago. In August of 2006, the Labrador Correctional Centre finally followed the example of prisons elsewhere in Canada and allowed prisoners in Goose Bay to build a lodge inside the centre to aid in their own rehabilitation.

The morning after my own initial experience with the sweat lodge, I woke up happy. During the night, we had received our first snowfall of the winter. I was quite convinced that my troubles were over and it was a bit of a letdown when, after a few nights, the old hag returned.

"Being inside a sweat lodge is like being inside a prayer," Penashue explained, when we discussed the matter later. "It's Mother Earth's womb. It's safe. But when you go outside, you are vulnerable again. You have to bring your heart in so when you go outside you are stronger."

Since then, I have returned to the sweat lodge and learned that it is a far more complicated process than I had first realized. It is not the answer to physical or spiritual problems, but it can lead you closer to one.

Some First Nations people feel that the sweat ritual is theirs, and they do not wish to have it appropriated by non-native people. They would exclude casual participants from outside the culture, participants like me. Apenam Pone, however, disagrees.

"We participate in your health system, so why shouldn't you participate in ours?"

In the same vein, Pone said he would also like to see sentencing circles opened up to non-Aboriginal offenders. He invited judges, doctors, and anyone else who deals with Innu to come and sweat with him.

I was later present at a sweat Pone held at the Charles Andrew Treatment Centre. Young residents from as far away as Pond Inlet took part, but it also drew people from the local community. As many as two dozen people stopped by on that Sunday afternoon.

The Innu tradition of the steam tent as a treatment for one individual has evolved in response to changing circumstances. If the whole community is suffering, everyone in it may need the medicine the sweat lodge offers, broadening the Innu sweating tradition to make it a truly communal event.

Bush Medicine and Home Remedies in Labrador

It's often assumed that medical treatment was unavailable in Labrador before the appearance of Wilfred Grenfell in the late 19th century, but medicine was not always the formal, scientific practice that it is today. As long as there were illnesses and injuries in the world, there were healers willing to try to cure them, so the practice of medicine in Labrador could be said to go back about 7,000 years, as long as people have lived in this area.

In the early days of Paleolithic and Neolithic man, prevention was considered the first and most effective method of practicing medicine, and prevention almost certainly meant incantations and charms, essentially magic words and amulets intended to ward off illness and accidents. Grave goods found in the Labrador Archaic Indian burial mound at L'Anse Amour and elsewhere give support to this notion.

Hot steam was probably early man's second line of defence. The cracked stones and cobbled hearths associated with steam tents or sweat lodges are often found in Labrador archaeological sites. Bloodletting, or "poking," as it was later known among the Inuit, was probably common also.

But when traditional charms failed to ward off sickness, and incantations and sweats failed to cure them, the notion that what went into the body could probably help was obvious, and someone—a person with a natural propensity for healing or magic—almost certainly looked to the plants and animals around them to find a solution.

Such was also the case in more recent times, when the direct ancestors of today's Innu, Inuit, and settler populations got sick. If illness and injuries struck despite efforts to prevent them, the Innu medicine man, the Inuit *angakok*, or the settler granny midwife or healer would fall back on herbal medicine.

Not a great deal is known about traditional use of herbs among Innu or Inuit. Anthropologist Frank Speck, who believed that studying modern Innu was an effective way to learn about early man, claimed that magic and charms were "more general among them than pharmacology," but Henry Youle Hind believed that Innu were more likely to try bush medicine before going to the conjurer, because the shaman was a dangerous and powerful person. Kaniuekutat—the late John Poker of the Mushuau Innu—believed that all people have the power to heal, but that if anyone other than a shaman employs that power, his or her own life is shortened.

Hind reports seeing Innu using gum from balsam spruce to seal up a cut from an axe, a practice that was known throughout Newfoundland and Labrador. He also documented the use of the root of blue iris and a decoction of red osier being used as a purgative. Spruce was used to treat frostbite, tamarack (also called larch or juniper) was employed to heal flesh wounds, and the roots of white water lilies, rushes, and thistle were also employed medicinally by the Innu.

William Duncan Strong reported that an Innu child with vomiting and diarrhea was cured when his parents plastered his belly with "fir pitch" and he noted that the Mushuau Innu would scratch a baby's back and face with glass and rub in salt to cure seizures. One Innu informant told him he had "consecrated salt that a priest gave him to cure cramps."

The *mukashan*, or caribou marrow feast, is still used by contemporary Innu to cure sickness. The long bones of the caribou are cracked open for the marrow, then broken and boiled to remove the grease, which is eaten in a strict ritual feast. At one *mukashan* which I attended, a caribou fetus which hung from the ridge pole of the tent was intended "to treat an old man who had a bad hip."

Steam is still used to treat illness in Labrador today among the Innu of Sheshashit and Natuashish. Often the person leading the sweat will blow hot air onto an injury using a funnel of birch bark, and tamarack tea is still commonly used as a cleansing agent, good for the blood and the kidneys. In serious cases of illness, St. Anne's oil, brought from a pilgrimage to St. Anne de Beaupré, is applied with a blessing. St. Anne is the grandmother of Jesus and, therefore, a powerful healing figure.

Traditional medicine among Labrador Inuit was displaced sooner in Labrador than in other parts of the Canadian Arctic because of the early presence of Moravian missionaries trained in European ways of treating illness. However, Inuit in Labrador almost certainly employed cures used farther north, such as tying a louse to a hair and walking it over the surface of a snow-blind eye to remove the film.

Some Inuit herbal cures have persisted into modern times, such as the use of raw Arctic willow to treat headaches and toothaches; the bark contains salicylic acid, which is the main ingredient in Aspirin. Ground juniper, a low growing bush with frosted blue berries, is brewed into tea to treat colds, flu, and scurvy; Arctic harebell to treat fever and influenza; purple saxifrage to relieve constipation; and cottongrass tufts are put into the ear to cure earache.

Once contact had been established with people coming into the country from outside, people from all three cultures adopted one another's medical cures. Aboriginal people used the slightly acidic water in pitcher plant leaves to clear up eye infections, and Europeans adopted that cure when suffering from smallpox. Europeans found Labrador tea, used both externally and internally, to be an extremely effective medicine.

George Cartwright, in the 1770s, used Labrador tea to cure a servant who was ailing after childbirth. Dr. Grenfell believed Labradorians used Labrador tea for its narcotic qualities, but virtually all who used it agreed that it was an extremely effective treatment for skin problems: chapping, burns, eczema, and inflammation. Labrador tea skin creams are available commercially today as "Green Beaver Boreal Face Cream" and as Lise Watier's "Supreme Ritual of Youth" products. It is also one of the ingredients in a prize-winning gin called "Ungava," which is made in Quebec.

Charms, religious or otherwise, were and are used to prevent and cure sickness in Labrador. A piece of lead carved into the shape of a heart would be chilled and dropped down the back to stop nosebleed. Copper wires around the wrist helped arthritis. A nutmeg, the knucklebone of a beaver, a fish doctor (a tiny copepod which attaches itself to injured fish), lodestones, and anodyne bracelets were all thought to be helpful. Crucifixes and religious medals, particularly medals of St. Anne, are favoured by the Innu. Today, with very little alteration, many charms have simply been designated as jewellry.

Grenfell himself liked to pepper his speeches with examples of folk charms, probably to stress the supposedly "primitive" nature of his patients (this being a sure way to coax the dollars out of amused patrons), and reported, for example, that a haddock fin cut from a fish before it touches anything except the water counteracts rheumatism. Grenfell would mockingly chant "Meenie, Miney, Mo" when asked to charm away a pain, before setting to work with his powders and potions or his surgeon's knife.

While most of the diseases suffered by Labradorians were common around the world, some, like water pups (blisters around the wrist), were location specific. Seal finger, an infection contracted by exposure to raw seal bones or pelts, is known from Alaska to Norway. Its cause has tentatively been identified as *Mycoplasma phocacerebrale*, an organism that was isolated during an epidemic of seal disease in the area of the Baltic Sea. In Labrador, it used to be treated with bread poultices containing roseroot (*tulligunnak* in Inuktitut or *Rhodiola rosea* in Latin), or if that didn't work, the affected digit was amputated. Today, seal finger is treated with tetracycline or similar antibiotics.

It is interesting to note that contemporary archaeologists working on old seal hunting sites in Labrador wear rubber gloves to prevent infection from the old blubber that contaminates the soil, which suggests bacteria that causes seal finger is persistent. The roseroot used to treat seal finger was one of the most important healing plants known in Labrador, as it was also used to treat toothache, fatigue, colds, and a variety of other illnesses.

According to medical historian John Crellin, the self-care

practices of European settlers in Labrador were not significantly different from those in Newfoundland. Besides the usual spring tonics and tamarack or Labrador tea poultices and concoctions, Labradorians looked to over-the-counter compounds, which they obtained from traders or schooner men. Often these commercial products were "improved" by being mixed with other elements such as fat, gunpowder, molasses, Sunlight soap, or juniper bark.

Castor oil was commonly used to induce or speed up labour, as was tea of senna leaves or pods, which was also used to treat colds. Friar's Balsam, "an alcoholic preparation of beuzoin, aloes, storac and balsam of tolu," was used for cuts and as an all-purpose medicine. Ammonia and camphor gave Minard's Linament a sharp odour thought to have a placebo effect brought on by the familiarity of the pungent scent. It was used internally and externally for headache, athlete's foot, neuralgia, sprains, and colds. Vicks Vaporub, around since 1890, was also appreciated for its strong aroma.

Given that until recently most Labradorians had few fruits or vegetables in their diets for much of the year, it is not surprising that Epsom salts, a laxative, were widely popular. The efficacy of Epsom salts is captured in the following epitaph, though whether it ever truly appeared on a grave marker is unknown:

Here lies I and my two daughters,
Kilt by drinking old bog waters.
If we had stuck with Epsom salts,
We wouldn't be lying in these here vaults.

Gentian violet, a triarylmethane dye used as a topical antiseptic, like iodine and Mercurochrome, stains the skin in a most satisfactory fashion. It was used to treat impetigo and thrush in children. A woman from Ontario reports that she was successfully treated with Gentian violet for a persistent yeast infection after her young doctor consulted with an older colleague who had worked for the Grenfell Mission. Redway's painkillers, Sloan's Linament, and Menare's tea were all popular self-help medicines.

Today, the Labrador population is well served by Labrador-Grenfell Health, with its modern hospitals, medevacs, and telemedicine programs, but Labradorians don't like to become too dependent on outside help. In a storm, at the cabin, or on the water, there are still medical problems that need the attention of a home-healer, so home remedies get passed on and remembered. As Elizabeth Goudie wrote in her autobiography, "You would be surprised what you can do without the doctor."

Labrador Burial Practices in Ancient and Modern Times

Two things that all cultures have in common are birth and death. Biology determines how people come into this world, a process that they have surprisingly little control over, but how they leave it is often determined by those left behind. Despite emotional attachment, bodies must be disposed of in some way.

Those ways differ considerably from one cultural group to the next, but it is surprising how consistently people invent or reinvent similar ways of coping with what for many is a frightening encounter with death. Amerindian, Eskimoan, and European graves can be found all over Labrador, but it is not always easy to identify them.

The acidic soil and discontinuous permafrost of Labrador makes it an unlikely place to find really ancient human remains, yet, ironically, it is the location of one of the world's oldest burials. In the dunes near the community of L'Anse Amour, archaeologists James Tuck and Robert McGhee found an Amerindian burial mound. After removing a thick overlay of tuckamore, three layers of boulders, and 2 feet of sand, they came upon the skeleton of a Labrador Archaic child of 12 or 13 years of age.

The body was face down with a large flat stone on its back, and it was stained with red ochre. Grave goods included knives or spear points, various amulets, and a bird bone flute. Radiocarbon dating indicated that the grave was built between 7,000 and 7,500 years ago. According to McGhee, "no people on earth were taking such pains in disposing of their dead in this manner at that time—a period that preceded the building of the Egyptian pyramids by more than 2,000 years."

At Rattler's Bight, in Hamilton Inlet, Bill Fitzhugh reported a small Maritime Archaic cemetery with nine red-ochre pit burials and grave goods including polished slate adzes and gouges, implements of Ramah chert and soapstone, sheets of mica, and copper pendants. Four rock burial mounds at Nulliak Cove contained similar Maritime Archaic grave goods and red ochre but also birch bark linings in the graves, suggesting that wood products were being moved north along the coast.

A cache of Intermediate Indian tools found at Daniel's Rattle contained end scrapers and a large corner-notched biface blade all made from local chert. The site, at the top of a large promontory with a broad view, is consistent with a burial site, and the cache is consistent with similar caches that have been interpreted as graves farther west.

Very little seems to have been written about more recent Amerindian burial practices, but we do get glimpses. In 1631, Jesuits recorded that when an Innu died, the body was removed from the dwelling through an opening made in the side of the structure. In winter, the corpse was placed on a platform in a tree and then removed for burial in the summer. Henry Youle Hind, writing in 1853, says Innu buried their dead 3 feet deep, wrapped in a blanket with grave goods such as weapons or tools. A dog might be killed and left in the grave and a small hut erected over the site with a window for food offerings.

By the 20th century, Innu grave goods were often of European origin: lamps, kettles, dishes, toys, knives, and clothes were laid on top of the grave after being broken "to liberate the spirit residing there." In winter, the bodies were simply laid out in the snow, presumably to be buried after the thaw. By the 1930s, a fence would be built around the grave and if the deceased had been an important hunter, "a pole, upon which are fastened bear and beaver skulls, is erected near the grave." If people died in the country, the remains might be buried there or, after a year or two, might be brought back to the community for Christian reburial.

Today, Innu generally bury their dead in Christian fashion, but they still erect enclosures or roofed structures over the graves. Mementos such as photographs, rosaries, and small gifts are put into the coffin by mourners and, in Sheshatshiu, mourners will blanket the body with spruce twigs. Religious shrines such as those evident on the road to Goose Bay might be erected if death was due to a car accident, and family members will often visit a favourite or significant place of the deceased to make offerings by pouring tea into the ground or by putting food into a fire. Innu do not appear to fear the corpse, or the spirit of the dead, and often report that they have seen a deceased loved one in the woods or out on the land.

Eskimoan people seem to have a very different attitude toward the dead. There are no known Pre-Dorset, Groswater Paleoeskimo, or Dorset Paleoeskimo burial sites in Labrador, although there is plenty of evidence of their residence here. Thule people, the direct ancestors of today's modern Inuit, moved into Labrador fairly late in the day and their graves are almost indistinguishable from those of the early contact era Inuit. Thule bodies were often either just left exposed on the land, put into crevices in the rock, or inserted into caches or boulder graves. Thule burial cairns have been found in Nachvak Fjord and boulder graves have been identified on Rose Island in Saglek Fjord. The Hebron area contains sod houses, middens, tent rings, and graves from both the Thule pre- and post-contact eras. Grave goods consist of gender-specific tools and other gifts.

Unlike the Innu, the Inuit traditionally abandoned bodies quickly, where they died, sometimes just laid on the open ground. Inuit bodies in Labrador were often placed close to cliffs or in crevices and then covered by boulders or rock cairns. Burials at Rose Island and Upernavik Island in Saglek Bay occasionally show evidence of secondary burial after some or all of the flesh had decomposed, and grave goods such as knives, hunting or scraping tools, amulets, ornaments, and objects that were probably gifts were left with the bodies.

Grave robbing by Europeans has probably altered the record of both Thule and Inuit burials. J.A. Jacobsen recorded that in 1880 he "had examined the graves at various places in Labrador and taken along everything suitable for a museum." He lamented that most of the grave goods had been deliberately broken. Wilfred Grenfell wrote that he got some unsalable old razors from the Moravian Mission store to "trade" for "a few ancient stone implements" found in some graves near Hopedale. By swapping the razors for the artifacts, Grenfell believed he was able to obtain grave goods without incurring the disapproval of the local Inuit but with little or no cost to himself.

In some cases, the bodies themselves were stolen. William Duncan Strong surreptitiously removed 22 Inuit bodies from the Moravian cemetery at Zoar to the Field Museum in Chicago in 1927. These were Christian Inuit with documented names and dates. The bodies were repatriated in 2011 after the intervention of the Nunatsiavut government.

In recent years, Inuit have adopted Christian burial practices, while still retaining an aversion to the dead that is not evident among today's Innu. Tent rings with skeletal remains, canvas-wrapped bodies, and opened or broken coffins are common sights in Inuit communities and campsites across the Canadian Arctic, but people seem to want to avoid handling the dead and to escape proximity to them so they are left as they are.

European graves, too, are now scattered all throughout Labrador. Dating back to the 1500s, the Saddle Island cemetery at Red Bay contains the remains of about 140 Basque. The graves are mostly pit burials, and the bodies were generally interred clothed. Some bodies, having been buried with shells containing calcium carbonate, were preserved and others, in wet and acidic bog which disintegrates bone but preserves wool, were not. In one case, a cap, stockings, red shirt, and blue trousers remained although the skeleton it had clothed had dissolved. Keys and other pieces of metal were found with the bodies, but there were no grave offerings.

Settler graves can still be found in seasonal communities around Labrador. The grave of Charles Williams, a native of Plymouth, at North River in Sandwich Bay, is interesting because of the archaeological dig related to his sod house. Another grave that attracts a lot of attention from tourists is that of Victor Croucher at Battle Harbour. Croucher died as the result of a bird-hunting accident while he was in his early 20s, but by then was famous as the subject of the most reproduced photograph in Newfoundland history—the little boy in the sailor suit posed between two giant cod.

Settler graves are generally pit graves with stone or wooden markers. An exception is the monument to George Cartwright in the cemetery at Cartwright, a marble tomb that does not contain a body but records his history in the community. A more modest monument to the stepson of Lord Strathcona is said to be tipped over in a pioneer cemetery in North West River, where he was raised. In some cases, gravestones have been placed in Labrador cemeteries to remember soldiers who died in World Wars I and II and are buried overseas.

Several Labrador cemeteries contain unusually narrow categories of people. The Military Cemetery at Goose Air Force Base contains the remains of military men and veterans, but a surprising number of the graves there are of young children or infants, victims of the polio and gastroenteritis epidemics of the 1950s. There are also numerous infants' graves bearing only the marker "Known unto God," the epitaph used on the graves of unknown soldiers. Local gossip claims these are babies born to young Labrador girls and American soldiers. The cemetery at Churchill Falls is similarly anomalous as it has only two adult graves and all the rest are those of children, mostly infants. Churchill Falls is a company town, so as soon as an employee retires, he or she has to leave.

A dead body can prompt feelings of fear, aversion, respect, and grief. Funeral feasts, gift offerings, taboos, body wrappings, casings or coffins, and internments such as are found in Labrador also turn up as mortuary practices around the world. The human remains at the Qafzeh Skhul Cave in Israel were buried with red ochre, as were Labrador's Maritime Archaic Indians. Irish wake houses had a small door used only to remove bodies, just as the Innu cut a separate opening in their tents to remove the dead. Many cultures wrap corpses in special clothing, skins, or shrouds, just as the Labrador Archaic people wrapped their bodies in birch bark and the modern Innu dress their dead men in white hunting clothes and their women in blue veils. These practices show the dead are all connected as humans rather than connected by specific cultural practices.

Drawing conclusions about how people lived by examining how they treated their dead is a practice that should be adopted with extreme caution. Graves tell us how people reacted to death, not how they interacted with the living, and while they do give us information about cultures, they tell only a very narrow part of their story.

L'ENVOY

What's in a Name: Labrador Ducks and Dogs

Most people who are interested in the north know that Labrador's name comes from the Portuguese for cultivator or labourer, *lavrador*, to acknowledge that João Fernandez of the Anglo-Azorean Expedition of 1501 was the first European to sight the unknown country. However, fewer are aware that the name was first applied to coastal Greenland, and later was extended to mean large parts of northern Canada and even parts of America, before being narrowed down to the Ungava Peninsula.

The name Labrador is applied to all sorts of things that in some cases have nothing to do with the Labrador Peninsula as we know it today. Heavy salted, hard, or semi-dried codfish are called Labrador fish because that was the way fish caught on the coast of Labrador were sent to market, but it is the cure, rather than the fish themselves, that comes from Labrador.

The *Dictionary of Newfoundland English* lists no fewer than 20 animals and birds that are prefaced with the name Labrador; some but not all of them are primarily or even secondarily associated with Labrador. An example of how the name gets attached to an animal is the Labrador retriever, a descendant of the Newfoundland dog, which originated on the island of Newfoundland. With its smaller size and shorter hair, the retriever was originally known as the lesser Newfoundland or St. John's dog, but when it was officially recognized by the English Kennel Club in 1903, it was given the name Labrador to distinguish it for show purposes.

The extinct Labrador duck lives on as study skins and taxidermied exhibits around the world. Ornithologist Glenn Chilton, author of *The Curse of the Labrador Duck,* has seen and examined all 55 examples that are known to exist and is the acknowledged expert on the bird. According to Chilton, the Labrador duck was thought to have bred in coastal Labrador and spent its non-breeding season feeding on mussels off the American east coast. None of the surviving examples were known to have been hunted in Labrador, none of their eggs have ever been identified, and Chilton and others have doubts about Labrador as their place of origin.

Labrador as the breeding place of the Labrador duck is usually attributed to the famous bird artist John James Audubon, who visited Blanc-Sablon in July of 1833. While there, his son saw some empty nests that an English clerk in the village identified as belonging to the pied duck, which was the name by which the Labrador duck was then known. Audubon described these nests as being similar to eider nests, but he didn't actually see them himself and his description of them was recorded many years later, not in the detailed journal he kept during his trip. The ducks that had made the nests had, by the end of July, gone south.

Michael Parsons attributes the extinction of the Labrador duck to the improvement in firearms in the 19th century. While overhunting was the cause of the extinction of the great auk, the Labrador curlew, and the passenger pigeon, the Labrador duck never had a population large enough to attract the attention of many hunters. According to Chilton, the duck's demise occurred in its non-breeding location, not in Labrador, when the human population of the east coast of America increased, and they were polluted into extinction.

It interesting to note that the Labrador duck or pied duck was also known as the skunk duck, presumably because of its black and white markings, but possibly also because its flesh "was strong smelling and fishy," not at all good eating.

Like the Labrador duck, the Labrador curlew is also extinct, though more recently as the last confirmed sighting was from a photograph taken in 1962 in Texas. A curlew is a species of sandpiper, and the Labrador curlew is one of many common names for the Eskimo curlew, *Numenius borealis,* or boreal curlew. The term

Labrador curlew is one that recently seems to have found favour for reasons of political correctness, but at least the curlew is known to have inhabited the Labrador Peninsula.

There is a Curlew Harbour in Labrador, although that may have been called for the Curlew family, some of whom still live in Labrador. Probably the common name for the Eskimo or Labrador curlew, which is also called a doe bird, fute, or prairie pigeon, should be the Inuit curlew. Their demise was the result of overhunting, altered habitat, and the extinction of a favourite food source—the Rocky Mountain locust, which disappeared when the American plains were plowed for agriculture. As a boy, Arctic explorer Captain Bob Bartlett contributed to the extinction of the Labrador curlew whenever he could, as, unlike the Labrador duck, they were excellent eating.

Labrador tea or Indian tea is found everywhere in Labrador, but it is also found throughout boreal North America, and its Latin name is not *Ledum labradoricum* as one might expect but *Ledum groenlandicum*, Greenland tea. The leaves were used in Medieval Europe to make ale and to spice meat, possibly even before Greenland was called Labrador.

The Labrador violet, unlike Labrador tea, carries the Latin name *Viola labradorica*, as does the Labrador poppy, *Papaver labradoricum*, and the Labrador lousewort, *Pedicularis labradorica*.

The Labrador flying squirrel is, again, a common name, but its Latin name backs up its claim to citizenship: *Glausomys* or *Sciuropterus sabrinus makkovikensis*, the Makkovik flying squirrel, a subspecies. The Labrador hare, *Lepus acticus Labradorius*, is also a subspecies, one of two Arctic hares that inhabit Labrador. The *Lepus articus bangsii* is the other.

Arctic hares, which most Newfoundlanders persist in calling rabbits, occupy the tundra, while snowshoe hares, *Lepus americanus*, prefer bogs and woods. The Arctic hares are twice the size of snowshoe hares and make a very substantial meal. Inuit have been known to catch them simply by throwing a jacket or blanket over them, but the hunter needs to be careful, as they have a powerful kick and sharp claws. They eat small birds and other kinds of meat, if they can get it.

Some of the animals, such as the Labrador vole and the Labrador savannah sparrow, are subspecies that carry the name *Labradorius* in their Latin monikers, but others, such as the Labrador jumping mouse or the Labrador marten, do not. The term *arcticus* or *borealis* suggests they live or breed in the north, but apparently the Labrador herring is no different from the Newfoundland herring, and the Labrador seal is identical to the seals found off the British Isles.

Internet users looking for Labrador-related information sometimes find themselves sidetracked into the lives of the saints, particularly to Saint Isidore, who in Spanish is known as Isidro Labrador, a 10th-century Spanish farmworker who was known for his piety toward the poor and animals. St. Isidore is honoured around the world on May 15, particularly in Spain, the Philippines, and Peru, and no fewer than 438 miracles have been attributed to him. His emblem is a hoe or a spade, and he is often depicted as plowing with the assistance of two angels. When, 40 years after his death, torrents of rain unearthed his body, it was found not to have suffered corruption, proof if it were needed that he was indeed a saint.

The last "Labrador" name to consider is Labradorite, a feldspar which is prized for its iridescent colour. The most significant source of Labradorite on the Labrador Peninsula is near Nain, where it is quarried, but occasional outcrops of it can be located elsewhere. In the Goose Bay area, one can find a beautiful example on a large rock bordering one of the snowshoe trails at Birch Brook Nordic Ski Club. To see it at its best, you need to pour some water on it, but in a pinch, urine might do the trick, although the position may be somewhat awkward for female geologists. Labradorite is found in many other countries such as Finland and Norway, but some jewellers argue that the Labradorite found on the Labrador Peninsula is superior to that mined elsewhere.

The term Labradorite has also led to the coining of another Labrador term: Labradoressence. In 1924, Ove Balthasar Bøggild described Labradoressence as "the peculiar reflection of the light from submicroscopical planes orientated in one direction (rarely in two directions); these planes have never such a position that they can be expressed by simple indices, and they are not directly visible under the microscope."

A term and definition such as that of "Labradoressence" would also be very useful to describe the effect on someone who comes to Labrador to work for a short while, falls in love with a Labradorian, and never leaves. The result may not be visible under a microscope but it certainly produces a beautiful radiance.

Index

Adams, Capt. Thomas 27
Adams, Lizzie 228
Advent tree. *See* Christmas tree 21
akenashau 208–210
alexander 54, 74–76
American man. See *inutsuk*
Amy, William Lacy 167
An Arctic Man 162, 164
Anauta 156–60
Andersen, Bertha 231–32
Andersen, Susan 230
Andersen, Uncle Jim 7
Andersen, William Sr. 15, 16
Arctic char 70–73
Arima, Eugene 8
Ash, Archibald 169
Ashini, Jean Pierre 206–7
atinakan see checkers
Atlas of Labrador Plants 90
Aunt Stana 162
aurora borealis 188–93
avalanches see snow slides

Baikie, Margaret 128
Baine Johnston 132, 153, 154
Banikhin Island 147
Banikhin, Frank 147–50
Banikhin, Wilfred 149
Banks, Sarah 123
Banks, Sir Joseph 123–26, 239
bannock x, 63, 209
Barbour, Florence Grant 19
barratry 29, 30
Bartlett, Abram 132
Bartlett, Robert (Bob) 132–36, 156, 186
Bartlett, Sam 134

Bartlett, William 43, 132–36
Bartlett, William Jr. 135
bats 99–103
Battle Harbour 3, 4, 34, 74–5, 153–4
    Grenfell Mission 166
    Marconi station 149
    ranger station 37–9
Battle Island 75
Beaudoin, Matthew 54
Beaumont Hamel 33, 167
Benefiel, Roberta 64
Best, Cortland 105
Bettelheim, Bruno 182
birch bark 114–17
birch beer 115
Birch Brook 61
Birch Brook Nordic Ski Club 88–90,
    102, 266
birch trees 113–18
Birches Gallery 9, 192
Bird, Cecil 56
Birdseye, Clarence 104
Black, Gilbert 232
Black Tickle 187, 229
Blackmore, Sarah Elizabeth Ford
    see Anauta 156, 157
Blake, Annie 228
Blake, Dale 159
Blake, Gilbert 232
Blake, John 169
Blake, Sylvia 104
Bluff Head 3
Bockstoce, John 186, 187
Bonneycastle, Richard 77
Borlase, Tim 192
Bourquin, Brother 43

Bradbury, Elise 154
Bradley, Ralph 149, 150
bread 62–65
Bright, Christiana 162, 165
Brown, Herb 9, 152
Brown, Robert George 169
Brown, Thomas 43, 44
Bruneau, Stephen 194, 195, 198
Buchheit, Manfred 153–55
Buckle, Rev. Francis 13
Buckle, Meagan 178
Buckner, Mary 159
Budgell, Anne 170
Budgell, Leonard 72, 176
Bunyan, Rev. John 12
Burdett, John 54
burial practices 255–60
Burns, Kay 184, 187
Burry, Lester 192
bush medicine 249–54
Butler, Kenneth C. 165
butterwort 97–98

C-CORE 198
Cabot, Lou 230, 232
Cabot, William Brookes 246
cairns 180–83
Campbell, Lydia 22
Cape Charles 147, 148
caribou cakes 104
carnivorous plants 96–98
Cartwright 13, 44–46, 138, 170, 187, 222, 232
Cartwright, Capt. George 14, 41, 60, 74, 92, 104, 105, 109, 110, 232, 239, 251, 259
Catholic Cadet Corps 166
Chaffey, Const. Leslie 37
Chard, Samuel 231, 232
Charles Andrew Treatment Centre 48, 49, 248
Chateau Bay 67, 123–26
checkers 203–7
Christian, Denny 197–98
Christmas
    in Labrador 19
    ornaments 20, 21
trees 19–21
Chubbs, Gertrude 229
Church Lad's Brigade 166
Churchill Falls vii, 208, 259
    development 209–10

Churchill River vii, ix–xi, 212
Cleary, Edmund 42
Collins, Duncan 171
Combined Councils of Labrador 91
Commission of Government 33
confederation 33, 34
Cook, James 125
Coombs, Will 230
Crane, Jean 62
Craze, Timothy 41
Crellin, John 79, 221, 225, 252
Croucher, John Thomas 154
Croucher, Victor 153–55, 258
Curl, John 170
Curl, Thomas 170
Curlew Harbour 265
Curwen, Eliot 43, 44, 185, 189

damper dogs 64
dandelion 77–80
Davies, Robert H. 148
Davis, Doris 56
Davis, Frank 9, 175
Davis, Jerome 31
Davis, John 9
Davis, Josh 53, 56
Davis, Lew 56
Davis, Margaret 53, 55, 56
Davis, Mercer 56
Davis, Tommy 4, 9
Davis Inlet 35, 93, 205, 230, 231, 247
Day, Robin T. 90
de Boilieu, Lambert 60
Diamond, Beverly 8
Dickers, Clara Broomfield 163
Dictionary of Newfoundland English 221, 263
dole 34, 35
Doyle, Alan 62
Drover, W.H. 144
Dumaresque, Mary 230, 231
Dyson, John 4

Ecke, Robert 223
Edmunds, Sharon 21
Effie Morrissey 135, 186
Elson, George 94
Elson, Mary Ann 229, 230
Encyclopedia of Newfoundland and Labrador 127
Enrichment of Flour Regulations 59
Erhardt, John Christian 40
Evans, James 117

fata morgana 184–87
Felsberg, Susan 31
Fequet, Betty Anne 88
fiddle
    European 8, 9, 10
    Inuit 7, 8, 9, 10
fiddle making 7, 8, 9, 10
Finney, Richard 140
firewood 14–17
Fitzhugh, Bill 256
Foray Newfoundland and Labrador 68
Ford, Augusta 230
Ford, George 156
Ford, Harriet Merryfield 156, 159
Ford, Henry 162
Ford, James 169
Ford, John 156
Forsythe, Dr. Lionel 46
Forteau 169, 178
Fox, Manasse 71
Francis Harbour 41
Frankel, Miles 234–37
Franklin Expedition 140
Freida, Frederick 168
Frenchman's Island 3
Fry, Natalia 229

Gaden, George Hugh 121–22
Gallivan, John 42
Gardiner, Rev. Michael 13
Gear, Edward 169
Ged, Alexander 27
Gedalof, Ze'ev 9, 10
George, Marjorie (Pye) 171
Gibbons, Cindy 75
Gillingham, Esau 46
Goodfellow-Baikie, Robin 89
Goodridge, William 215
Goose Bay vii, x, xi, 55, 64, 68, 69, 77, 208, 214, 247, 257, 266.
    See also Happy Valley-Goose Bay
Goose Cove 175
Gordon, Rev. Henry 28, 44
Gosling, William 43, 107
Goudie, Elizabeth 15, 254
Goudie, Horace 104
Goudie, James 170
Goudie, Jim 15
Goudie, John 137
Goudie, Sally 229
granny midwives 227–33
Grant, James 128, 129

Great War *see* World War I
Gregory, Lynn 49
Grenfell Mission 15, 22, 45, 55, 127, 166, 231, 234, 253
Grenfell, Wilfred 14, 15, 19, 22, 67, 79, 133, 156, 170, 189, 221, 225, 227, 249, 258
    judicial decisions / as magistrate 28–32
grey jay 91
Groves, Daniel 169
Gull Island viii–x

Hamel, Harold 67
Hamel, Miriam 37
Hammond, Roy 143, 144
Happy Valley 185, 223
Happy Valley-Goose Bay 4, 32, 61, 72, 75, 82, 83, 87–90
Hardisty, Isabella 127–31
Hardy, Marion R. 9
Harp, George 177
Harper, Kenn 167
Haven, Jens 66, 121–22
Hawkes, E.W. 8, 40, 41, 181, 190, 229
Hay, Gilbert 192
Haynes, Hayward 5
Heard, John O. 6
Hebron 8, 20, 176, 177, 257
Hedderson, Harry 169
Henriksen, Georg 107, 204, 246
Hicks, John 81
Hind, Henry Youle 25, 92, 185, 189, 240, 250
Hind, William 92
History of Newfoundland 127
Hobbs, William 186
Hogan, Corp. John 38
Holeiter, Deiter 88
Holloway, Henrietta Palfrey 242
Holloway, Robert Edwards 153, 154, 186
Holloway, Robert Palfrey 242
home remedies 249–54
Homfeld, Henry 78
Homfeld, Meta 78
Hood, John E. 3, 5
Hopedale 21, 42, 43, 175, 182, 240, 258
    ranger station 34, 37
Hopkins, Clarice 54
Horwood, Harold 4, 5, 37, 46, 133, 145
Howard, Euen 131
Hubbard, Mina 94, 106, 156

Hudson, Scott 184
Hudson's Bay Company 15, 71, 72,
    127-29, 133, 137-41, 143, 156,
    161-64, 171, 176
Hunter, Judy Pauline 144
Hynes, Sheila 19

*I Want to Know if I Got to Get Married:
    A Doctor on the Grenfell Mission*
    234
Iceberg Alley 194
icebergs 194-99
Icebergs of Newfoundland and Labrador
    194
Igloliorte, Jim 28
Igloliorte, Susie 11
Igloliorte, Suzannah 175
Innu viii-x, 36, 47-50, 79, 143-45,
    186, 208-11, 216, 218
    see also Elizabeth Penashue, Francis
    Penashue, Apenam Tanien Pone
    atinakan 203, 204
    bats (legends) 101
    birthing practices 228, 229, 232
    burial practices 114, 256, 257
    checkers 205-7
    food traditions 57-60, 61, 69
    grey jay stories 92, 93
    iceberg 195
    relief 35
    medicine 250-52
    mukashan (food) 58
    Mushua Innu 145, 146
    northern lights 189-90
    porcupine 106-8
    spruce 109, 111
    sweat lodge 244-48
    use of birch bark 114-16
    Uauitshitun Alcohol and Drug
    Awareness Program 48
Innu Nation 47, 145
International Grenfell Mission
    see Grenfell Mission
Inuit 12-13, 40-42, 79, 122, 126,
    139-41, 161-65, 175-77, 181,
    182, 265
    See also Anauta, John Shiwak
    birthing practices 228-29
    burial practices 257-58
    Christmas traditions 20
    food traditions 57-60, 66, 70-72
    ice and iceberg legends 196-97

medicine 249-51
music 7-10
Northern lights 189-90
tautirut (Inuit fiddle) 8
relief 35
uses for moss 239
inutsuk (inukshuk) 180-83
Ivany, Gladys Stone 19

Jackman, Lawrence 108
Jackson, Chick 157
James, John Anley 169
Jarvis, Dale 3
Jenkins, Larry 192
Johns, A.C. 110
Johnson, Pauline 156
Joy, John 48, 99

Kaniuekutat see Poker, John
Kearley, Wade 72
Keddie, Mrs. 54
Kennedy, John C. 148, 167
Kennitok, Mark 46
Kerr, J. Lennox 28, 30
Kohlmeister, Ida 177

L.A. Learmonth 141
Labrador
    local food 57
    use of name 263-67
Labrador by Choice 105
Labrador City 64, 179
Labrador Corrections Facility 48
Labrador Court of Sessions 41
Labrador Creative Arts Festival 101
Labrador flag 109
Labrador Inuit Association 159
Labrador Life xii
*Labrador Memories: Reflections at
    Mulligan* 128
Labrador tea 251, 256
labradorite 190, 266
Lake Melville 89, 90, 216
lamb's quarters 82-83
Larsen, Henry 140
Lavallee, Jamie 179
Law Society of Newfoundland 48
Learning, Jemima 67
Learmonth, Lorenz Alexander 137-41
Learning, Betty 192
Learning, Jim 16, 17
Legion of Frontiersmen 166

LeMare, Isaac 232
Lethbridge, Chelsey 55
Lindsay, Marguerite 44, 45
Linstead, Maggie Arkell 222
liquor trade 36
Liverman, David 175, 178
Loder, Millicent Blake 21
Lodge Bay 3
Lord Strathcona: A Biography of Donald Alexander Smith 128
Lower Churchill viii, ix, 208, 210
Luther, Jessie 189
Lyall, Amos 163
Lyall, Bob 177
Lyall, Ernest Wilson 161–65
Lyall, Ernie 140, 178
Lyall, John 162
Lyall, Margaret McNeill 230
Lyall, Miriam Igloliorte 11, 13
Lyall, Sam 230

MacDonald, Donna 128–30
Makkovik 31, 42, 132, 136, 163, 164, 229–32
Manak, Mabel 228, 229
Maritime Archaic Indians 256, 259
Marshall, Tom 27
Martin, Bishop 12
Martin, Harry 45
Martin, John 44
Mary's Harbour 74, 150, 234
matjes herring 147–50
McCarthy, Sara 99–102
McGhee, Robert 255
McKenzie, William 169
McKinnon, Kimberly 192
McLean, Audrey 153
McLean, Wallace 38, 167
McNeil, Rupert 133
McNeill, Susan 230
Mealy Mountains 54, 185, 212–15
Memorial University School of Music 7
Memorial University viii
Mercer, Frank 5, 37, 46
Merkuratsuk, Emilia 190
Merrick, Kate Austin 67
Meshkana 205–6
meshkanau 209, 210
Metcalfe, Bill 176
Methodist Guards 166
Michelin, Rose 72
midwives 227–33

Miller, Alice 183
Millman, Lawrence 190
Mista Shipu vii
Montague, Louie 16, 23, 111, 192
Montague, Shirley 192
Moodie, Suzanna 79
moonshine 3
Moorhouse, Shirley 192
Moravians, Moravian missionaries 7, 20, 27, 35, 123, 163, 175–77, 240, 251
  Christmas traditions 21, 22
  food traditions 42–45, 61
  interest in botany 123–26
  musicians 8
Moravian Brethren 8, 43, 104
Moravian Mission 7, 11, 15, 35, 258
Morry, Howard 168
moss see sphagnum moss
Mowat, Farley 141, 161, 165
Mud Lake 15, 31, 101, 138–141, 166
Mueler, Francis Saunders 62
Mukashan 58, 107
murder 40–46
Murphy, Ruperta 133
Museum of the Flat Earth 184
mushrooms 66–69
Musical Forests Inc. 9
My Life with Trees 113

Nain 20–22, 28, 142, 145, 166, 175–78, 182, 196, 229, 266
  ranger station 34, 37, 38
  fish plant 70–72
Native Cookery and Edible Wild Plants of Newfoundland and Labrador 82
Natuashish viii
Newfoundland Highlanders 166, 168
Newfoundland Ranger Force museum 39
Newfoundland Ranger Force 33–39
Newfoundland Regiment 143, 166, 168, 169
Newman, Terry 9, 10
Niger 27, 123–25
Nitsman, Sybella 21
Nooquashock 232
North River 53–56, 258
North West River 62, 72, 89, 111, 127–131, 153, 170, 184, 213, 229, 259

O'Brien Theatre 192
O'Brien, Edward 35, 36
Okak 46, 88, 126, 176–78, 190
Old Frederika 229

Old Pauline 229
Old Smoker 3–6
Oliver, Flossie 62
Oliver, Stanley 101
Oliver, Uncle George 6
Onalik, Herman 8
One Pilgrim's Journey 13
Osbourn, John 82
O'Shea, Kathleen 62

Paddon, Harry 167, 170, 171
Palliser, Joe 38, 39
Pamak, Rose 182
Paradise River 62
Pardy, Leslie 192
Pardy, Manuel 170
Parry, William 185
Partridge Bay 3
Peacock, Doris 176
Peacock, F.W. 5, 8, 20, 46, 57, 58, 196
Peary, Robert 134, 156
Peck, E.J. 158
Penashue, Elizabeth vii–xi, 57, 92, 111, 112, 116, 117, 206, 212–15, 217, 245
 Labrador walkabout 208–11
Penashue, Francis 116, 206, 209, 210, 212–15
Penashue, Max 244–48
Penashue, Peter 50, 214
Penney, Mark 154
Penney, Mavis 154, 155
Phillips, Frank 108
Pike, Patricia 19
Pilgrim's Progress 11–13
pitcher plant 96–98
Pitseolak, Pete 19
pitsik 72
Point Amour 61, 68, 198
Poker John 107, 205–6, 250
Pone, Apenam Tanien 47–50, 247, 248
Poole, Alex 229–31
Poole, George 237
porcupine 104–8, 115
potherbs 81–83
Pottle, Levi 170
Powell, Ben 105
Prohibition 28
Prowse, D.W. 127
Pye, Gerald 75
Pye, Pearl 75, 148

Radar Hill 216–18
Ramah 176

Ramah chert 256
Rawluk, Wieslaw 68
Red Bay 9, 75, 149, 232, 258
Reed, George Hutchinson 4
residential school 163, 164, 214
Rich, Cajetan 117
Rich, Joseph 92
Rich, Justine 101, 116
Rich, Katie 247
Rich, Scott 192
Richie, Bill 4
Rideout, Sharon 154
Rideout, Tom 49
Rigolet 57, 71, 74, 127, 128, 131, 157
Roberts, Tim 36
Rollmann, Hans 8, 12, 27, 66, 121
Rooms Provincial Art Gallery 4
Ross, John 140
Rowley, Graham 139
Royal Canadian Mounted Police 33
Royal Newfoundland Constabulary 33
Royal Newfoundland Regiment 33
Rumbolt, Alie 231
Russell, Bob 236
Ryan, Ginny 101

St. Lewis Bay 110
Sampson, Chris 192
Sampson, Harry 149
Sandwich Bay 37, 53, 59, 258
Saunders, Alex 176, 180–82
Saunders, Doris 67, 192
Saunders, Gary 94, 113, 115, 117
Saunders, Gilbert 38
Saunders, Jim 5
Saunders, Una 104
Saunders, Margaret 230
Savage, Candace 93
scapulamancy 107
Schneider, H.G. 20
Score, Joseph 41, 42
scotch lovage 74–76
sea stacks 180–83
seal finger 252
Seaward, Edward 168
Sheshatshiu 47, 62, 111, 206, 213–18, 244, 247, 257
Sheshatshiu Band Council 217
Sheshatshiu Group Home 214
Shiwak, Jack 104
Shiwak, John 167
Sillett, Jerry 28

Simms, George 188
Simpson, George 128, 129
Smallwood, Joseph 143
Smith, Donald Alexander 127–31
Smith, Nancy 75
Smith, Nelson 75, 147
Smoker Gillingham 4, 5
Smoker, James 4
Smoker, Jane 4
snow slides 175–79
Speck, Frank 92, 144, 145, 186, 189, 204, 207, 250
sphagnum moss 238–43
spruce, spruce boughs 109–12
St. Anne
    feast of 216–18
St. John's Native Friendship Centre 192
Stefansson, Vilhjalmur 158
Stick, Leonard B. 33
Stirling, Terry Bishop 241, 242
stove cakes 64
Strathcona, First Baron
    see Smith, Donald Alexander
Strong, William Duncan 92, 101, 115, 250, 258
Sturrock, D.G. 140
Strathcona 29, 31, 130, 234, 235
sundew 97
sweat lodge 244–28
Swile Cove 3

tautirut see Inuit fiddle 8
Taylor, Garth 121–22
Terriak, John 182
The Songs of Labrador 192
Them Days 9, 15, 21, 36, 53, 62, 67, 75, 78, 121, 148, 154, 167, 170, 175, 229
Through Newfoundland with a Camera 186
Thule 257
Ticoralak 3
Tocque, Philip 117
tonewood 9, 10
Torngat Fish Co-operative Society 70
Toumishey, George 169
Townley, Ruth 142
trapper, trapline
    food traditions 63
Truth and Reconciliation Commission 214
tshemetentshian 207
Tuck, James 255
Tucker, Otto 78
Turnavik 43, 132–136
Turnbull, Minnie 229
Turner, Lucien 7, 190, 204, 228, 246
Tweegok 232

Uvloriak, Karoline 177

violin-making 8
Voisey, Emma Dicker 67
Voisey's Bay 35, 67, 73, 108, 142, 143, 170, 210, 246

Wabush 32
Wadden, Marie 212
Wakefield, A.W. 166
Wakefield, Marjorie 138, 139
Waldo, Fullerton L. 29
Wallace, Dillon 106
Webber, Sarah 229, 230
Welbourn Bay 101
White Eskimo 4, 5, 37, 46, 146
White Harbour 142
White, Margaret 154
White, Richard 170
White, Richard Jr. 141–46
White, Winston 145
wildflowers 87–90
Wildflowers of Newfoundland and Labrador 90
Williams, Charles 54, 55, 258
Williams, Dorothy 55
Williams, Griffith 59, 60
Williams, Rod 38
Williamson, Tony 108
Women's Patriotic Association 238, 241
Wood, Barb 192
wooding 14–17
World War I 143, 162, 166–71
World War II 34, 79

Yeoman, Elizabeth 215
Young, Rob 154

Robin McGrath was born in Newfoundland in 1949, one of the famous "castor oil babies" of the anti-confederate movement. She took her PhD at the University of Western Ontario, and was an associate professor at the University of Alberta where she specialized in Aboriginal and exploration literature, for which she did extensive research in Canadian Arctic communities over several decades.

The author or editor of 24 books, 30 book chapters and several hundred articles, newspaper columns, and reviews, Robin's work has appeared in countries such as Finland, Denmark, Sweden, the United States, Ireland, Inner Mongolia, and Australia as well as Canada. She has won a number of literary awards including the Henry Fuerstenberg Poetry Prize, the Geldert Medal, and the Helen and Stan Vine Award for Canadian Jewish Fiction.

Robin is a social commentary columnist for *The Northeast Avalon Times*, and a feature writer for *Labrador Life*. Her books include the novels *Donovan's Station* and *The Winterhouse*, poetry collections *Escaped Domestics* and *Covenant of Salt*, and *Salt Fish and Shmattes: A History of the Jews of Newfoundland and Labrador*. Robin lives in Harbour Main, Conception Bay.